D1567717

Ada: the design choice

The Ada Companion Series

There are currently no better candidates for a co-ordinated, low risk, and synergetic approach to software development than the Ada programming language. Integrated into a support environment, Ada promises to give a solid standards-orientated foundation for higher professionalism in software engineering.

This definitive series aims to be the guide to the Ada software industry for managers, implementors, software producers and users. It will deal with all aspects of the emerging industry: adopting an Ada strategy, conversion issues, style and portability issues, and management. To assist the organised development of an Ada-orientated software components industry, equal emphasis will be placed on all phases of life cycle support.

Some current titles:

Portability and style in Ada
Edited by J.C.D. Nissen and P.J.L. Wallis

Ada: Languages, compilers and bibliography
Edited by M.W. Rogers

Ada for multi-microprocessors
Edited by M. Tedd, S. Crespi-Reghizzi and A. Natali

Proceedings of the Third Joint Ada Europe/Ada Tec Conference
Edited by J. Teller

Proceedings of the 1985 Ada International Conference
Edited by J.G.P. Barnes and G.A. Fisher

Ada for specification: possibilities and limitations
Edited by S.J. Goldsack

Concurrent programming in Ada
A. Burns

Ada: Managing the transition
Proceedings of the 1986 Ada-Europe International Conference
Edited by P.J.L. Wallis

Selecting an Ada environment
Edited by T.G.L. Lyons and J.C.D. Nissens

Ada components: Libraries and tools
Proceedings of the 1987 Ada-Europe International Conference
Edited by S. Tafvelin

Ada for Distributed Systems
Edited by C. Atkinson, T. Moreton and A. Natali

Ada in Industry
Proceedings of the 1988 Ada-Europe International Conference
Edited by S. Heilbrunner

Ada: the design choice

Proceedings of the Ada-Europe International Conference
Madrid 13–15 June 1989

Edited by
ANGEL ALVAREZ

DIT-UPM (Departamento de Ingeniería y Sistemas Telemáticos)
Madrid, Spain

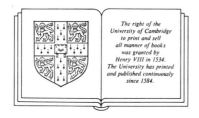

CAMBRIDGE UNIVERSITY PRESS

Cambridge

New York   Port Chester   Melbourne   Sydney

Published by the Press Syndicate of the University of Cambridge
The Pitt Building, Trumpington Street, Cambridge CB2 1RP
40 West 20th Street, New York, NY 10011, USA
10 Stamford Road, Oakleigh, Melbourne 3166, Australia

First published 1989

Printed in Great Britain at the University Press, Cambridge

Library of Congress Cataloging in Publication data available

British Library Cataloguing in Publication data available

ISBN 0 521 38130 4

CONTENTS

PREFACE

The unprecedented size of Ada compilers is a clear indication that they are more than just simple language translators. They are also software tools which enforce diverse programming methodologies and, more concretely, design methodologies. This is of the upmost importance considering the massive size of many of the applications that are being built with Ada. In order to keep the complexity of these applications within manageable intellectual bounds, they must first be designed with sound methodologies.

To make adequate use of the compilers, and the language itself, the design methods which are embodied within Ada need to be systematically experimented and, where deemed insufficient, augmented with the use of additional methods and support tools.

A sign of the high interest design issues favour within the Ada community was the large number of abstracts (73) received for this Conference. With the help of the referees, the Programme Committee had to solve the difficult task of choosing 24 contributions, which are the ones making up this volume. The Programme Committee was formed by

H. Davis
S. Heilbrunner
J. Kok
H.-J. Kügler
B. Lynch
M. Mac an Airchinnigh
J.-P. Rosen

The Programme Committee is most grateful to the referees and to the sponsoring organizations as well as to the many individuals who made this Conference possible. In particular, it wants to thank Ada-Spain and J. B. Pérez-Aparicio for the local arrangements, and Cambridge University Press for their cooperation in publishing these proceedings in their Ada Companion Series.

Angel Alvarez
Programme Chairman

Part 1 Language Extensions

ADA++
A Class and Inheritance Extension for Ada

J. P. Forestier, University of Nice,

C. Fornarino, INRIA Sophia Antipolis,

P. Franchi-Zannettacci, INRIA Sophia Antipolis.

LISAN University of Nice
Sophia Antipolis
06561 Valbonne Cedex France
E-mail pfz@cerisi.cerisi.fr

INRIA
Sophia Antipolis
06565 Valbonne France
E-mail fornarin@lynus.inria.fr

Abstract.
We present ADA++, a superset of Ada, supporting real object oriented design and constructs. ADA++ provides a model for classes and inheritance fully compatible with the Ada language. The inheritance mechanism is solved in the spirit of the Ada language, as a static type-checking using an extended version of the usual overloading resolution algorithm.

The ADA++ language is embedded in a user-friendly environment, ADALOOK, a graphical class-browser.

1. Reusability and Convivial Programming Environments

The production of modern software for large computer applications can benefit from both advanced techniques issued from Software Engineering and tools created for Artificial Intelligence.

Considering the programming needs, the Ada language [LRM (83)] becomes, owing to its normalization, an unavoidable tool for industrial developments. It enhances some fundamental program qualities such as modularity, security, efficiency, portability, etc.

Considering the design phase, the Ada language appears to be less suitable [Booch (1987), Perez (1988), Touati (1987)] than its rivals coming from object oriented programming (OOP) (Smalltalk [Goldberg & Robson (1983)], Loops [Bobrow (1983)], C++ [Stroustrup (1986)], Eiffel [Meyer (1987)]). The most important feature provided by OOP is the facility for re-using entities previously existing such as modules, types, operations, etc. This paradigm leads to architectures based on composition and adaptation of pre-existing software ICs [Cox (1986)] (using a class hierarchy and specializations). Such a methodology notably decreases the cost of the design and improves programs reliability and consistency by enforcing intensive use of shared modules.

Finally, focusing on the programming environments, the Ada world (MAPSE,APSE) appears to be rather conservative compared to the convivial philosophy resulting from the Lisp world (graphical browsers in Smalltalk or Loops, etc).

This work is the starting point for the study of a joint Ada/Lisp programming and design environment based on the three paradigms mentioned above:

- procedural programming in standard Ada,
- object oriented design and programming using classes and inheritance,
- graphical interactive environments including icons, menus, windows, etc.

The solution selected to implement such an environment is based on the use of both standard Ada mechanisms (types, packages, generics, tasks, etc) and some mechanisms borrowed from strongly typed OOP (classes, methods, inheritance). This choice leads to an elegant and powerful answer to the problems stated by [Meyer (1986)]. Furthermore, this association makes it possible later specific developments well suited for real time or deductive programming [Buhr (1984), Yonezawa & Tokoro (1986)].

This paper presents ADA++, a pre-processor for Ada in the spirit of (C++ [Stroustrup (1986)], Eiffel [Meyer (1987)], ObjectiveC, ClassicAda [SPS (1988)], InnovAda [Simonian & Crone (1988)]) which allows the use of some OOP paradigms above standard Ada. ADA++ provides Ada with a full model for class definition and multiple inheritance scheme on abstract objects (section 2.).

This superset of Ada is fully compatible with the language and moreover, it preserves the programming philosophy of Ada. The initial constructs are embedded in the OOP mechanisms of ADA++. In order to extend classical overloading on types we choose a limited polymorphism (called *subtyping* in [Cardelli & Wegner (1986)]) and we also avoid dynamic binding (section 3.). The technical part of this paper is devoted to the overloading+inheritance resolution algorithm for translating ADA++ into Ada (section 4.). The expressive and reusability power of ADA++ is demonstrated by an example shown through our specialized browser ADALOOK [Forestier & al. (1988)] (section 5.).

2.   Ada and Object Oriented Programming

Many recent works [Cox (1986), Meyer (1986), Stroustrup (1987), Snyder (1986), Touati (1987), Stefik & Bobrow (1986)] and several issues in programming languages [Meyer (1987), Stroustrup (1986), Bobrow (1983), Bobrow & al. (1988), Goldberg & Robson (1983)] showed that object oriented programming may provide a powerful and efficient answer to the reusability problem resulting from complex software architectures.

[Booch (1987)] gave a methodological answer to this question, where some features of the Ada language such as private types, packages and genericity enhance the facility for structuring software upon abstract data, instead of procedural manipulations. However, we think with [Cox (1986)], that such a methodology will gain if supported by dedicated languages and environments and we agree with [Meyer (1986)], saying that Ada gives only weak solutions for such a functionality. Genericity, and more generally Ada type definition rules, allow reusing in an a-priori way (the designer must imagine what kind of future use can be done with the objects). On the contrary, the inheritance technique, that we propose to introduce in Ada, is an a-posteriori way of thinking and provides means for adapting already existing objects for new usages.

2.1   Class and Inheritance Paradigms

Let us synthesize from some well-known related works [Cardelli & Wegner

(1986), Bobrow & al. (1988), Goldberg & Robson (1983), Shriver & Wegner (1987)] the gist of "strongly typed object oriented programming", which settles the framework of ADA++.

The OOP paradigm consists of:

- **objects**, which act as responsible actors and determine with **methods** the behavior of an entire software by exchanging **messages**,
- **classes**, which define data, operations, and messages available for one type of objects,
- **inheritance**, which computes inherited behavior between classes with respect to a given class hierarchy.

In the setting of this extension for Ada, we are not concerned with dynamic aspects of OOP, so method identification will be achieved by subprogram typing resolution, messages will be partially simulated by subprogram calls and binding will obviously be static.

An **object** is a data encapsulation, with internal hidden information and an external abstraction defining the state of this object and its set of suitable operations.

We shall use the term **slots**, as in Clos [Bobrow & al. (1988)] to denote the structural components (private or not) of objects.

A **class** defines an abstract data type for similar objects, called **instances** of the class. The instances of a given class share the same internal representation, the same logical structure, and the same set of operations.

A class may inherit, from one or more parvent classes, additional slots and operations for its instances. The directed acyclic graph, induced by the dependencies between classes, is called the **inheritance** hierarchy graph. Reusability of software is a consequence of the fundamental mechanism used for defining new classes from others and called **specialization**.

Following [Cardelli & Wegner (1986)] object oriented languages can be considered as extensions of procedural languages supporting:

(i) data abstractions,
(ii) object types,
(iii) type inheritance.

Finally, an object oriented language is strongly typed if every object (instance of a class) has a type. As mentioned above for messages, we only consider here the static case, so our extension will be statically strongly typed, i.e. each object will be typed at compile-time.

2.2   Ada as an Object Oriented Language

The Ada language has been designed to offer powerful mechanisms to deal with the first point (i). So, private types, packages, separation between specifications and bodies and more generally modularity and genericity, provide a comfortable framework to express data abstraction. All these features must be fully preserved by an acceptable extension for the language.

On the other hand, Ada gives weak and partial support for the two other points (ii) and (iii) and this has fundamental consequences on programming methodology [Hendler & Wegner (1986)].

Considering object types, subprograms and packages are not first-class entities in Ada [Wegner (1983)]; we improve this by giving to every ADA++ object, a type associated with its class definition.

Focusing on the third point, the facility for Ada programmers to create new abstract types from existing ones holds in subtypes and derived types. The relations betwen types resulting from these constructs appear to be very limited compared to the class model of Smalltalk, Loops, etc; particularly, there is no means in Ada for creating a type, either by modifying the structure of another type, or by gathering definitions from several ones.

ADA++, as a superset of Ada , supports data abstraction, provides a full model for type inheritance and extends the type definition of Ada, while preserving the static philosophy of the language.

3.   ADA++: Classes and Inheritance in Ada

ADA++, an Ada-based language which supports a class and inheritance model for abstract typed objects, is fully compatible with Ada syntax, semantics and methodology.
The added reserved words are :

- **class** for class definition (see section 3.1),

- **from** for class hierarchy definition (see section 3.2),

- **slot** for object component definition (see section 3.3)

- **sendsuper** for the call of a method defined in a parent class.

We present below the syntax and semantics of the main features of ADA++.

3.1   Classes vs Packages

A class in ADA++ defines an abstract data type for objects, i.e. the data structure and the operations. It defines the logical data structure of the instances by slots, according to the Clos terminology; slots are strongly typed either by any Ada type or by a class. A class also defines the locally allowed methods for its instances.

At first glance, classes can be seen as classical packages and objects as records of slot-components; although ADA++ classes and objects are presently implemented via Ada packages and records; inheritance mechanism gives them a new operational semantics (see section 3.2).

As for usual packages, a class definition consists of two parts: specification and body; the syntax is mapped from the package declaration [LRM 7.1] :

```
class_specification ::=                          class_body ::=
    class identifier                                 class body identifier is
        [ from class_indentifier_list ] is               [ declarative_part ]
        { basic_declarative_item }                   [begin
        [slot_declaration]                               sequence_of_statements
        { basic_declarative_item }                       [ exception exception_handler
        [ private { basic_declarative_item } ]              { exception_handler } ] ]
    end [ class_simple_name ];                       end [ classe_simple_name ];
```

The static semantics of classes is directly deduced from package declaration rules but, unlike packages, a class does define a type (the class identifier) for all the objects instances of this class.

A class may inherit logical structure and methods from a list of parent classes, this is the specialization paradigm on classes [Snyder (1986)]; we give in the next part the inheritance mechanism, which makes this paradigm operational.

3.2   Class Hierarchy and Multiple Inheritance

The **from** option in a class declaration, defines the list of parent classes (the Supers in Loops terminology) from which this class directly inherits.

The inheritance mechanism allows that objects in a class (so-called descendant) share the semantics defined by any parent class (so-called ancestor), so that this class specializes its parents classes.

The set of all relations between classes defines a directed acyclic graph, the inheritance hierarchy graph; this graph is the basis of the inheritance mechanism and we will show in section 4. how we use it, together with the overloading resolution, to solve ADA++ type checking.

ADA++ inheritance implies multiple inheritance on both slots and methods for the instances.

The inheritance process in ADA++ is fully compatible with general visibility rules in Ada (hiding, overloading, renaming, etc.), so the available methods for the objects are resulting either from the scope of standard units, or from the inheritance rules on the class hierarchy, or from mixed ways when both systems are needed to correctly type a method (see example 4.2).

The ambiguities arising from multiple schemes are treated with the Ada philosophy: overloaded entities must be solved in a unique way by the algorithm describe in section 4.2.

3.3   Slots and Objects

Slots are the components of the type associated with a class definition; they define the logical data structure for the instances in this class. As for usual records, each slot in a class has a specific name and stands for a typed value.

```
slot_declaration ::=                    list_slots ::=
    slot                                    component_declaration
        list_slots                              {component_declaration}
    private                                 | null ;
        list_slots — — private slots
    end slot
```

The slot declaration defines the set of local slots for every object within a class; as explained in section 3.2, objects also include inherited slots from the parent classes of the definition class. Objects are instances of a unique class and consequently they are typed by this class; they are declared with the following syntax:

```
identifier {, identifier } : [constant] class_name [:= expression]
```

where the usual Ada rules apply.

Objects consist of the set of all local or inherited slots in its class and record type pre-defined operators such as "=", "/=", etc are available for the objects; particularly the selection operator "." allows access to the slots where they are visible.

The slots declared in the private part are only reachable in the class declaration or by methods in this class. Note that these slots are inheritable for descendant classes (they may exist in the logical structure of the instances of descendants classes), but they are not directly accessible outside of the class declaration.

3.4   Subprograms as Methods

In ADA++, methods in a class are operators or subprograms; for conceptual reasons, we consider that if a method is defined in a given class, the first argument or the result argument must be an instance of this class.

Instead of the usual execution of methods by sending messages to objects in dynamic object oriented languages, we give to ADA++ a procedural semantics.

The two major reasons for this choice are the static philosphy of Ada and the efficiency of static type checking.

Thus, in ADA++ the methods are not strongly related to a class as in Smalltalk; the class gives them extended visibility scope via the inheritance mechanism and classical rules for packages in Ada.

The multiple inheritance scheme can be stated as follows: a method is correctly typed for a set of actual parameters (and result) if it does exist and is visible with a set of formal parameters, where each of them is respectively typed by a parent class of the corresponding actual parameter.

The identification process for methods can be sketched by the following steps:

(a) determine the actual parameter types of the method.

(b) determine the unique definition corresponding to these types.

Note that, as in Ada, (a) and (b) are mutually recursive and that inheritance and overloading are interleaved in both steps.

3.5   Generic Classes

Like packages, classes can be generic in ADA++; the syntax declaration follows from generic package declaration [LRM 12.1]:

```
generic_specification ::=
        generic_formal_part class_specification
```

The instantiation is made by:

```
generic_instantiation ::=              generic_class_actual_part ::=
     class identifier is new                generic_class_association
        generic_class_name                    { , generic_class_association }
        [ generic_class_actual_part ]
                                       generic_class_association ::=
                                            generic_formal_parameter
                                              => generic_actual_parameter
```

The actual and formal parameters are exclusively associated by names, the inherited parameters have indeed no effective positions.

The following remarks establish the well-foundness of our construction between classes and generic units:

A class may inherit from one or more generic classes; in this case the inheriting class becomes generic and inherits from formal generic parameters of the parent generic classes.

A class, as any Ada type can be used as actual parameter (corresponding to a formal private type parameter) for a generic instanciation and thus an ADA++ generic unit (subprogram, package or class) can be instanciated with a class type; this facility notably increases the expressive power of the language and has no equivalent constructs in other languages.

4.   Implementation of ADA++

ADA++ is currently implemented as a pre-processor translating ADA++ source into standard Ada source. According to figure 1, the pre-processor consists of two steps:

  - A first step from ADA++ to ADA-, a syntactically correct Ada source , where class and slot constructs have been translated into packages and records and where statements and expressions might be ill-typed with respect to Ada identification rules.

- A second step from ADA- to Ada using a new algorithm for type checking instead of the usual overloading resolution.

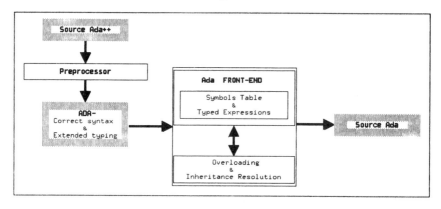

- Figure 1 -

4.1   The Overloading+Inheritance Resolution Algorithm

The translation process from ADA++ to Ada consists of two phases:

- a type-checking for ADA- expressions and statements,
- a type-conversion when inheritance arises.

The type-checker algorithm is based on a modified version of the usual overloading solver for Ada [LEVI (1988)]. ADA++ visibility rules determine, for each expression and statement, two sets of allowed types:

- Regular types resulting from the Ada overloading resolution,
- Inherited types induced by the ADA++ class hierarchy.

Method selection is treated as type determination and classical hiding rules apply in this case. To be correct, an expression must support, with respect to its context as in standard Ada, exactly one type.

The type-conversion for inheritance generates system-defined function calls (SUPER) which allow to apply methods typed by a class A to objects of a class B, descendant of A in the class hierarchy. We use the SUPER functions to make ADA++ statements well-typed in Ada when this conversion is not ambiguous.

This solution has three advantages:

- the selection for methods is done at compile-time,
- the selection of methods results from a typing process according to all the arguments [Bobrow (1988)] (instead of the unique *self* argument in Smalltalk),
- the algorithm is general and could be used to extend in the same way any language supporting strong static typing and ad hoc polymorphism in the sense of [Cardelli & Wegner (1986)] .

We give the algorithm for function calls only; this form can be easily generalized to the other forms [Persch (1980)]. So, we use the following abstract syntax:

> function_call : NAME $\times$ EXP2 $\to$ EXP1
>
> where EXP1 stands for the result parameter of the function, EXP2 for the actual parameters, and NAME for the function name.

The whole algorithm can be expressed by the computation of two semantic attributes on the abstract syntax tree associated with a program: A_TYPES, a set of available types (computed bottom-up) and C_TYPES, a set of constrained types (computed top-down).

Definitions

(i) A_TYPES and C_TYPES are sets of signatures (S) attached to the EXP nodes in the tree and given by Ada visibility rules for the NAME nodes. We denote by N.A the value of the attribute A in node N.

(ii) A signature S for a function f defines the typing of f as a word on T*, where T is the finite set of defined types in the program, i.e. $S = T_0 T_1 T_2 ... T_n$, where n is the arity of this definition for f. We denote by S[0] the result type of a signature S and by S[i] the ith parameter type and we use N.A[i] to denote the set of parameter or result types in the attribute A for node N.

(iii) We also use a coercion predicate $\Rightarrow$ between types, induced by the inheritance hierarchy graph in the following sense:
$T_2 \Rightarrow T_1$ holds iff T_1 may inherit from T_2
and consequently objects of type T_1 can be converted into type T_2 by a SUPER conversion.

Bottom up pass

As in Ada, this pass computes the set of available types for functions by using a specific intersection operation between the signatures and parameter types; but, for ADA++, we also consider during this pass the possibility for any type to be converted to another parent type in the class hierarchy.

> EXP1.A_TYPES = S in NAME.A_TYPES such that:
>
> for every i$\neq$0:
>
> either S[i] is in EXP2[i].A_TYPES[0]
>
> or S[i] $\Rightarrow$ T , for some T in EXP2[i].A_TYPES[0]

Top down pass

As the previous one, this pass eliminates the mismatched signatures. In a well-typed tree, each node must hold a C_TYPES attribute with only one signature.

EXP2[i].C_TYPES = S in EXP2[i].A_TYPES such that:

either S[0] is in EXP1.C_TYPES[i]

or T $\Rightarrow$ S[0] , for some T in EXP1.C_TYPES[i]

Remark

The compatibility of ADA++ with standard Ada results from the following fact: if the $\Rightarrow$ relation is empty (inheritance is not considered), then the standard overloading resolution rules apply.

4.2   Overloading and Inheritance : A Simple Example

Let us analyse how the previous algorithm works in the context defined by the following declarations:

```
with INTEGER_IO; use INTEGER_IO;      with S_INT; use S_INT;
class S_INT from INTEGER is           ...........
     -- a class unit for some extended  type N_INT is new INTEGER;
     -- integer inheriting from INTEGER  function "/" ( X: INTEGER; Y: N_INT)
     -- and using INTEGER_IO                 return S_INT;
end S_INT;                            function "/" ( X: INTEGER; Y: N_INT)
                                          return N_INT;
                                      procedure P (X: N_INT; Y: INTEGER) ;
                                      procedure P (X: INTEGER; Y: N_INT) ;
                                      ...........
                                      I: S_INT;
                                      N1,N2: N_INT;
                                      ...............
                                      begin
                                        P ( ( 3 * N1 ) , ( I / N2 ) ); -- (1)
                                        PUT ( I ) ; -- (2)
                                        PUT ( N1 ) ; -- (3)
                                      ...............
                                      end ;
```

The usual resolution on the procedure-call (1) gives an error, since there is no definition for "/" with S_INT as first parameter type. Using the overloading+inheritance resolution, the following holds:

(3 * N1) is typed N_INT $\times$ N_INT $\rightarrow$ N_INT

(I / N2) is typed (INTEGER$\Rightarrow$ S_INT) $\times$ N_INT $\rightarrow$ S_INT

and the whole statement (1) is typed N_INT $\times$ (INTEGER$\Rightarrow$ S_INT)

This example shows how subtyping is embedded in the standard Ada constructs such as "with", overloading and derived types.

Furthermore, let us see how we solve in this case an usual non desired Ada feature. Contrary to PUT(N1) in (3), which requires a new instantiation of the generic TEXT_IO by N_INT, the statement PUT(I) in (2) is correctly typed by inheritance.

4.3   Subtype conversion

The type conversion resulting from inheritance is computed by a set of system-defined functions, SUPER, generated where needed by the pre-processor.
Each class defines as many SUPER functions as parent classes; we intensively use the overloading facility for this purpose and the type conversion is achieved by nested calls of the SUPER functions.

Coming back to the previous example, this process transforms the initial statements (1) and (2) into:

```
     P ( (3 * N1) , SUPER( (SUPER (I) / N2) )) —— (1')
     PUT (SUPER (I)) —— (2')
where SUPER : S_INT → INTEGER
```

This algorithm is a revisited version of Levi's algorithm [Levi (1988)] for a subset of ADA++.

5.   ADALOOK: A class browser for ADA++

ADALOOK is a graphical interactive programming environment for ADA++. Following the spirit of the browsers of Smalltalk, Loops, etc, ADALOOK integrates the main paradigms of OOP and, more specifically, the superset ADA++. It provides the user with four main facilities:

- A user-friendly browsing for software architecture, using graphics and icons to handle software components such as packages, tasks, classes and their dependencies (with, new, from).
- A multi-form editing, where the consistency between different forms (Ada or ADA++ source, internal trees, graphics, code, etc) is insured by the system.
- A semantic analysis, which provides the user with semantic information and control on manipulated objects according to a set of rules defining the language and the involved applications.
- A dialogue with the operating system, which insures consistency of ADA++ entities with standard tools (compilers, loaders, debuggers, etc).

ADALOOK [Forestier & al. 88] is currently implemented upon AIDA [Devin & Duquesnoy (1987)], using LE_LISP [Chailloux (1987)] and X_WINDOWS.

Let us now demontrate the expressive and reutilisability power of ADA++, giving a description of a class hierarchy. The example below describes the design of a class DAG (Directed Acyclic Graph) from specialization of previously existing classes: LIST, SET, VERTEX, SET_OF_NODE, GRAPH, GRAPH_ACYCLIC, GRAPH_ORIENTED.
LIST is a generic class with one private type (for its elements) as generic parameter.
SET is a class which inherits from LIST; it is consequently a generic class. SET specializes the method INSERT in such a way to prevent duplication in a set.
VERTEX is a class which defines a vertex by his name and a set of adjacent vertices.

14   Forestier et al : Class and Inheritance Extension

This class imports the class SET and instanciates this one with the name of the vertex. VERTEX provides some methods to denote a vertex, to add a link between two vertices, etc.

SET_OF_NODE is an instanciation of the class SET with the type VERTEX as element type.

GRAPH, descendant of the class SET_OF_NODE, imports the class VERTEX and specializes the methods which add a link, a vertex, etc.

GRAPH_ORIENTED and GRAPH_ACYCLIC are two descendants of the class GRAPH. They both redefine the method which adds a link: the first one indicates that edges are oriented and the second one verifies that there is no cycle in the graph.

The class DAG inherits from both classes above and specializes the method which adds a link using the two inherited methods.

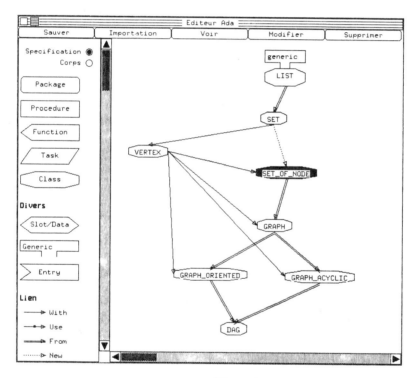

- Figure 2 -

Acknowledgements

This project is developed in collaboration with Ilog and Thomson CSF. It is supported by GRECO-CNRS in programming.

References.

D. G. Bobrow (1983). The LOOPS manual. Rank Xerox, Inc., Palo Alto, USA.

D. G. Bobrow, L.G DeMichiel, R. P. Gabriel, S. E. Keene, G. Kiczales, D. A.Moon (1988). Common Lisp Object System Specification. Draft submitted to X3JI3 march 1988 (ISO/IEC JTC1/SC 22/WG 16 LISP N. 10).

G. Booch (1987). Software componant with Ada structures, tools and subsystems. The Benjamin/cumming Publishing Company, Inc.

R. Buhr (1984). System Design with Ada. Prentice-Hall.

L. Cardelli, P. Wegner (1985). On Understanding Types, Data Abstraction, and Polymorphism. ACM Computing Surveys V. 17, N. 4 (Dec).

G. Chailloux (1987). Le-lisp V15.21 Le manuel de référence (1987). ILOG - 9, rue royale, 75008 PARIS.

B. Cox (1986). Object Oriented Programming : an evolutionnary approach . Addison Wesley.

M. Devin, P. Duquesnoy (1987). Aida: Le manuel de référence. ILOG - 9, rue royale, 75008 PARIS.

J.P. Forestier, C. Fornarino, P. Franchi (1988). ADACOP: Programation Objet Conviviale pour Ada. Conférence francophone Ada, Bruxelles.

A. Goldberg, D. Robson (1983). SMALLTALK-80 The language and its implementation. Addison Wesley.

J.A. Hendler, P. Wegner (1986) Viewing Object-Oriented Programming as an enhancement of data abstraction methodology. Proceeding of the 9th Annual Hawai International Conference on System Sciences.

D. Levi (1988). Problèmes de réutilisation lié au typage, application à une extension de langage Ada. Thèse de doctorat, university of Nice (France).

LRM Ada, ANSI/MIL-STD1815A (1983). Reference Manual for the Ada programming language. US Departement of Defense 1983.

B. Meyer (1986). Genericity versus Inheritance. OOPSLA 86 Special Issue of Sigplan Notices.

B. Meyer (1987). The Eiffel User's Manuel. Interactive Software Engineering Inc. Goleta, USA.

E. Perez Perez (1988). Simumulatig Inheritance with Ada. ACM press Ada letters V.8 N.5 1988.

G. Persch, G. Winterstein, M. Dausmann, S. Drossopoulou. (1980). Overloading in Preliminary Ada . Sigplan Notices V.15 N.11 Nov. 1980.

B. Shriver & P. Wegner (1987). Research Directions in Object-Oriented Programming. The MIT Press Series in Computer Systems. Cambridge, Massachusetts. London, England.

R. Simonian, M. Crone (1988). InnovAda: True Object-Oriented Programming in Ada. Journal of Object-Oriented Programming. V. 1 N. 4 (nov/dec 1988).

A. Snyder (1986). Encapsulation and Inheritance in Object-oriented Programming Langages. OOPSLA 86 Special Issue of Sigplan Notices.

SPS (1988). Classic-Ada is a software tool developed by Software Productivity Solutions, Inc., P.O. Box 361697, Melbourne, Florida 32935. USA.

B. Stroustrup (1986). The C++ programming language. Addisson-Wesley.

B. Stroustrup (1987). What is "Object-Oriented Programming" ?. ECOOP 87. Bigre + Globule N.54

H. Touati (1987). Is Ada an Object Oriented Programming Language. Sigplan Notices V.22 May (1987).

P. Wegner (1983). On the unification of data and program abstraction in Ada. Proceeding of the 10th Annual Symposium of Programming Langages. ACM New York.

A. Yonezawa et M. Tokoro (1986). Object Oriented Concurrent Programming. MIT Press Series in Computer Systems (1986).

DYNAMIC BINDING AND INHERITANCE IN AN
OBJECT-ORIENTED ADA DESIGN

C. M. Donaldson
Software Productivity Solutions, Inc.
Indialantic, Florida 32903 USA

Abstract: This paper describes an object-oriented design language and toolset, collectively called Classic-Ada.™ The language includes all of Ada and a set of extensions to support dynamic binding and inheritance in an approach loosely modeled after Smalltalk. These extensions are automatically translated by the toolset into compilable Ada code. The paper presents some of the advantages provided by such an approach, particularly increased reuse and adaptability.

Introduction

Object-oriented programming languages (OOPLS) have been used successfully for several years for artificial intelligence, simulation, human-computer interaction and programming environment applications. In fact, many of the ideas behind object-oriented programming have roots in SIMULA, a simulation language developed in the late 1960s (Dahl and Nygaard, 1966). Products such as C++, Objective-C, FLAVORS and Loops are all popular examples of object-oriented languages and development environments.

The basic primitive in object-oriented languages is an object--a set of encapsulated data and operations that manipulate the data. A class is a prototypical description of a type of object, and includes operations (methods) and data common to all subclasses and instance objects (an instance object is a specific object of a class). Booch (1987) describes how class and instance objects may be represented in Ada, using generics, packages that export private types, instances of private types and packages that serve as abstract state machines.

Abstraction and specialization are supported in object-oriented languages with inheritance. Inheritance allows new, specialized objects to be built from generalized class objects, instead of being entirely recoded. A class object inherits methods and data from its parent class, or superclass. An instance object exhibits the behavior defined and inherited by its associated class. Ada provides support for limited, static forms of inheritance through the use of generics and derived types.

Interaction among objects is accomplished through requests for operations, or sending of messages to objects that perform the desired operations. Upon receipt of a message, an object responds by invoking the appropriate operation (method). Object-oriented languages support dynamic binding, permitting execution-time determination of which object invokes a method. In Ada, subprogram calls are statically bound during compilation.

How does Ada fit in with all this hOOPla? Strictly speaking, Ada is not an object-oriented programming language (see Wegner 1987, Seidewitz 1987 and Stroustrup 1988). There appears to be a growing consensus that a "true" object-oriented programming language must minimally support data abstraction, information hiding, dynamic binding and inheritance.

There has been discussion in the literature on how to simulate, in Ada, the inheritance and dynamic binding capabilities of object-oriented programming languages. Two recent reports discuss the use of exported records and derived types to simulate inheritance. Quanrud (1988) describes a process of exporting and redefining records as derived types to inherit operations, noting that there seems to be "no easy way to add variables to those already defined for an object," thus limiting one's ability to add new operations for an object. Perez (1988) provides extensive examples on how to implement a "simulation" approach to inheritance. Of recent interest also is an article resulting from the Arcadia project at the University of California at Irvine, describing an object-oriented design of a User Interface Management System (UIMS) for a software environment. The developers designed the UIMS using inheritance and dynamic binding and implemented a prototype with "an imperfect and somewhat labor-intensive mapping to the implementation language [Ada] ..." (see Young and Taylor, et al., 1988).

Ada provides language support for limited inheritance and static (but not dynamic) binding. The "simulation" approaches discussed do not significantly reduce the amount of source code that must be written (a proven benefit of object-oriented programming languages). In addition, we are uncomfortable with the increased cognitive complexity introduced into the design process by such approaches. We've concluded that the most accurate and convenient way to incorporate inheritance and dynamic binding in an Ada design is to use an object-oriented design language that directly supports dynamic binding and inheritance, and is automatically translated into Ada code.

Classic-Ada Language and Toolset

As a result of internal research and development, we have developed an object-oriented design language and supporting toolset, collectively called Classic-Ada. The language incorporates all of Ada and adds a few additional constructs for:

- Class objects to encapsulate methods and state behavior
- Superclass declarations to specify inheritance
- Class and instance methods to define operations for class and instance objects
- A **send** statement to support message passing between objects and dynamic binding of operations to objects
- Object "handle" mechanisms for creating new instance objects and referencing existing objects
- Instance variables to describe properties or states of instance objects

These constructs are supported by nine additional reserved words: **class, method, destroy, superclass, send, self, instance, instantiate** and **super**. Classic-Ada predefines the following set of "object handle" mechanisms: a type Object_Id (used to declare variables that point to instance objects), a constant for referencing class objects (*class_name*.class_object) and the functions **instantiate** (used to create new instance objects), **self** and **super** (used by an object to refer to itself and its superclass, respectively). The latter functions return the type Object_Id.

Classic-Ada class objects have specifications and bodies, very similar to Ada packages, and also contain class and instance methods, and instance variables, to be used by instance objects of the class and inherited by subclasses. Class objects may contain Ada subprograms, data types and variables, generic instantiations and exceptions, and are translated into Ada packages by the Classic-Ada processor.

The inheritance facilities add some visibility rules which seem contradictory to those rules familiar to an Ada programmer. Instance variables, which are declared only in class <u>bodies</u>, are visible to subclasses and are referenced without qualification. Class and method names are globally visible and can be referenced anywhere within a program by their simple names and without a **with** clause.

An instance object represents a specific object of a class. The behavior of an instance object is defined by the instance methods and variables defined and inherited by its associated class. The inherited methods and state of an instance object are implemented by Ada code that resides in the appropriate class object, thereby eliminating coding redundancy. Instance objects, represented as dynamic Ada data structures, are created with the **instantiate** function and can be eliminated with the **destroy** statement, which uses the host Ada compiler's unchecked deallocation facilities.

Both class and instance objects are active in a Classic-Ada design, a concept that is difficult to appreciate at the beginning, as it would appear that class objects simply serve as "templates" for instance objects. However, class objects also respond to messages, typically to create and initialize instance objects but also in cases where subclasses add behavior by overriding inherited methods and then invoking the overridden methods of superclasses. Class objects can also maintain information about the existence of their instances and perform "global" broadcasts to update instance objects, delete them, etc. Thus, an entire set of operations can be performed by the application with a single request (invocation of the class object's method).

Class and instance methods are invoked upon receipt of a message **send.** The first parameter of a **send** is an object handle (a variable of type Object_Id), a identifying the object to which the message is sent. The second parameter of the **send** is the method to be invoked. Subsequent parameters correspond to actual parameters being passed to the method, if any. Because the object is identified as a variable parameter of the **send**, messages are dynamically bound to objects at execution-time. This allows the same **send** statement to invoke the same operation for different objects during execution, depending on events in the application.

In Ada, operations are statically bound and thus must be specifically coded for each anticipated event, typically through the use of **case** or **if then else** logic. If a new object is added, the existing code must be modified, recompiled and relinked. In Classic-Ada, the addition of a new object will require no change to existing code. The new object, once translated by Classic-Ada, may be compiled and linked in with the existing application.

If an object receives a message requesting invocation of a method it does not have, the message is propagated up the class inheritance hierarchy until it is recognized by an object or, if none exists, a predefined exception, Method_Not_Found, is raised. A method defined in a superclass may be <u>overridden</u> in a subclass if it is redefined with the same name and same parameter profile. Methods are typically overridden in order to provide more specific functionality for a particular class.

Classic-Ada supports <u>differentiation</u> of methods, allowing variants of a method to be defined with the same name but different formal parameter profiles. This is distinctly different than overloading of subprogram names in Ada, where the compiler distinguishes among the overloaded subprograms by their parameter types. In fact, Classic-Ada prohibits methods with the same name and same formal parameter names in the same order, but with different base types in the parameter positions.

Using Inheritance and Dynamic Binding with Ada

Classic-Ada has been used to develop a proprietary User Interface Management System (UIMS), which is a collection of reusable components for building application user interfaces. The UIMS includes high-level facilities for building and manipulating windows, menus, forms, various kinds of graphics, etc., and works with both Digital Equipment Corporation (DEC) VT100 (character-based) terminals and workstations running XWindows.

The UIMS has been applied to a variety of software tool developments (also designed using Classic-Ada). Principle advantages gained by using the UIMS include the ability to rapidly prototype user interfaces and to build application code that is truly independent of the user interface. The architecture imposed by UIMS has the user interface driving the application, such that the underlying application model has no knowledge of how it is displayed.

Let's now step through a small example of how inheritance and dynamic binding capabilties provided by Classic-Ada can be applied using facilities of the UIMS. Figure 1 illustrates a subset of a UIMS inheritance hierarchy used in this example.

The class Graphic Object defines methods and instance variables common to various geometric shapes that may be displayed on the screen or in a window. The class objects Vertical Scroll Bar and String Rendering inherit methods such as initialize, enable, disable, hide, show, resize, move, etc., from Graphic Object. The String Rendering class object defines methods for rendering string data on a display surface; the

Integer Rendering class is a subclass of String Rendering and overrides some of the inherited methods of String Rendering.

Figure 1. Sample Inheritance Hierachy

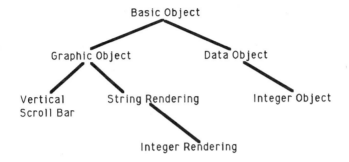

Here is a class specification for Integer Rendering:

```
WITH Cartesian;
CLASS Integer_Rendering IS
    SUPERCLASS String_Rendering;

    -- Create a new Integer_Rendering instance object

    FUNCTION Create (
        Data_Object : Object_Id; Surface : Object_Id;
        Extent : Cartesian.Box) RETURN Object_Id;

    METHOD Create (
        Data_Object : Object_Id; Surface : Object_Id;
        Extent : Cartesian.Box; An_Object : OUT Object_Id);

    -- Initialize a newly created Integer_Rendering object

    INSTANCE METHOD Initialize (
        Data_Object : Object_Id; Surface : Object_Id);

    -- The user has edited the rendering, update the
    -- corresponding data object

    INSTANCE METHOD Update_Data (Valid : OUT Boolean);

    -- The data object has changed value, update the
    -- .rendering

    INSTANCE METHOD Update;

    -- Delete object receiving this message

    INSTANCE METHOD Delete (Extent : OUT Cartesian.Box);

END Integer_Rendering;
```

Notice that Integer_Rendering provides both a function and a method Create. This allows the application to use static binding of the Create operation when the object is known. Because Classic-Ada is a hybrid OOPL, the designer can choose static binding when dynamic binding isn't needed.

The class Data defines methods and instance variables for all data objects managed by the UIMS. The UIMS separates data from its rendering, so that multiple renderings of an object can be easily created, managed and added to an application's user interface. The actual storage representation of a data object (i.e., integer, real, etc.) is defined in terms of subclasses of Data (for example, Integer). An application's user interface manages the attachment of rendering objects to data objects.

Figure 2 illustrates our small example application, the Vertical Bar (Vbar) demonstration. The VBar demonstration presents to the interactive user a vertical bar that is defined by three values: its length, which is the outside rectangle; its value, which is the inside rectangle shown in black; and an offset, which is the space at the top between the length and the value. When the application is invoked, the vertical bar is initialized with a length of 100, a value of 50 and an offset of 0.

Figure 2. Vertical Bar Demonstration

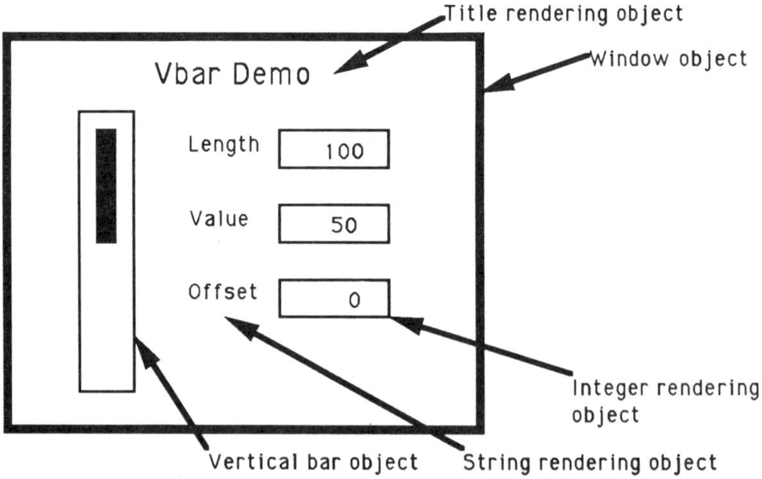

Users can interactively manipulate the appearance of the vertical bar by changing the values for the length, value and offset (the rectangles in which the values

appear are editable fields and are traversed using arrow keys from the keyboard). Each
time a new value is input, the appearance of the vertical bar adjusts automatically.

Each of the items shown in Figure 2 are instance objects. The words
"Vbar Demo" represent an instance of the Title Rendering Object (a subclass of String
Rendering); the presentations of "Length," "Value" and "Offset" are instances of the
String Rendering Object (the words are themselves String objects). The vertical bar
shown is an instance of the Vertical Scroll Bar object and the window is an instance of a
Window object (not shown in the inheritance hierarchy). Each of the fields in which the
values are provided are instances of the Integer Rendering object.

Suppose in the example that the user currently has the cursor at the Value
input and hits the "up arrow" key to indicate a movement up to the Length value input.
The sequence of events in the application are shown in Figure 3.

Figure 3. Communication Among VBar Objects

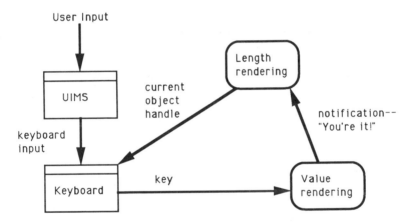

The UIMS is constantly monitoring user actions; thus, the user's input
from the keyboard is sent from UIMS to the Keyboard object (a package in this design).
Keyboard maps the escape sequence to a key type ("up arrow") and sends this key to the
current object (in this case, the Value Rendering instance). The **send** statement is:

```
SEND (Keyboard_Cursor, Process_Key, Key => Up_Arrow,
      Control => False, Alternate => False);
```

where Keyboard_Cursor, a variable of type Object_Id, is a handle to the object that
currently has the cursor. Keyboard_Cursor's value is passed in as a parameter to

Keyboard when an object receives the cursor (the object calls a procedure Set_Keyboard_Focus in Keyboard).

Keyboard uses this same send statement to pass keys to Length Rendering, Value Rendering and Offset Rendering--this is an example of dynamic binding in Classic-Ada. Keyboard has no knowledge of what objects can have the cursor, it simply receives handles to these and passes keys as appropriate. New objects can be added and can receive keys from Keyboard with no change to code in Keyboard.

Process_Key is a message that Keyboard sends to the current object (in this case, Value Rendering). Process_Key is an instance method defined in String Rendering (thus inherited by Integer Rendering and defined for use by Value Rendering). Process_Key is invoked, causing a message to be sent to Length Rendering requesting that it accept the cursor. Length Rendering accepts the cursor and calls Set_Keyboard_Focus in Keyboard to give it a handle to the object that now has the cursor (Length Rendering).

Conclusions and Future Directions

We have found inheritance and dynamic binding to be useful in reducing the overall amount of code that must be written, significantly reducing the amount of code that must be recompiled when a new object is added to an application, increasing the amount of code that can be reused across applications, and enabling us to build applications that are easily modified and extended.

Learning how to apply inheritance and dynamic binding has taken time. The UIMS, for example, underwent two complete design revisions before we were satisfied with the resulting implementation. The process of generalizing and specializing classes to form an optimal inheritance hierarchy is very iterative and often it is a pragmatic decision on whether to move an operation up to a superclass. Use of dynamic binding dramatically impacts an application's architecture; laying out an application's inter-object communications is a skill that we are still learning.

The current toolset includes an object generator, builder, dictionary and reporting utilities. The object generator checks the Classic-Ada syntax and semantics and generates Ada source code that implements the application. The builder generates the Classic-Ada executive for linking into the application; the executive supports dynamic binding of messages to objects at run-time. To support incremental object processing, the dictionary maintains class and method definitions for all Classic-Ada units processed by the object generator. Reporting utilities include an inheritance hierarchy listing, a dictionary of method definitions, a mapping of Classic-Ada methods to generated Ada procedures and an execution-time trace of message sends.

Plans for the future include the addition of interactive browsing utilities to identify and manage inherited state and operations, possibly multiple inheritance and the addition of persistence to store objects in a Classic-Ada database.

References

Booch, G., Software Engineering with Ada, Benjamin-Cummings Publishing Company, copyright 1983. Menlo Park, Ca.

Booch, G., Software Components with Ada: Structures, Tools, and Subsystems, Benjamin-Cummings Publishing Company, copyright 1987.

Dahl, O.J. and Nygaard, K., "SIMULA--an Algol-based Simulation Language," Communications of the ACM, Vol. 9, pp. 671- 678, 1966.

Perez E., "Simulating Inheritance with Ada," ACM Ada Letters, Volume VIII, Number 5, September/October 1988, pp. 37- 46.

Quanrud, R., Generic Architecture Study, Final Report 3451-4-14/2, prepared by SofTech, Inc., for U.S. Army CECOM, Ft. Monmouth, New Jersey, January 1988.

Seidewitz, E., "Object-oriented Programming in Smalltalk and Ada," OOPSLA 87 Proceedings, pp. 202-213.

Stroustrup, B., "What is Object-Oriented Programming?", IEEE Software, May 1988, pp. 10-20.

Wegner, P., "Dimensions of an Object-Based Language Design," OOPSLA 87 Proceedings, pp. 168-182.

Young, M., Taylor, R., and Troup, D., "Software Environment Architectures and User Interface Facilities," IEEE Transactions on Software Engineering, Volume 14, Number 6, June 1988, pp. 697-708.

Language Extensions to Allow Rapid Mode Shifting in the Ada Programming Language

Jan van Katwijk, Hans Toetenel

Delft University of Technology Faculty of Technical Mathematics and Informatics 132 Julianalaan Delft, The Netherlands

Abstract.
The Ada language has been designed with applications in the real-time domain in mind. In this paper it is argued that language extensions of Ada are inevitable in order to achieve some features important in the real-time domain, in particular mode shifting. We propose two models for extending the language, one based on termination semantics, modelled in terms of exceptions and exception handling. The other one based on resumption semantics. We discuss a syntactical framework in which the semantics are made clear.

1. Introduction

The Ada language (1983) has been designed with applications in the embedded systems domain in mind. Ever since its actual use, comments are made on problems with its effectiveness in applications in the aforementionned domain. Generally three areas of concern are identified: (i) (potential) problems with the efficiency of the implementation of various tasking constructs (see for an overview of problems and some performance data e.g. Huijsman et al (1988), Katwijk & Toetenel (1988), (ii) problems with the distribution of Ada tasking programs over multiprocessor systems and computer networks (see e.g. Atkinson (1988)) and, (iii) limitations in the way tasks may influence each other (see for an overview of the problem area e.g. the report of a workshop on Real-time Ada issues (Workshop (1988))). One of the topics in this workshop was concerned with extensions to the Ada language required for allowing tasks to influence each other such that a smooth modelling and implementation of *rapid mode shifting* is possible. It was generally felt that, in order to accomplish such features, language extensions were inevitable. The nature of language extensions of such a kind, though oriented towards expressing changes of control, deviates from the existing constructs influencing change-of-control such as *if-then-else* statements and *case* statements.

In order to address rapid mode shifting, we developed some language extensions that were presented at the aforementioned workshop. Based on experiences with these extensions and results of the workshop, we redesigned these extensions. These resulting language extensions are the central topic of this paper. We exemplify the need for language extensions with which tasks have possibilities to influence each other first. Next, a set of straight-forward language extensions addressing this problem are discussed (these language extensions were the main topic of a previous paper by Toetenel & Katwijk (1988)) and the limitations of the extensions are given. The main topic of this paper is a second set of designed language extensions to address the problem of tasks influencing each other. We discuss the relative merits of these extensions and we present an example of their use.

At Delft University of Technology we have developed a prototype implementation of almost the whole Ada programming language (the so-called Ada-— implementation (see for details Katwijk (1987)). Although the implemented language has some restrictions, it includes the full Ada tasking semantics. The implementation of Ada tasking has got quite some attention in this implementation; the annotated listing of the tasking kernel used is separately presented by Toetenel & Katwijk (1989). One of the obvious advantages of having such an implementation is that it gives a perfect vehicle for excercising implementation techniques and language extensions.

We prototyped the language extensions that are proposed here in order to get some experiences in their practical use. Our first conclusions are fairly positive and optimistic. Apart from the syntactical appearance the proposed extensions seem to be sufficient.

2.   The need for asynchronous transfer of control

A general issue in real-time applications is the ease with which a so-called *mode shift* within an executing task can be executed. The main characteristic of such a mode shift is that a program performing a certain activity is forced to switch quickly into doing something else as a reaction on some external stimulus. Reaction within an acceptable time limit on the external stimulus that triggered the mode shift is often required by the event causing the external stimulus. A particular case where mode-shifts often are required as a means to solve a problem, is in real-time applications when there is an explicit dependency of program parts on time constraints. In particular, cyclic tasks e.g. often have the property that the actions specified to be performed within a cycle, have to be performed *within* a given amount of time. Not obeying the constraint on this time limit may give rise to timing-error conditions. Recovery from such an erroneous situation is usually implemented using a construction similar to a mode shift: the task object is brought into some form of *error mode*, in which an attempt is made to recover from the consequences of the error and - possibly - to repair the cause of the error.

The Ada language in its current form enforces the use of polling in implementing a mode shift. Although polling may lead to an acceptable solution in situations that are *not* time critical, for most time-critical applications the method leads to an unacceptable overhead. Polling is usually implemented in terms of conditional entry call and conditional selective wait constructs. It is believed that the application of these constructs is rather expensive in terms of time (this assumption is acknowledged by empirical results as reported by e.g. Katwijk & Toetenel (1988)) and a situation in which the overhead is deemed unacceptable is soon reached.

The only mechanism provided by the Ada programming language for a task to *asynchronously* affect the behaviour of another task (a prerequisite for being able to directly model mode shifts in the language) is the *abort* statement. A first order approximation to the implementation of an asynchronous change in control can be obtained by aborting a task and replacing it with a new instance. Such a solution is hardly appropriate, it is crude and - as discussed by various authors, e.g. Baker (1988) - it does not always give the desired results.

Another solution that at first side seems applicable is to have a distinct task object for each mode a task can be in, and to manipulate the priorities of the task objects to achieve the desired effect. A task object that implements an active mode will run with a high priority, tasks corresponding to modes that are not currently active, will get a low priority. Drawbacks of such a solution are twofold. First, even tasks with a low priority may become active if no other tasks are eligible (implying that the task representing the prohibited mode will execute sooner or later). Second, dynamically changing of priorities is not supported in the Ada language.

In order to allow the implementation of rapid mode shifting, other approaches are required. If language extensions are considered, extensions supporting some form of asynchronous interruption of the flow of control come first in mind, due to the nature of the problem.

A historical survey shows that two different points of view are apparent when discussing interruptions of the flow of control by exceptional events (see e.g. Ghezzi & Jazayeri (1987)). One view supports implicitly called units as procedure calls on receiving a signal, with control returning to the point where the exception occurred (i.e. a *resumption* model). In the other view an exception is reacted upon by *terminating* the currently executing unit with a transfer of control to an exception handler (i.e. a *termination* model). The latter model is the one adopted for handling exceptions in the Ada language. An approach in this spirit seems therefore a suitable basis for extending the Ada programming language.

In the remainder of this paper we present two lines of solutions, the first one is based on a termination model, using the existing mechanism of Ada exceptions. The second line is based on a resumption model.

3.   Asynchronous transfer of control: a simple approach

It is a tempting thought to extend the notion of exceptions to allow the raising of an exception in another thread of control. Syntactically, such an extension may look like:

raise *exception_name* **in** *some_task*

In this extended raise statement the notion *exception_name* identifies the exception to be raised, the notion *some_task* identifies the thread of control that is to be interrupted by the exception.

The semantics of raising an exception in another thread of control are, roughly speaking, the same as the semantics of ordinary exceptions. Whenever such an exception is raised, control in the receiving thread of control is transferred to an exception handler enclosing - in the same sense as with ordinary exceptions - the point where the exception is raised. The acting thread of control continues it execution as though a *null* statement was executed.

This solution seems perfectly reasonable from the actor's point of view: once a condition is detected prescribing the notification of another task, a remote exception is raised. On the other hand, from the server's point of view this solution may not be desirable at all. The occurrence of exceptions is completely unpredictable and the server does not have any possibility at all to prevent a dictated change in the flow of control which results from an exception raised by an actor.

Other problems, discussed in detail by Toetenel & Katwijk (1988), have to do with semantics, e.g. what is the meaning of an exception raised by another thread of control when the server is itself in the process of handling an exception, prior to dispatching the latter?

In general, the structure of a server, anticipating a remote exception, will be as depicted below.

```
task body example is
begin
  loop
    begin
      -- | do some periodic actions
      -- | actions to be performed
    exception
        when some_exception   => ...
          -- | normal handling of exceptions
        when special_exception => ..
          -- | react on mode shift
          -- | repair whatever is to be repaired
    end;
  end loop;
end example;
```

As may be clear from this structure, the computations to be performed in a cycle may get lost completely once an exception is raised by another thread of control. Our experiences convinced us that it is essential to allow the server side to choose how to react upon the stimulus. The presented solution seems therefore, in its current form, too crude. Toetenel & Katwijk (1988) discussed several extensions to the plain model in some detail. These extensions had in common that their purpose was to limit the sensitivity of a thread of control for remote exceptions. Possibilities were created for tasks to allow - either explicit or implicit - selective listening, i.e. the possibility that in some region of text or span of time a thread of control would be deaf to remote exceptions.

The implementation of the above model turned out to be straight-forward. A prototype implementation - including both the syntactical and the semantical extensions - took only a few days.

Nevertheless, a solution along these lines remained unsatisfactory. Experiments with the extended exception mechanism convinced us that, although perfectly adequate from the actor's point of view, exceptions raised by other threads of control introduce an asynchronicity that is undesirable from the server's point of view. Having the control flow radically changed on unpredictable moments and positions, from elsewhere and not based on the semantics of the instructions executed by the current thread of control, leads to uncontrollable and unpredictable situations. Managing the asynchronous interruption of a thread of control turned out to be a main bottleneck. In spite of all extensions that were proposed and that were aiming at a greater degree of controlability, it was hard to keep the reaction on the external stimulus under control.

4.   A second approach to modeling asynchronous transfer of control

A close look at the language extensions and the way these extensions are used to implement mode shifting, shows that the desired sequence of events is: (1) an asynchronous event draws the attention of the server to a certain event, and (2) the event is transformed in a synchronous event as quickly as possible, to allow communication to take place between the server and the actor over the cause of the event, and (3) if possible, the server is allowed to continue at the place where the asynchronous event was noticed.

The desired sequence of events resembles the interrupt model as applied in e.g. PL/I (see for a description e.g. Ghezzi & Jazayeri (1987)). This interrupt model is known to be dangerous, in particular, care must be taken not to allow a transfer of control from the interrupt handling routine to other places.

We propose extensions to the Ada language, based on the interrupt model. These extensions will be formulated as much as possible in terms of the Ada primitives. This approach leads to rather rigid syntactical structures. Our aim is however to concentrate on the semantics of the extensions. We leave it up to others to find a suitable syntactic framework to express these extensions.

The extensions create the possibility for any thread of control to interrupt another thread of control and provide a framework to have synchronous communication between the interrupted and the interrupting threads of control to take place. This synchronous communication is expressed in terms of existing Ada language constructs. If taken literally, it may suffer from a performance problem.

At the actor side we introduce the construct:

```
    raise in taskname
/ select
    taskname. error_entry (parameters)
    else
    statements
    end select/;
```

The construction is - with purpose - almost completely expressed in terms of existing Ada language constructs. The *raise* statement acts as an interrupt statement. Once the receiving thread of control (identified by *taskname*) is interrupted, the actor and the receiver - possibly - are made ready to *synchronously* transfer data from and to each other. At the interrupting side, this synchronous transfer of control syntactically - and to a large extent semantically - takes the form of a conditional entry call. The *else* clause will be executed if the interrupted thread of control has no associated *selective wait* construct. The statements in the *else* part can be used to react on the unwillingness of the server to accept a request for communication.

To allow service, the structure of a potential server task is extended with a *remote exception handler*. Syntactically, the handler appears following the regular exception handlers in a task body (We associate such an exception handler to a task body only, it makes no sense to have an interrupt handler associated with inner blocks or procedures.) An outline of the syntactical structure of the extensions is given below:

```
    remote  [[conditional_selective_construct]
        statements exception_handler]  end remote
```

In more detail:

```
    task body  ...
    .. declarations
    begin
    ... statements of the task body
/ exception  ...]       -- exception handlers
-- the extensions to the task body follow here
-- with extra indent
        / remote
          / select
            accept error_entry  do
                user-provided statements
            end;
          or else null;
          end select;
        /
```

> ... *statements for further interrupt handling*
> **exception**
>   **when others** => **null** ;
>   **end remote**]
> **end** ;

The keyword *remote* identifies the handling place in the code of a task body of the interruption of the thread of control. The construct is terminated by a - syntactically superfluous - specification of *end remote* in order to indicate that program continuation differs from the textual program order.

Whenever an interrupting exception is received, the (optional) code following the keyword *remote* is executed after which the thread of control is resumed where the exception was caught. The code in the *remote* body is such that a single entry call may be served after which some statements may be executed. If an entry call is served, care must be taken that no exception raised during the handling of the rendezvous causes a transfer of control in the server after handling the *remote code*. Therefore, an exception handler, catching all kinds of exceptions, is obligatory. This exception handler is associated to the construct to ensure that no transfer of control - either erroneous or planned - outside the handler takes place. Further processing of data in the interrupted mode of the task may be performed by the statements following the conditional selective wait construct.

During handling of the rendezvous, the actor and the server may communicate data that is important for deciding the cause of the need for this mode shift. Based on this information, the server may alter the values of actual parameters such that a controlled switch in operation at the actor side may take place. A certain amount of synchronization between actor and server takes place, the server may e.g. restore the conditions for the normal mode of control of the actor.

Notice that care is taken to allow for situations in which the actor does *not* want to communicate data with the server and for situations where the server does not want to communicate data. The server side contains a conditional selective wait construct, so that in cases where the actor only executes a

raise in *task_name*

construct, no locking occurs at the server side. For cases where the actor wants to communicate data with the server while the latter does not want to take part in this communication and no selective wait construct is specified at the server side the actor side contains a conditional entry call.

It will be clear that the syntactic form of the proposed language extensions is rather rigid. The expressiveness of the constructs that are used in the extensions, is less than that of the same constructs in other places, basically because there are no alternative constructs in those places. Syntactical shorthands, using other keywords, are required.

5. Rapid mode shifting: an example

In this section we briefly discuss the solution for a problem mentioned by Toetenel & Katwijk (1988). In that paper paradigms were derived for expressing solutions to the problem of rapid mode shifting using remote exceptions.

The example comprises an implementation for the problem stated in the next informal and incomplete specification:

A real-time system consists of a sensory device which records discrete measurement values, resulting from monitoring an analogous signal. The recorded values may alter very quickly (e.g. within 1 ms). Assumed is a range within which the values are "correct", and outside this range the values can be considered erroneous or even fatal. The monitored signal must be sampled with a rate as high as possible. Once the signal starts to deflect it is assumed that it cannot recover without repair from some controlling device.

The system contains a hierarchical sub-system consisting of mutual autonomous layers, that is processing independently from the sensory device provided that the recorded values are correct. If these values start to deflect, some layer of the sub-system must be informed, on which this layer will shift its current mode of execution to a new mode in which it will try to repair the cause of deflection of the signal. It will use different repair strategies for both erroneous and fatal signals. If the recovery succeeds, it will re-enter its normal mode of execution, otherwise it will alarm a more advanced sub-system followed by re-entering its normal execution mode.

An encoding of the solution to the above mentioned problem expressed in the Ada programming language using the extensions presented in the previous section, is given below.

We distinguish between three modes of operation, expressed in terms of Ada values as:

type *MODE* **is** *(GREEN, RED, ALARM);*

GREEN indicates the normal mode of operation for the system and its sub-systems; **RED** indicates an erroneous value of a signal, in this mode of operation code is executed to repair the deflection of the signal; and **ALARM** indicates a fatal value. In this mode of operation code has to be executed to adjust the signal source.

The structure of the solution is straight-forward, a task called *SAMPLER* periodically samples a sensor device. As soon as the sampler has detected an *erroneous* or a *fatal* result value, an asynchronous activity is initiated in which the *LEVEL_X* task (implementing a task in which a rapid-mode shift is to be performed) is interrupted to take actions on the erroneous value. Having detected an erroneous or a fatal value, sampling will stop until a repaired value is received, indicating (i) the corrected value, and (ii) the fact that the sampling device is repaired. Waiting is implemented, taking advantage of the rendezvous being synchronous.

```
 1 task body SAMPLER is
 2 begin
 3   -- | initialising the sampling
 4   loop
 5     RESULT := SAMPLE (...);
 6     -- | process resulting values
 7     if ERRONEOUS_OR_FATAL (RESULT)
 8     then
 9       -- | place interrupt and pass result value
10       raise in LEVEL_X
11       select
12         LEVEL_X. ERROR (RESULT);
13       else null;
14       end select;
15     end if;
16   end loop;
17 end SAMPLER;
```

The outline for the LEVEL_X task body is given below. As soon as a remote exception is caught, a (conditional) selective wait construct is executed to obtain the data involved from the sampling task. The code in this repair "mode" dispatches between erroneous and fatal values and attempts a repair of the value and the sensory device. If no repair is possible, a remote exception is executed to put yet another task into a repair mode.

```
18 task body LEVEL_X is
19 -- | appropriate declarations
20 begin
21   loop
22     -- | do normal actions
23   end loop;
24 -- | exception handlers, if any
25 remote
26   select
27     accept ERROR (X: in out value_type) do
28       if ERRONEOUS (X)
29       then
30         -- | repair the erroneous signal and pass it back
31       elsif FATAL (X)
32       then
33         -- | repair the signal and pass it back
34           if no repair is possible
```

```
35          then
36              raise in LEVEL_Y
37              select
38                  LEVEL_Y. ERROR (X);
39              else null;
40              end select;
41          end if;
42        end if;
43      end
44    or else null;
45    end select;
46        exception
47            when others = > null;
48        end remote
47  end LEVEL_X;
```

6.   Conclusions

In this paper we proposed some language extensions for the Ada programming language to support rapid mode shifting in real-time applications. The appearance of some of the proposed constructs would improve by providing a less rigid syntactic framework. Providing another syntactical framework, less rigid than the one suggested here, would also provide the opportunity to move some of the semantics - and the associated overhead of the presented forms of data transfer - to a run-time system. However, providing such a framework is, however, not the topic of this paper. We believe that the strength of the model is that the server is itself allowed to decide whether or not to react upon a request for a mode shift and, when expressing its intention, how to react upon the occurrence of an interruption of the thread of control. We believe that *any* solution - irrespective of its details - should obey this rule.

The extensions have the following properties: (i) it is fairly straight-forward to design an implementation strategy such that no overhead is incurred when the extensions are not invoked; and (ii) responding to a asynchronous event is followed by transforming the event to a synchronous one, so that subsequent actions can be expressed in available language constructs.

We must realize that some care must be taken in implementing mode shifting. Mode shifting must be seen as a reaction on an exceptional situation, whereby attempts are made to minimize the penalty for applying the construct when it is not used. As such it may be compared with exception handling within a single thread of control.

A precise definition of the semantics of the constructs still has to be given. A first question is: should it be allowed to respond on a remote exception when handling a remote exception? A related question is: should a task be allowed to raise a remote exception within its own thread of control?

These questions and others should be addressed prior to incorporating features as this one to the Ada-9x language.

7.   References

References.

Atkinson, C. (1988). Programming distributed systems in Ada in: IFIP/IFAC Working conference on Hardware and Software for Real-Time Process Control, Warsaw Preprints Vol I pp 37 - 50.

Reference Manual of the Ada Programming language (1983). U.S. Gouvernment, AJPO.

Baker, T. (1988) Improving immediacy in Ada In: (Workshop 1988)

Burns, A. (1985) Concurrent Programming in Ada. The Ada Companion Series, Cambridge University Press.

Ghezzi, C. & Jazayeri, M. (1987) Programming language concepts, Wiley, second edition.

Huijsman, R.D., Katwijk, J. van & Toetenel, W.J. (1987) Performance Aspects of Ada tasking in embedded systems Microprocessing and microprogramming 21 pp 301 - 310.

Katwijk J. van (1987) The Ada- compiler, On the design and implementation of an Ada compiler, PhD Thesis, Delft University of Technology, Faculty of Mathematics and Computer Science.

Katwijk, J. van & Toetenel W.J. (1988) An Ada Tasking implementation, Proceedings of the IFIP-IFAC conference on "Hardware and Software for Real-time process control" Warsaw. Preprints Vol I pp 15 - 36

Toetenel, W.J. & Katwijk, J. van (1988) Asynchronous transfer of control in Ada, In: (Workshop 1988)

Toetenel, W.J. & Katwijk, J. van (1989) An Ada tasking kernel: annotated listing, Report 89-XX; Reports of the Faculty of Mathematics and Computer Science, Delft University of Technology, Delft, The Netherlands.

Workshop (1988) 2nd International Workshop on real-time Ada issues, Manor House Hotel, Moretonhamstead, Devon England 31 may - june 3.

Part 2 Real Time Design

DRAGOON: An Ada-based Object Oriented Language for Concurrent, Real-Time, Distributed Systems.

Andrea Di Maio, Cinzia Cardigno
TXT S.p.A., Via della Guastalla 2, 20122 Milano (Italy)

Rami Bayan, Catherine Destombes
GSI Tecsi, 6 Cours Michelet, Paris La Defense (France)

Colin Atkinson
Imperial College, 180 Queen's Gate, London (U.K.)

Abstract. DRAGOON is a design and programming language that enriches Ada with the typical features of an object oriented paradigm and can be automatically translated into Ada. This paper describes how it can be used to design concurrent, distributable and dynamically reconfigurable applications.

Introduction

The design and implementation of large real-time software systems is a very challenging and critical task, due to the increasing complexity of such systems in terms of functional and efficiency requirements. The problem is further complicated by the distributed nature of many targets and by strict reliability requirements that introduce a need for the capability of dynamic reconfiguration. The most effective way of keeping down the cost of these applications is by encouraging the reuse of software components at different levels: design, coding, testing. Reuse will therefore become increasingly important in the future in order to produce competitive and reliable software.

A recent trend in developing large real-time applications of this kind is *object oriented design*, the advantages of which are quite well-known: data abstraction, information hiding, low coupling and strong cohesion of components, and so on. Several such methods and notations have been proposed which specifically consider Ada as the target language (Booch 1986), (Berard 1985), HOOD 1987). While these methods significantly improve the potential for reuse in Ada, they only represent a partial solution to the problem. Moreover they do not address the difficulties of distribution and reconfiguration at all. A much more powerful paradigm for increasing the reusability and extensibility of software is the object oriented programming model exemplified by languages such as Smalltalk 80 (Goldberg & Robson 1983), Eiffel (Meyer 1988), C++ Stroustrup 1986).

As well as promoting good programming practices such as modular design and separation of concerns, object oriented languages offers two main features for software reuse. The most important is *inheritance* which is essentially a mechanism for sharing knowledge amongst the various objects of a system. It enables the functionality of a new class to be defined by inheriting (i.e. reusing) the routines and state variables of previously defined classes, and either extending or restricting this set in some way to yield more specialisation. The other feature, known as *polymorhism*, depends on the fact that a subclass generally inherits all the methods and attributes of its parents, and can therefore be used in any context where one of its ancestors is expected. Consequently an instance variable defined to be of a given class can alternatively be set to refer to an object of any its descendants.

In view of the strengths of object oriented languages from the point of view of software reuse and extensibility (Wegner 1984) it would clearly be useful if this style of programming could somehow be supported in Ada. At first sight this goal seems to be unattainable, because although certain characteristics of object oriented languages can be simulated using packages and generics, Ada provides no direct support for the fundamental object oriented features of inheritance and polymorphism. Worse than that, Ada's strict typing scheme seems to be completely incompatible with polymorphism.

Although, these features cannot be programmed directly in Ada, it is possible to implement them in a higher level notation which maps into Ada. The DRAGON Esprit project (Gatti et al. 1988) has developed a technique by which a fully object oriented language, called DRAGOON (Distributable Reusable Ada Generated from an Object Oriented Notation), can be automatically mapped into standard Ada for execution. As well as providing inheritance and polymorphism DRAGOON (Di Maio & al. 1988) aims to support distribution and dynamic reconfiguration in a fully coherent, object oriented framework.

Although DRAGOON is a self contained programming language in its own right, since it is mapped into standard Ada it can equally well be regarded as a *design language* for developing Ada programs. Moreover, since DRAGOON is largely based on Ada, and the new object oriented features designed according to the Ada style, DRAGOON may also provide some useful ideas for the future evolution of Ada.

The DRAGOON Notation

The most important aspect of DRAGOON is that it provides a coherent framework for handling all aspects of programming, thus avoiding differences between implementation language, configuration language and operating system command language.

A major respect in which DRAGOON extends the power of Ada is in the possibility of declaring **classes** as the basic software components for modelling applications.

A class can be seen as an implementation of an *abstract data type*. In fact defining a class means describing the set of the subprograms (also called *methods*) that are visible and callable from outside. The details concerning the implementation of the class are hidden from external view and given inside a *class body* that encloses all those aspects that cannot be accessed from outside. An instance of a class is called a *dragoon object* and it is created by invoking a predefined method. A class can declare both subprograms and *instance variables* that either refer to objects of basic or user defined types or *dragoon* objects. The instance variables are enclosed in the body of a class and represent the *state* for all the instances of that class. The only way to access and/or modify the state of dragoon objects is by method calls. Furthermore, dragoon objects can communicate only via method calls.

From the reuse point of view, DRAGOON adds some value to the already powerful mechanisms offered by Ada: together with full-fledged genericity, DRAGOON supports inheritance and abstraction.

Inheritance, an essential feature of object-oriented paradigms, allows a class (called *heir* or *descendant*) to inherit all the features of another class (called *parent* or *ancestor*). The heir is more than a copy of its parent: it can add, modify and/or rename some of the features of the parent class. DRAGOON supports *multiple* inheritance since a class can inherit from more than one parent.

To illustrate, consider class DAISY_PRINTER, offering methods RESET and PRINT, and class GRAPHIC_DEVICE, offering method GRAPHIC_PRINT; class LASER_PRINTER, inherits from both DAISY_PRINTER and GRAPHIC_DEVICE, modifies and extends the methods of the parent classes (see fig. 1).

```
class DAISY_PRINTER is
    introduces
        procedure RESET;
        procedure PRINT( F: in FILE);
end DAISY_PRINTER;

class GRAPHIC_DEVICE is
    introduces
        procedure GRAPHIC_PRINT( F: in FILE);
end GRAPHIC_DEVICE;

class LASER_PRINTER is
    inherits
        DAISY_PRINTER, GRAPHIC_DEVICE;
    redefines
        RESET, GRAPHIC_PRINT;
    introduces
        procedure LOAD_FONT;
end LASER_PRINTER;
```

In the example class LASER_PRINTER inherits all features (i.e. subprograms and instance variables) of DAISY_PRINTER and GRAPHIC_DEVICE: it redefines (i.e. provides a new body for) RESET and GRAPHIC_PRINT and adds the new method LOAD_FONT.

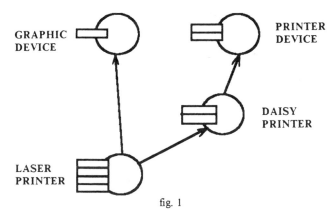

fig. 1

In the design process a higher degree of **abstraction** is obtained by omitting implementation details of a class, which is then called *abstract*. Methods of an abstract class are declared as *deferred* (i.e. the implementation of the methods is not given in the class body but is deferred until definition of descendant classes). Therefore classes can be refined and specialised in further steps, making full use of inheritance.

Abstraction is not to be confused with Ada genericity: designing a generic component implies specific implementation choices (e.g. algorithms of generic subprograms), whereas abstraction allows classification hierarchies to be organised without implementation details. This provides an additional support for reuse, preventing premature design and implementation decisions. To specify what should be expected from any implementation, DRAGOON allows the programmer to declare, at any abstraction level, those constraints which must be verified by a class (*class invariants*) or by the methods of a class (*pre-* and *postconditions*). These constructs are useful aids both when writing abstract classes (at the design level) and during execution (at run-time), where they complement the exception mechanism.

For example, an abstract class PRINTER_DEVICE could have been defined as a parent of DAISY_PRINTER (see fig. 1):

```
class PRINTER_DEVICE is
   introduces
      procedure RESET is deferred;
      procedure PRINT(F: in FILE) is deferred;
end PRINTER_DEVICE;

class DAISY_PRINTER is
   inherits
      PRINTER_DEVICE;
   completes
      RESET, PRINT;
end DAISY_PRINTER;
```

A consequence of inheritance is **polymorphism**, that adds dynamic binding to a strongly-typed language like Ada: this property allows an instance variable to refer to objects of different classes at run-time, provided that such classes are related by inheritance.
If a class SPOOLER declares an instance variable of class DAISY_PRINTER,

DAISY : DAISY_PRINTER;

(SPOOLER is said to be a *client* of DAISY_PRINTER), then at run-time it can refer to either a daisy printer or a laser printer. Therefore:

DAISY.RESET;

will execute the method of a daisy printer or of a laser printer according to the actual value of DAISY.
Polymorphism is also very important for reconfiguration purposes.

Although introducing novel features, DRAGOON enables reuse of normal Ada packages (unless they declare tasks). The recommended structure of the package should be that of a **template package**, that is a package offering subprograms and/or types but no objects (i.e. a package without a state). Non-template packages could impact distributability of the application (see below) (Atkinson et al. 88).

By combining the object oriented paradigm with sound Ada features DRAGOON gets the best of the two styles, avoiding the extremes of pure object oriented languages (e.g. the unnatural asymmetry of simple binary operations). Therefore, DRAGOON permits the use of conventional variables and subprograms of primitive data types such as REAL, INTEGER, CHARACTER etc. This has the important additional advantage of allowing the reuse of professionally produced mathematical subprograms currently under development for Ada.

The DRAGOON Concurrency Model

A concurrent application is generally modelled by independent activities that must communicate and synchronise, and often share resources, to reach a common goal. The programming paradigm must, therefore, provide proper features to describe processes (i.e. independent threads of control) and the way in which they synchronise (Strom 1986).

DRAGOON allows a class to be *active* by describing its thread of control in the *thread* section of its body. This is a sequence of statements whose execution is to be initiated upon object creation. If the thread section is empty, the class, and the corresponding instances, are said to be *passive*.

Active objects belonging to the same application will often ask for the same services: provisions must be made to rule the interactions of different threads of control. In particular those objects that offer methods to other potentially active objects must protect their internal state, that can be affected by method calls as well as by execution of their own thread of control (Yonezawa & Tokoro 1987). Protection is achieved by superimposing **behaviours** on classes, in other words by specifying the policy ruling the method calls.

With conventional programming languages (including Ada), when dealing with concurrent systems, programmers must consider both functional and behavioural aspects at the same time. This often prevents reuse of potentially reusable components, because their behaviour is tied with the needs of the concurrent application they were developed for.
In DRAGOON the problem is solved by separating the method interleaving policy of the component from the functionality of the methods. In practice one finds that only a limited variety of such *behaviours* is required. DRAGOON, therefore, provides a mechanism called **behavioural inheritance** by which a behaviour can be superimposed on the methods of a (non concurrent) class.

In the DRAGOON environment, there is a catalogue of **behavioural classes** (provided by experienced system engineers) that contain only descriptions of behaviours (e.g. mutual exclusion, serialisation, bounded re-entrancy). When designing a concurrent application, the DRAGOON programmer selects a non-concurrent class from the library and, by behavioural inheritance, he assigns it a behaviour, thereby obtaining a new concurrent class which obeys that particular concurrent discipline.

It is then possible to reuse the functionalities offered by the same non-concurrent classes in different concurrent applications, just by inheriting from different behavioural classes. Note that, when using the mechanism of behavioural inheritance, the properties of polymorphism, that enable the concurrent behaviour of a supplier class to be changed without its clients having to be modified, still hold.

In order to meet the requirements of different application areas, behavioural classes are supported which either rely on Ada tasking implementation or use a specific run-time support for efficiency purposes. Behavioural classes, however implemented, are specified by system engineers using **deontic logic** (Goldsack 1988), a quite powerful and simple formalism to express axioms based on *history functions* and *deontic operators*.

For instance, a behavioural class MUTEX describing mutual exclusion among methods can be expressed as follows:

```
behavioural class MUTEX is
   ruled  OP;
   where
      per(OP) < = >  act(OP) =  0;
                - - deontic logic specification
end MUTEX;
```

where OP defines a set of mutually exclusive methods. A mutual exclusive behaviour can then be assigned to class DAISY_PRINTER by building a concurrent class MUTEX_DAISY_PRINTER which inherits functionalities from DAISY_PRINTER and behaviour from MUTEX (see fig. 2):

```
class MUTEX_DAISY_PRINTER is
   inherits DAISY_PRINTER;
   ruled by MUTEX;
   where
      RESET, PRINT: OP;
end MUTEX_DAISY_PRINTER;
```

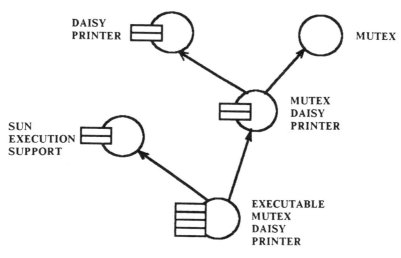

fig. 2

DRAGOON Design Approach for Distributed Systems

In the object oriented paradigm the application is made of several independent entities (objects) which communicate by exchanging messages. This view matches naturally the requirements of distributable software applications which are conveniently designed in terms of abstractions of network nodes, called *virtual nodes* (Atkinson et al. 88). These are the smallest units of distribution, and since communication between them is potentially remote, they are best made as weakly coupled as possible. According to this model, it is easy to see that the concept of object corresponds closely to that of virtual node.

In a distributed environment multi-tasking is generally handled across machines *externally* at the operating system level by allowing concurrently executing programs to interact through operating system mechanisms (e.g. Unix pipes, VMS mailbox). This implies that the user is forced to decide from the very early design stages about distribution issues. It also makes maintenance very difficult to achieve should these modes of interaction need to be changed. With DRAGOON the designer disregards distribution issues in the early stages of design, where he is concerned only with the logical aspects of the application that is written in terms of communicating objects. Instance variables can either refer to local objects, that are private to their clients and will never be remote from them in any distributed version of the logical application, or refer to external objects which can be shared by more than one client: in this case the server object is a distributable entity which could, for some particular configuration, be on a different machine from its clients.

When the hardware topology is known, integration teams decide how to split the logical application into different executable programs. In a heterogeneous system different executable images will be needed to correspond to the various types of processors in the network. Consequently DRAGOON introduces the concept of an **Execution Support Class** (one for each type of machine) which can be inherited by any non abstract class. This inheritance allows the DRA-GOON preprocessor to generate the required distributable objects, but also extends the object interface with the methods provided by the execution support of the desired machine.

The previous printer object could be made into an independently executable object by inheriting class SUN_EXECUTION_SUPPORT (see fig. 2).

```
class SUN_EXECUTION_SUPPORT is
introduces        - - For example
    procedure LOAD;
    function  IS_LOADED return BOOLEAN;
end SUN_EXECUTION_SUPPORT ;

class EXECUTABLE_MUTEX_DAISY_PRINTER is
    inherits
        MUTEX_DAISY_PRINTER, SUN_EXECUTION_SUPPORT;
end EXECUTABLE_MUTEX_DAISY_PRINTER ;
```

Such methods of the execution support class correspond to the capabilities offered by a given system to manipulate these objects. Therefore this mechanism gives visibility of the underlying execution and distribution system to the application. An application configuration manager would invoke method LOAD of the executable object, for example, to load its binary code onto the machine.

Similarly, in order to interface the application to events which either occur at the hardware level (interrupts) or are detected by the execution and distribution system (such as site failures or a wake up of a new site), DRAGOON introduces the concept of **Physical Node** (PN) classes offering methods which are directly called by the hardware or by the underlying system. They can have a' visibility of other objects through instance variables. PNs are developed by integration teams when the topology is known and are not taken into account by the logical application.

```
class SUN_PN is
    introduces        - - For example
        procedure SITE_STARTUP;
        procedure NEW_SITE(SITE_ID : in T_SITE_ID );
        procedure SITE_FAILURE(SITE_ID : in T_SITE_ID );
end SUN_PN ;

class PRINTERS_CONFIGURATION_MANAGER is
    inherits
        SUN_PN;
        ...
end PRINTERS_CONFIGURATION_MANAGER ;
```

Dynamic reconfiguration is achieved by changing the values of various instance variables referring to external objects when a certain situation is detected. If a PN object is responsible for changing such an instance variable, this is dynamic *Physical Reconfiguration*. In the other cases we speak about dynamic *Logical Reconfiguration*, where reconfiguration has been taken into account from the very beginning in the original logical application (such as a consumer taking inputs from a new producer in a starvation situation with a previous producer).

In the previous example of a PRINTERS_CONFIGURATION_MANAGER physical node, method SITE_STARTUP would load all printers it is responsible for, by invoking method LOAD on proper instance variables of class EXECUTABLE_MUTEX_DAISY_PRINTER.

Physical dynamic configuration is thus achieved at the application level with the physical nodes mechanism. Configuration strategies are made easier to write with the uniform object oriented style adopted for all classes of the application: application classes, execution support classes and physical nodes classes. This also improves maintenance flexibility by separating the application writer's concerns from the hardware topology problems.

Ada Transformation

As with other object oriented design approaches targeted to Ada, the transformation from DRAGOON into Ada is based on the correspondence between classes and abstract data types. However, to support the features of a full object oriented programming language such as DRA-GOON considerable enhancements and extensions to this simple principle are required. In particular, some mechanism is needed for overcoming the apparent incompatibility of DRAGOON polymorphism and Ada's strong typing scheme.

In the simplest form of the abstract data type approach, the attributes of a class are collected into a record type, and the methods mapped into subprograms each with an extra formal parameter to receive the state on which the method is to operate. The invocation of a particular object's method therefore corresponds to the application of the subprogram to the appropriate state record.

While this approach is adequate for implementing method invocation, it does not support reference semantics of instance variables - that is, the ability to dynamically assign objects to different instance variables. For example, an instance variable DAISY of class DAISY_PRINTER can refer to many different instances of this class during the life of a program, by means of assignments of the form :

$$\vdots$$
$$DAISY := PRINTER\_1;$$
$$\vdots$$
$$DAISY := PRINTER\_2;$$
$$\vdots$$

Where DAISY, PRINTER_1 and PRINTER_2 are instance variables of class DAISY_PRINTER.

To accommodate this feature of DRAGOON, the attributes of a class are mapped into access types rather than a static record. Instance variables can, therefore, be represented by access variables to which various objects (records) can be assigned dynamically.

Inheritance /Polymorphism

Much more difficult to support in Ada are the inheritance and polymorphism properties of DRAGOON. Since the heirs of a class generally enrich the inherited properties, and possess at least all the methods of the parent, the typing rules of DRAGOON allow instance variables of a particular class to refer also to instances of its subclasses. Therefore, the above assignments are not only allowed when PRINTER_1 and PRINTER_2 refer to instances of class DAISY_PRINTER, but also to instances of subclasses of DAISY_PRINTER, such as LASER_PRINTER.

Clearly, the strong typing rules of Ada rule out the direct assignment of a LASER_PRINTER record to a DAISY_PRINTER instance variable. One way of overcoming this problem would be to model DAISY_PRINTER objects and LASER_PRINTER objects as variants of a single variant record type. This would certainly allow assignments of this kind to take place within the rules of Ada's typing scheme. However, this variant record strategy has severe compile time overheads, because whenever a new class is added to an inheritance hierarchy, all the clients of all its ancestors have to be recompiled to recognise the new, extended variant record type.

This overhead is completely unacceptable in an environment designed to promote reuse, so a completely different strategy is adopted in DRAGOON. Instead of representing the state of an object by a single record, it is represented by a "linked list" of records, each node in the list storing the state added by a subclass in the inheritance hierarchy. Since all user-defined inheritance hierarchies in DRAGOON conceptually have the class APPLICATION_OBJECT as their root, the first node in every such state list is of the Ada type APPLICATION.STATE. Therefore, all instance variables in DRAGOON are of the same Ada access type, referring to records of type APPLICATION.STATE. This enables any object to be assigned to any instance variable, although DRAGOON places certain restrictions on those assignments allowed.

The class to which a particular state list belongs is determined by following the state records' HEIR fields, which point to the next state record in the list, and the OFFSPRING_NO fields which identify the branches in the inheritance hierarchy. In order to produce the appropriate linked list structure for a particular class, a CREATE function is defined which uses UNCHECKED_CONVERSION to link the new state record onto the parent class's linked list structure. The use of UNCHECKED_CONVERSION, however, is completely invisible to the client Ada code. In the case of multiple inheritance, when a class has more than one parent, the state lists of the parent classes are combined into a more complex "ring" structure.

Dynamic Binding

Inheritance also has a large impact on the implementation of methods. As mentioned above, since the class LASER_PRINTER redefines the method RESET inherited from DAISY_PRINTER, the polymorphism rules of DRAGOON mean that the version of RESET invoked by a particular method call depends on the preceding dynamic assignments. This is what is called dynamic binding in object oriented contexts, and requires a run-time choice of which implementation of the method to invoke.

To cope with this requirement, two Ada subprograms, rather than one, are produced for each DRAGOON method. One of the subprograms actually contains the Ada code implementing the body of the DRAGOON method. This is contained in an inner package called SELF, along with the "implementing" subprograms for the class's other methods. The other subprogram is responsible for performing the run-time selection of the various currently existing implementations of the method. The body of the "selection shell" is defined as a separate sub-unit, so that it can be recompiled with minimum impact to cope with addition of new versions of the method to the system.

Concurrency and Distribution

As described above DRAGOON has extended the basic inheritance model of object oriented programming to handle concurrency, distribution and reconfiguration. These can be handled in a fairly straightforward way using Ada's tasking model.

Naturally, the thread of an active object is implemented as a task. To handle the dynamic creation of multiple active objects, the thread is mapped into a task type which is instantiated by the Ada procedure corresponding to the pre-defined START method. The access value of the task type is stored in a special field in the class's state record. In order to allow the task to manipulate the state of the object it requires an initialisation entry which receives the object's state list as a parameter.

The behaviour of an object can be handled in a similar way, by a dynamically created task whose access value is stored in another special field in the state record. Unlike the thread task, however, the behaviour task represents a kind of "structured semaphore" providing a number of methods analogous to SIGNAL and WAIT operations. The method selection shells call these methods immediately before and after invocation of the implementing method, in order to ensure the specified behaviour.

The DRAGOON distribution model is based on the use of special surrogate tasks to perform local calls on behalf of remote callers. To allow for the possibility that any instance variable in DRAGOON may refer to a remote object, DRAGOON has also adopted the DIADEM (Atkinson et al. 1988) strategy of using "remote access types" to provide globally unique identifiers for each object. The reference to each object is tightly coupled to the identifier of the encapsulating executable object, and so can be passed over the network in safety.

The transformation was designed making provisions for different implementations of basic synchronisation and remote communication primitives. Therefore, although an implementation heavily relying on Ada tasking can be selected, others and possibly more satisfactory implementations can be adopted with minimal impact on the automatic preprocessing tools. In fact the implementation of such primitives has been restricted to certain package bodies, so that alternative implementations can be easily substituted when required.

Acknowledgements

The authors wish to thank all the partners of the DRAGON consortium and in particular Steve Goldsack (Imperial College), Sigrid Kutzi (DORNIER System), Martin Wirsing (University of Passau), Egidio Astesiano (University of Genoa) and Stefano Crespi-Reghizzi (Politecnico di Milano), for their contributions to the definition of DRAGOON.

This work has been partially funded by the Commission of the European Communities under the Esprit programme.

References

Atkinson, C., Moreton, T. & Natali, A. (1988). Ada for Distributed Systems. Cambridge University Press.

Berard, E. (1985). Object Oriented Design Handbook for Ada Software. EVB Software Engineering Inc.

Booch, G. (1986). Software Engineering with Ada. Second edition. The Benjamin/Cummings Publishing Company.

Di Maio, A., Cardigno, C., Genolini, S., Crespi-Reghizzi, S., Bayan, R., Destombes, C., Atkinson, C. & Goldsack, S. (1988). DRAGOON: the language and its implementation. Deliverable DRAGON/WP1.T6/TXT/11.1

Gatti, S., Cardigno, C., Di Maio, A., Crespi-Reghizzi, S., Bayan, R., Destombes, C., Kaag, F. & Atkinson, C. (1988). Draft Definition of the Object Oriented Notation. Deliverable DRAGON/WP1.T5/TXT/10

Meyer, B. (1988). Object-Oriented Software Construction. Prentice Hall.

Goldberg, A. & Robson, D. (1983). Smalltalk-80: The Language and its Implementation. Addison-Wesley.

Goldsack, S. (1988). Specifying Behaviours. Internal Report (DRAGON/WP1.T6/IC/1).

HOOD Manual (1987). Issue 2.1.

Strom, R. (1986). A Comparison of the Object-Oriented and Process Paradigms. SIGPLAN Notices. Vol. 21, no. 10

Stroustrup, B. (1986). The C++ Programming Language. Addison-Wesley.

Wegner, P. (1984). Capital Intensive Software Technology. IEEE Software. Vol. 1, no. 3. pp. 12-45.

Yonezawa, A. & Tokoro, M. (1987). Object-Oriented Concurrent Programming. The MIT Press.

A PRACTICAL REAL-TIME DESIGN METHOD FOR ADA

P.M. Molko
Jet Propulsion Laboratory, 4800 Oak Grove Drive, Pasadena,
California 91109

K.S. Ellison, Ph.D.
Jet Propulsion Laboratory, 4800 Oak Grove Drive, Pasadena,
California 91109

Abstract.

This paper describes the methodology used for the design phase of the Real-Time Weather Processor (RWP) System, being developed for the Federal Aviation Administration in Ada under the Department of Defense (DOD) Standard, DOD-STD-2167A. After selecting Ada as the programming language, the challenges were to choose a design approach that (1) would take advantages of the features of the language; (2) would provide ways to handle the design aspects of real-time systems; and (3) could be documented in an acceptable tailoring of DOD-STD-2167A requirements. All of these goals were achieved by combining the best features of several existing design approaches, tailoring them for the RWP Project, validating them during a training phase, and then using the methodology during the recently completed preliminary and detailed design phases. This paper describes the methodology, how it was selected and validated, and how the staff was trained. Most importantly, it provides the lessons learned by both the design team and management staff.

Introduction.

The Ada programming language offers the software designer a variety of useful features that facilitate good software engineering practices. For real-time systems development, the Ada concurrency and process communication require a different approach than conventional language and executive combinations. The Ada language uses a tasking model (the rendezvous), which differs from conventional operating system tasking concepts. Combining many principles such as abstraction, information hiding, and hierarchical decomposition into a coherent methodology for a design team to apply in an actual project is a difficult task. The risks associated with using a methodology that the staff may not be experienced in, must be balanced against the benefits expected to be gained. The process can be successful if time is allocated to select and document the method, train the staff in a combined Ada language and methodology training program, validate and refine the method during the training process, and oversee its application during the actual program design phases.

This paper is organized as follows: Section 1 gives background information on the RWP Project; Section 2 provides an overview of the design methodology and information on the training program; Sections 3 and 4 describe the steps in the methodology. The final section provides a set of lessons learned.

Acknowledgment.

The work reported in this paper was performed for the Jet Propulsion Laboratory, California Institute of Technology, under NASA Contract NAS7-918.

1.   **Project Overview.**

The Real-Time Weather Processor (RWP) System is being developed by the Jet Propulsion Laboratory (JPL) under a National Aeronautics and Space Administration (NASA) contract with the Federal Aviation Administration (FAA). The RWP is one of the weather information programs being developed to improve air traffic control and airway facilities services as part of the FAA's National Airspace System Plan (DOT FAA 1987).

An RWP System will be located in each of the Center Weather Service Units at Air Route Traffic Control Centers. The RWP will receive weather data from current and new weather data sources and provides automatic distribution of pertinent weather information to meteorologists and air traffic controllers.

The Project is being developed using Revision A of the Department of Defense's development standards, DOD-STD-2167A, and its associated Data Item Descriptions (DIDs) (DOD 1988), which contain document outlines for required documents. The standards were tailored, not only because of the choice of Ada, but also to accommodate the RWP design methodology and an incremental development approach. The system is being developed as a series of builds, each providing additional system capability.

2.   **Design Method Development And Overview.**

2.1   **Design terminology.**

The first requirement on the design methodology is to provide a mapping between the 2167A terminology and the Ada terminology.

DOD-STD-2167A requires that software be organized in a hierarchical structure of Computer Software Configuration Items (CSCIs), Computer Software Components (CSCs), and Computer Software Units (CSUs).

Following are the definitions chosen by the RWP and the mapping to Ada. The RWP is being developed as one CSCI. There are two levels of CSCs, a Top-Level CSC (TLCSC) and a Sub-Level CSC (SLCSC). The TLCSCs are defined over functional boundaries. They map primarily to the functional entities in the Software Requirements Specification, with several added to collect implementation entities such as common utilities and a layer to encapsulate the operating system functionality and inter-process communication. A SLCSC is a set of Ada compilation units and their secondary units. A CSU is a separately testable component. RWP therefore chose the package as the Ada component to map to a CSU. Nested packages are not allowed. All procedures, except main programs, are contained in packages.

2.2   **Combining selected portions of methodologies.**

The methodology is documented in the RWP System Development Handbook (JPL 1988) and is based on the following:

a)   General Object-Oriented Development (GOOD) methodology (Seidewitz and Stark 1986) used by the NASA Goddard Space Flight Center. This methodology provided an approach to transitioning from a structured analysis of requirements to an object-oriented implementation. Ward and Mellor's structured analysis methodology (Ward and Mellor 1985) was used to document software requirements using functional decomposition and Data Flow Diagrams (DFDs). Ward and Mellor's (1985) implementation modeling techniques were not used because they do not provide guidance in using the Ada tasking model and packaging concept.

b)   Grady Booch's object-oriented design methodology

(Booch 1983).   Object-oriented design provides a systematic way of applying principles of data abstraction, encapsulation, and information hiding to an Ada implementation.

c)   George Cherry's Pictorial Ada Method for Every Large Application (PAMELA[tm]) (Cherry 1985). Concepts used from the PAMELA methodology include the distinction between process modules, which have independent threads of control and may conserve local state, and procedures, which have no independent thread of control and cannot conserve local state information.

d)   Nielsen and Shumate (1987) provided additional design principles.   These included the edges-in approach utilized in structured design (Buhr 1984), as well as a set of steps for creating the middle portion of the design.

The Ada language itself is used as a Program Design Language (PDL) to obtain the benefits of providing an early validation of the preliminary design and an easier transition to detailed design and coding. During preliminary design, only the Ada package specifications were written, thus avoiding premature implementation of the design.

2.3   **Training, methodology validation, and refinement.**

Because the entire staff had to be trained in both Ada and the RWP design methodology, the training program was spread over twelve weeks.

It consisted of the following for the software design team:

a)   1 week of VAX/VMS orientation.

b)   3 weeks of Ada: 1/2 day lecture, 1/2 day hands-on problem solving.

c)   2-day seminars on each of the following: Object-oriented design principles; the NASA Goddard GOOD methodology; the RWP design methodology and using Ada as a PDL.

d)   6 to 7 weeks working in small teams to solve RWP-specific case studies, using the RWP design methodology.

The training of other staff members, including FAA staff, was based upon the level of knowledge needed to perform tasks. As a result of the training period, the methodology was refined and updated and presented to the staff prior to starting the actual RWP preliminary design phase. In addition, mini-tutorials were held prior to beginning each step of the design process to reinforce its principles.

3.   The RWP Methodology For Preliminary Design.

During the system design phase, in addition to determining the partitioning of hardware and software, the software architecture framework should be designed. The mechanisms which tie the system together are documented in a Software Architecture Concepts paper.

The two areas which must be addressed are System Services and System Monitor and Control. System Services provide the way in which applications of the system communicate with each other, access data, perform logging and algorithms common to the rest of the software. System Monitor and Control must address how the components of the system will work together to perform start up, shut down, fault detection, and recovery. The framework must be in place prior to having design teams perform the next level of design.

The preliminary design phase consists of four steps. Each step refines the design produced at the previous step and incorporates any changes to products of previous steps. Formal inspections, using the Michael Fagan inspection methodology (Fagan 1976), are held to review the products of each step. A formal Preliminary Design Review is held at the conclusion of the phase.

Products are developed which serve to document the design at each step and serve as a vehicle for informal reviews. In addition, some of the products are incorporated into deliverable documents, so that documents are produced incrementally. The four steps are:

1.   Identify top-level CSCs.

2.   Identify sub-level CSCs.

3.   Produce formal documentation for each sub-level CSC.

4.   Describe abstract algorithm of each sub-level CSC.

3.1   Step 1 - Identify top-level CSCs.

Top-level CSCs are the major functional entities of the system. They are derived by analyzing the system-level data flows. For a real-time system, begin at the external interfaces and work in, identifying the major processing done to handle each interface.   There should be no more than 5 to 9 TLCSCs for understandability.

The following are products of Step 1:   a) Grouping of functions in the system-level data flow and their allocation to TLCSCs; b) Requirements allocation to TLCSCs.

3.2   Step 2 - Identify sub-level CSCs.

Sub-level CSCs primarily show the concurrency required in the system.   Constraints due to hardware and the environment are considered. A SLCSC may also be identified to package services.   The DFDs from the functional analysis phase are used in this process to determine functions and entities that should be SLCSCs.   The process of transitioning the functional analysis into a design is called "recasting" the DFD.   Some of the criteria that determine what constitutes a SLCSC include:

a)   Concurrency: Must the processing be done as a separately scheduled process?   This is usually required to handle external events or because processing must be done periodically.

b)   Object-oriented design: Is this entity an object which contains state data and provides operations on that data?   Is this an entity which cannot be accessed simultaneously by concurrent processes?

c)   Encapsulation and information hiding: Is this a service which will be used to make applications independent of the specific operating system or off-the-shelf software being used in the system?   Note that these do not usually show up on a DFD but are required to insulate applications from dependencies on hardware or operating systems.

There are two types of SLCSCs.   The first is an object.   An object is a data type (or a collection of data) together with operations on that data.   The documentation of an object SLCSC includes a description of that object in terms of an abstract definition of the state data.   The description of the object should not be its implementation, but rather how it is to be used.   The operations on the object are specified as procedures and/or functions, with a description of the effect of the operation on the object.

The second type of SLCSC is a process.   It is best described as a classical (input, processing, output) entity. Usually the inputs and outputs are via system calls rather than procedure or task entry calls. There is no state data. Because object-oriented design approaches present objects as Ada packages where the procedures/functions are the operations, a "process" SLCSC cannot be described in terms of the processing performed on the inputs to produce the outputs.

A SLCSC may be a combination of the two types. It may have some processing which is best described in terms of input, processing, output and, in addition, encapsulate some state data upon which a user can operate via procedure calls.

The following are products of Step 2: a) A diagram for each TLCSC which shows the Ada tasks; b) A description of the assumed environment; c) A description of each SLCSC which provides its functions and interface mechanism, the requirements allocated to it, rationale for making the SLCSC a task or service, error handling and special processing.

3.3   Step 3 - Document purpose of each sub-level CSC.

The purpose of Step 3 is to formally describe each SLCSC using Ada as a PDL. Much of the information is placed in Ada commentary. The PDL is compilable and establishes the interface to each SLCSC.

The following are products of Step 3: a) For entities which are objects, the conceptual view of the data is described with Ada commentary in the package prolog. The operations on the data are Ada specifications of procedures and/or functions. Parameters of the procedures are documented in type definition packages, using the "TBD" type definitions package when refinement of the data type can be postponed until detailed design. The effect of the operations on the conceptual data is described in the procedure/function prologs; b) For process entities, the conceptual view of that processing is described with Ada commentary in the package prolog; c) For entities which are a combination, both types of commentary are described in the package prolog.

3.4   Step 4 - Describe abstract algorithm of each sub-level CSC.

This step supports development of the hardware resource allocation information, estimates of source lines of code, and modeling of the system using a discrete even simulator.

To verify the design, it is necessary to make assumptions about the implementation of each package so that a worst-case scenario can be modeled. Modeling can help identify areas of the software that must be carefully implemented. Modeling can also verify decisions about allocation of the software to hardware and provide help in developing the resource allocation information. The abstract algorithm is oriented towards the processing required per input for each operation of the object, or for a typical input to a processing entity.

The following are products of Step 4:   a) Implementation assumptions; b) An estimate of the number of Ada statements per step in the algorithm for each operation of the package; c) An estimate of the source lines code and memory requirements.

4.   Extending the Methodology to Detailed Design.

For the detailed design phase, the design process is continued by adding two steps which result in defining all CSUs which make up the CSCI.

4.1   Step 1 - Establish the "select" logic of each task.

In the first step, the concurrent entities identified in preliminary design are expanded. One SLCSC in preliminary design may turn into several tasks in detailed design. Tasks may be introduced for functions which are performed periodically, or to queue data to provide a looser coupling than the Ada rendezvous. Decisions are made as to which entities are callers and which are called. This requires examining the entity diagram for tasks that communicate with the subject task, in addition to the abstract algorithm of the task. The relationship of execution order is also examined between tasks that interact in order to determine if there is a potential for deadlock or starvation.

The following are products of Step 1:   a) Updated diagrams reflecting any changes in caller/calling relationships; b) An Ada package diagram of the internal relationships of the CSUs within the SLCSC.

4.2   Step 2 - Specify the implementation view of each sub-level CSC.

This step provides the information needed to eventually code each SLCSC. It also identifies the CSUs by step-wise refinement of the SLCSC.

For entities which are input, output, processing entities, specify the processing algorithm by step-wise refinement. Data-type definitions for the input and output which were at an abstract level during preliminary design are now completely specified.

For entities that are objects:

a)   Define the implementation of the state data of the object.

b)   Define the implementation of the operations by describing them in terms of their manipulation of the actual object.

c)   State the mapping from the implementation to the conceptual view. This mapping includes how initialization conditions of the object will be implemented and how the consistency rules will be maintained.

d)   Verify that the mapping is consistent and complete.

The following are products of Step 2: a) PDL for the package bodies, procedure bodies, and task bodies, as well as the Ada select logic in the task bodies. The general guideline is one line of PDL for each 7-10 lines of Ada code.

These steps complete the detailed design phase.

5.   **Lessons Learned and Summary.**

The completion of the design phases provided the RWP team with both a reinforcement of the approach taken and with additional lessons learned.

a)   It is important to provide adequate schedule time to decide upon the methodology to be used, document it, train the staff and the customer, and practice it using a case study team approach. In this way, the methodology and its support tools can be validated and refined prior to their use on the project.

b)   The methodology should consist of measurable steps, each step resulting in engineering products or documentation which can be reviewed in stages. Setting intermediate goals throughout the design phase also allows management to determine that progress is being made.

c)   Keep the methodology <u>and</u> support tools rather simple. Too many new and complicated tools can make designers frustrated and cause them to concentrate on things other than the design itself. The tools used in RWP were a word processor for textual descriptions, a text editor and the Ada compiler to generate and validate the PDL, and Adagen[tm] (Adagen 1988) to graphically portray the Ada design.

d)   Appoint a person in charge of the methodology who understands it, trains people, and provides continued support in both answering the team's questions and in making sure the method is followed.

The design methodology documented in this paper combines many important design principles which have matured over the last decade with several emerging design concepts. It is a practical method for real-time systems design.

The synergism of the methodology with many features of the Ada language allow a large portion of the preliminary design to be represented by compilable Ada, making the transition to the detailed design and coding phases a much smoother one.

References.

Adagen User's Manual, Mark V Systems Limited, Encino, California, May 18, 1988.

Booch, G., _Software Engineering with Ada_, Benjamin Cummings, Menlo Park, California, 1983.

Buhr, R.J.A., _System Design With Ada_, Prentice-Hall, Englewood Cliffs, New Jersey, 1984.

Cherry, G. W., and Crayford, B.S., _The PAMELA Methodology_, Thought[**] Tools, Reston, Virginia, November 1985.

Fagan, Michael E., Design and Code Inspections and Process Control in the Development of Programs, Technical Report TR00 2763, IBM Corporation, Poughkeepsie, New York, June 10, 1976.

Jet Propulsion Laboratory, _RWP System Development Handbook_, JPL D-3959, July 7, 1988.

Nielsen, K., and K. Shumate, Designing Large Real-Time Systems with Ada, Communications of the ACM, August 1987.

Seidewitz, E., and M. Stark, General Object-Oriented Software Development, NASA Goddard Space Flight Center, SEL-86-002, August 1986.

U.S. Department of Transportation (DOT), Federal Aviation Administration (FAA), National Airspace System Plan, April 1987.

U.S. Department of Defense, Defense System Software Development, DOD-STD-2167A, February 29, 1988, including the associated Data Item Descriptions (DIDs).

Ward, P.T., and Mellor, S. J., Structured Development for Real-Time Systems, Vols. I, II, and III, Yourdon Press, New York, 1985.

PRACTICAL EXPERIENCES OF ADA AND OBJECT ORIENTED
DESIGN IN REAL TIME DISTRIBUTED SYSTEMS

Neil W. DAVIS

Malcolm IRVING

John E. LEE
Logica Space and Defence Systems Limited, Cobham,
Surrey KT11 3LX, England

1.   INTRODUCTION

This paper describes some of the work performed at
Logica, which has the eventual aim of producing an Object
Oriented (OO) approach to software system development. It
reports on our experiences in the use of Object Oriented
Design (OOD) and Ada in the requirements analysis and design
of distributed real time systems.

Section 2 summarizes our background in OOD and
outlines our view of the status of OOD. Section 3 traces our
experiences on a number of projects with the introduction of
OOD. Section 4 describes the lessons learnt and our
conclusions together with an outline of further work needed
are in Section 5.

2.   BACKGROUND

OOD is very different to the traditional
functional/data flow approaches to design. It requires
software engineers and managers to be reeducated. The
claimed benefits are that OOD has the potential to improve
software quality by using more natural structuring
techniques which make the designs more understandable,
components and systems easier to design and verify,
components reusable, prototyping practical and designs
extendable. In many ways it is similar to hardware
component technology where the structure of the system is
based on the objects (components) rather than the individual
functions performed. These combined properties have the

potential to make software systems more reliable and
maintainable.

The authors have experience of using OOD on
several projects and believe these claims to be correct.
However, we see that Object Oriented Design in itself is
only a partial answer. It is a good foundation on which to
build a comprehensive, engineering approach to software
system development.

The problem at present is that OOD is still not a
mature method. There are no detailed procedures or
documentation requirements to guide designers through a
major project. The European Space Agency (ESA) has taken a
lead in this area by commissioning the development of an
Object Oriented Design method which it has called
Hierarchical Object Oriented Design (HOOD) (see HOOD (1)).
The HOOD method now has a user manual, a training course, a
prototype toolset and a number of software engineers
(including the authors) across Europe with experience of
using the method on a trial basis on real projects.

Our work to date has not been fundamental research
into the theory of methods but a practical approach to using
the best ideas from a number of techniques based around a
small set of Object Oriented principles.

Logica is a large system and software house which
produces a wide range of computer systems in areas as
diverse as industrial control, defence, space, data
processing, banking, research, communications and
government. Through the production of some of these systems
we have become users of many current development methods.
Some of these methods have features which contribute to the
work described in this paper.

We cannot avoid the fact that large software
system development is a complex and difficult task, which
should not be trivialized. Better methods and tools are
needed. Proper detailed and structured documentation is
needed. Highly structured data about a system must be
recorded. Formalized and mathematically formal notations

must be used. Methods must not only be supported by CASE
tools but must be designed with automation in mind.

An example of a possible method for OOD, to
implement some of the above is described in Davis et al (2).

3.   IMPLEMENTATION EXPERIENCE OF OOD

3.1 Introduction

The main type of approach that the authors have
being using is the object based style of OOD for systems to
be implemented in Ada, following Booch (3).

This may be described as the diagramming style, in
which stylised diagrams are used to show the encapsulation
of data structures with the routines which manipulate them
and to show the control and data flows between objects.
However as outlined in Davis et al (2) and in many other
references the diagramming style does not use the other OO
concepts of classes, inheritance and dynamic binding and
hence loses their associated benefits.

The experience has been based on the participation
in major projects in both space and defence industries, both
within Logica, and in a consultancy role to other companies.
We therefore feel that the problems encountered may be
typical of industry as a whole or at least of those trying
to use Ada on large multi-team projects.

The space experience was gained during work on the
Columbus space project for the European Space Agency, (ESA).
Our involvement was in the control of subsystems and
payloads in a distributed architecture, in the simulation of
space applications and in defining the software support
environment. The project involved contributions from
contractors throughout Europe. For this reason a complex
software development environment and management
communication system was required. It was within this
environment that large Ada software projects were to be
developed, in particular, using object based methods.

This project has completed the requirements
assessment phase, during which OOD techniques were used to

produce a conceptual software architecture. It is currently entering the initial design phase and is expected to continue to use OOD techniques to consolidate the architecture produced.

The defence experience was on a large distributed computer system project, based on previous similar projects implemented using a high-level language (HLL) similar to Coral. It was started before Ada became established, the requirements being written and the contract being placed on the basis of the previous implementation.

There was then a change to the use of Ada and OOD, agreed between the contractor and the customer, when it became apparent that it would be of long term benefit. This project is now in the implementation phase, deliveries being scheduled to start in 1989.

This section describes these experiences both in terms of the 'waterfall' software lifecycle and the project and organisational issues. The problems encountered and lessons learnt are discussed. In the subsequent sections our work to provide a solution to some of these problems is described.

3.2   Constructing a System Design

In order to give an understanding of the steps taken to produce a system design we outline a generic algorithm which is consistent with the projects currently known to us. It should be noted that our emphasis will be on the software issues involved.

Step 1:   look at customers requirements;

Step 2:   add more detail to these requirements to produce a number of requirement specifications for each contractor;

The following two steps are optional, dependent on whether the intention is to produce re-usable modules for subsequent use within the project, or for other projects.

Step 3:   look in product library of functions

Step 4:   if present then use library function
           else is new function generally useful?
               if true then put in library
               else implement as project specific

The approach up to here is functional, whereas in the following steps an object based method is applied.

Step 5:   transform requirements into a software
           architectural design (AD) using an object based
           approach.

For this step one possible approach we have implemented is the ESA HOOD algorithm as follows:

> - a - statement of problem: to give in one sentence a precise definition of the problem;

> - b - requirements analysis: to provide the information necessary to allow an experienced designer to produce a possible solution. This particular phase of HOOD was not considered as design but used to clarify all points that at this stage were not clear.

> - c - elaboration of problem: a textual presentation of approximately ten sentences to elaborate a solution to the problem previously defined. The purpose

is to establish a bridge between the solution the designer has in mind and the requirements.

- d - choosing objects: identification of the key nouns which will be used to represent the objects at this level of design.

- e - choosing operations: identification of the key verbs which will be used to represent the operations associated to the objects chosen above.

- f - combining operations with objects: the aim is to group the objects and operations to help establish a formal description of the object interfaces as well as a graphical description.

- g - graphical representation: the HOOD method introduces a graphical representation showing the nature of the object with their visible operations, data flows , exceptions and control flows between objects.

- h - object description skeleton: sketches the object description, interfaces between objects, and gives an Ada-PDL control structure description for each operation. This is equivalent to the detailed design phase.

- i - translation to Ada: the above steps are
translated into Ada as follows:

Ada units

object	- package or task
operation	- procedure, function or task entry
exception	- exception
class definition	- abstract data type or generic package
class object	- type of package
instances	instantiation

3.3 Experience of life-cycle related issues

Requirements (steps 1 and 2). The customer's
requirements on which the projects were based were written
as English text, based on pre-contractual data supplied by
the contractors and on requirements used on previous
projects.

The transition from customer requirements to a
system requirement specification requires a considerable
amount of work on the requirements to change them into a
form from which a design may be produced. The fundamental
problem is that the requirements may be categorised into
several types e.g. functional, operational, design aims,
interfaces and possibly performance. These are all at
different 'levels', some relating directly to the design of
a specific part, others general. For example in some cases
one requirement might impact the whole design (eg safety
requirements), in another just one aspect of one part (eg on
pressing a particular switch the display shall...)

The decomposition of these requirements into
requirements which were more consistent in their level of
detail and more related to the architectural design of the
overall system was undertaken by the contractors. One of the

methods used to try to achieve was to apply structured
analysis and design techniques (SADT).

Transition between requirements and design (step 2 to 5).
Here an object based approach has been used to gain a better
understanding of the requirements and to start to define an
architecture. Although SADT and an SADT tool set provided a
consistency check and traceability between requirements and
design, the method did not prove satisfactory for
identifying missing or alternative requirements. Asking
'what if' type questions also proved difficult due to the
nature of the graphical presentation of the SADT diagrams.

An analysis of the requirements met greater
success using an object based method following
identification of the major objects, operations and control
flows. For the space projects in which we were involved we
used the HOOD method on a trial basis. However, the step
from requirements to HOOD required considerable intuition
and a non-trivial number of iterations to generate what
seemed a 'good' design. The initial obstacle that the
authors faced being the change in attitude required to
produce an OOD when the functional decomposition approach
had been the standard method.

However, once a consistent design was achieved the
HOOD graphical representation proved much more conducive to
further requirements analysis than the SADT diagrammatic
presentation.

Unfortunately, a systematic form of traceability
between the requirements and design was hidden when using
HOOD. The solution adopted, albeit temporarily, was to use
SADT retrospectively to check consistency, after the
decomposition of requirements against objects had been done.
The real problem is that current requirements analysis
approaches structure the requirements around functions. This
tends to result in an artificial view of the system. A more
natural approach is to structure the requirements around
entities relevant to the system.

Reusable software libraries (steps 3 and 4). Care must be
taken if a decision is made to make reuse of existing
software. On economic grounds examples are known where
several different implementations for different projects
used a 'common' library of software modules and also a
common set of hardware modules. The problem encountered was
that these common functions were evolving whilst the system
design was going on. Thus, because of the incomplete nature
of the system design the hardware-software split was not
clear, nor was the fault recovery strategy, and insufficient
performance trade-offs had been carried out.

This type of problem can be exacerbated following
a change to another language such as Ada unless these common
modules received extensive revision. On one project it was
found that these common modules had not received adequate
attention and were too dependent on the original functional
split leading to many design and interface difficulties.

So, whilst reusability may be an aim, a
considerable amount of 'up-front' time needs to be spent in
defining the re-usable items, in defining a suitable AD
which can use them to meet the requirements and in
prototyping to check that this can be done in a sensible
way. This time seems rarely to be available, and certainly
requires a change in the funding of projects, until
libraries are built up.

The problems are associated with the functional
decomposition style. Functions tend to be bound into their
immediate context. An OO approach naturally produces
components which have a low level of coupling.

Constructing an architecture (step 5). It is in this phase
that OOD needs more guidance on how to identify objects and
produce a 'good' design. Steps are being taken, such as the
HOOD method (HOOD (1)), to provide a systematic, well
documented, approach to constructing an architecture.
However HOOD is immature at present, because it lacks a
specification language for expressing the operations

interfaces and behaviours at the AD stage. This is an
extremely important step and is essential if the meaning of
each object is to be made precise.

At this early stage in the application of OOD
methods in industrial projects there appears to be a
confusion between the historical functional decomposition
method and OOD. An OOD expert is needed in the design team
at this stage in order to avoid this problem.

HOOD and other similar methods tend to promote
object nesting. This is usually to enable the design to
proceed in a top down fashion, with the higher level objects
being abstractions of lower level detail. However an OO
approach tends to be more bottom up in style. Individual
concepts and entities are considered as separate objects
which provide a service to any other object. Issues of
nesting and clustering of objects should be taken later as
an implementation step, when the design is complete, in full
knowledge of design details, programming language
characteristics, constraints and performance issues.

A consequence of this is that OO designs tend to
have many objects (often greater than 10) at the same level.
Such designs can be difficult to communicate amongst large
teams. This is potentially a negative impact of true OOD.
However a good browsing tool might alleviate the problem.

We have encountered a number of major problems in
this area. For example, high level management do not as yet
fully (if at all) understand the differences between the
functional and OO approaches and are thus not entirely
appreciative of the problems encountered. For example, the
change from another high level language (Coral type) and FD
to Ada and OOD could be viewed as a change to 'just another
language'. On one project this manifested itself in the
desire to retain existing architectural design work from
previous projects rather than start again.

Another problem is that standards are still
evolving and therefore development work is continuing in a
changing environment. Only time will satisfactorily overcome

these problems. The HOOD method mentioned above is only in
its early stages but is a good attempt at producing an
object based approach. However, it has a number of
weaknesses. For example it does not include the concept of
class inheritance. In addition further work is required on
the earlier HOOD phases i.e. Steps 5(a) to 5(c) to provide a
systematic transition from requirements to a high level
design.

   In spite of the many problems, we have seen real
applications where OOD has made a much 'better' design
possible. An example, in the MMI area is described below.

Detailed design and testing (step 6). Staff training (see
Training) in most cases ensured that at the detailed level
OOD is adequately understood. For instance our experience
suggests that whereas difficulties had been encountered at
higher levels, the detailed design and coding appear to use
OOD quite effectively. At this level the full force of OOD
has been utilised with use of data abstraction, information
hiding etc.

   It is not too surprising that once the detailed
design and coding phase has been reached that fewer problems
are met. OOD tends to shift the problems into the initial
phases of design. Thus putting greater pressure on the
senior analysts and reducing the number of difficulties
faced by the programming staff.

   For example, it is our experience that once the
object definition skeletons were written the coding phase
progressed quickly. Further, because of the number of checks
on the compilation of Ada modules the time to perform unit
testing compared with previous experience decreased greatly.

   Testing at unit level is usually less
problematical after the use of OOD. However, in the case
where reuse was insisted upon, although not rigorously
planned for, the testing of some of the low level objects
has been found to be difficult (probably because the
original design was not object oriented). It has often been

found necessary to test groups of 'objects', and the low
level test specs often reflect this.

In the case of the MMI design, OOD was found to be
an advantage, since there were onerous requirements for the
way in which the MMI subsystems (of which there were
several, all identical) interfaced with the application
programs, which were running on different processors in the
system. When certain scenarios eg faults, operational
changes etc were activated the operators would move from one
MMI subsystem to another. The requirement was for their
displays to 'move' with them. Latterly an object oriented
approach to MMI was adopted to attempt to 'hide' these
complexities from the applications and to facilitate the
design, implementation and also the testing of the MMI
software.

Operational maintenance. Again a warning if OOD methods and
functional methods are mixed. On one project of which we
have experience which is not yet in an operational phase,
maintenance of the 'completed' software, even during the
development is already proving difficult. The library being
produced consists of both hardware and software functions,
and is continually being changed, updated and refined. This
is partly because of an unclear system design, partly
because of lack of control. Each new release necessitates a
lot of retesting/ modification of many other functions. If a
proper OOD had been done, there would have been simpler
interfaces between functions, and less retesting would have
been needed.

Real time issues. In the projects we have experienced we
have found that the system design does not give much
attention to real time issues, there being no current model
for system performance evaluation. All of the testing to
date has been on the host machine, whereas the target will
be a distributed microprocessor system, interconnected with
a local area network (LAN). The lower levels of the design

eg LAN software, operating system etc are to be implemented
in C for performance reasons. If insufficient trade offs are
performed the problems encountered moving between host and
target will prove extremely costly.

There is as yet little evidence that OOD will be a
major factor in the real time performance, since many of the
real time problems are often contained within low level
objects eg complex mathematical functions. However, the
concept of data abstraction is likely to cause
inefficiencies unless the interfaces (operations) are
carefully defined (and refined) compared with the normal
scenario of using common data (with all of the problems this
entails). In addition the current experience with the Ada
rendezvous, which would be the natural way of communication
between objects suggests that it is too slow.

3.4   Experience of support issues

Management. In the management of large projects
the splitting of the work between the teams is a major
problem, both contractually and technically.

The splitting of an FD is a problem because the
number of interfaces to the other functions is often very
large. The interface problems cause design problems and
later testing and integration problems.

OOD leads to a more natural decomposition into
work that may be distributed amongst project teams. To
control this work it has been necessary to introduce a
system architects office responsible for the overall
integrity of the system. The system architects prepare
individual specifications for each object and a system
interface control document. Team leaders are then
responsible for the development of the objects in accordance
with the requirements and interface control documents. The
system architects also participate in the design reviews and
are responsible for the resolution of any problems or
queries.

Standards/ QA /PA. The use of both Ada and OOD in large
industrial projects is relatively recent. The standards for
documentation and for the design methodology are currently
being written and are not properly integrated with each
other. Standards are evolving during the time at which the
requirements analysis and AD are being done. This may lead
to inconsistencies in style and other more serious errors
until the standards reach maturity. This places an
additional burden on the developers and requires increased
vigilance from the QA and PA teams.

Tools are now in their development phase and it
will be some time before an integrated set will be available
to assist in the rather labour intensive diagrammatic OOD
methods. Using these tools it should be possible to trace
and verify the transition between the requirement assessment
and the AD, which is a source of much concern in the
development process.

Most of the QA staff have yet to adapt from the
use of the functional decomposition (FD) methods and were
therefore not able to help with the transition to Ada and
OOD. It is important therefore that not only the developers
of projects receive training in OOD but also support staff.

Training. Training has so far, been based on Grady Booch
style OOD and is given to relatively junior programming
staff only. (These have most recently been at college and
might have heard of and used OOD/Ada and other software
engineering techniques.)

In all the cases in which we have become involved
this appears to have been successful with the low level
design and code reflecting OOD well. However there often
appeared to be a gulf in appreciation between these
programming staff and their project managers and the more
senior staff who did not understand OOD and thought of
OOD/Ada as 'just another language and design method'. Thus
when OOD/Ada is introduced to a project started with say
Coral, although the programming staff realise what is needed

is a complete rethink of the AD the managers may not allow enough time or resources for this with potentially disastrous consequences.

Training must extend to all levels (including support staff such as QA, maintainers etc). OOD and Ada change the nature of the software lifecycles and development procedures fundamentally. Much work is required to optimise the use of modern pracrtices. Awareness at all levels will we hope lead to a more efficient software development.

<u>Estimating program sizes.</u> To manage any project we must be able to estimate its size and cost. This section deals with our experiences and with the problems found.

It quickly becomes apparent that estimating the size of a software project is fraught with uncertainties. Clearly, the larger the project, and the more contractors, the more scope for inconsistencies and wildly varying cost estimates.

Boehm provides a number of COnstructive COst MOdels (COCOMO) of which the most detailed depends on the choice of type of project, number of lines of code and fifteen parameters (see Boehm (4)).

To estimate the number of lines of code a conceptual architectural design was produced early in the project using HOOD, an object based method. The final estimate was based on data structures constructed and a bottom up estimate from the each of the operations on the objects. This was input into a Logica implementation of the COCOMO model (SYCO).

On another Space related project an existing software project written in 'C' was converted to Ada using HOOD. The factors of interest here was that for a project providing the same functionality but using object based methods, 1.34 times as many lines of code was produced and the amount of documentation was 2.35 times greater, a factor not included in the COCOMO model.

The HOOD design has been used as a basis for software size estimates. This has been done by associating a number of lines of Ada code and data with each operation, together with a number for the object itself. We have found that an object is a convenient unit against which to make estimates. These estimates would be associated with the object at initial design stage and updated as the design progresses. Thus the object remains the unit of estimation throughout the development, with the actual code size eventually recorded.

We have found the code generation to be much simpler, when Ada and HOOD have been used, than when using FD. This is partly due to the design having less interface complexity. This leads to the belief that the estimates produced may be more accurate.

4   LESSONS LEARNT

The following lessons learnt from our experience of OOD are extracted from the above sections. The lessons learnt which can or could be addressed by improved methods are summarised in Section 4.1. Others are overall management or support lessons or ad hoc rules with little relevance to OOD methods are summarised in Section 4.2. The lessons learnt are describe in 'bullet point' form.

4.1 OOD lessons which may be addressed by methods.

The following lessons can and we believe should be addressed by better OOD methods and tools. An example of such a method is described in Davis et al (2).

-   Analyse how system requirements should be constructed to make transition to design smooth.

-   Transition to OOD from requirements needs considerable engineering judgement and is difficult.

-   OOD is better than SADT for 'what if' questions

- SA and OOD can both provide insights into engineering problems

- Traceability between requirements and design is essential and for large systems needs tool support

- Use of a specification language with OOD is needed to describe the syntax and semantics of each object at the AD stage.

- Object nesting should be avoided in the early stages of design. Decisions about nesting and clustering should be taken as an implementation step.

- OOD provides a good framework for detailed design phases and can make them easier than with FD.

- OOD avoids the need for users to see implementation details.

- The use of OOD tends to leave the identification of performance problems until late in the life cycle. Earlier prototyping is needed to flag real time problems at an early stage.

4.2 OOD lessons related to management and support.
We believe that, although these lessons cannot be remedied directly by better tools, they are nevertheless important. If acted upon they will help the transition of OOD from philosophy to method.

- Recognition that OOD still needs further development and analysis before a systematic method for its implementation will be available

- Requirements documents should be structured around entities, rather than around functions

- Mixing software libraries from FD and OOD is a recipe
  for disaster.Interfacing functional and object oriented
  programs leads to high maintenance costs

- OOD requires considerable skill in producing a software
  architecture. This means that it is important to use
  designers with experience of OOD in these activities.

- Project management and QA as well as the various
  technical levels all need OOD/Ada training

- With adequate training OOD can be used successfully. Do
  not dismiss the amount of training required.

- Standards for design and documentation are still
  evolving for OOD. This makes the design more difficult.

- Re-use of software is expensive and not to be
  undertaken lightly. It requires more Configuration
  Management and retesting effort than otherwise. It can
  have a large impact on the system which can cost far
  more than if it were implemented without re-using
  software. This contrasts with experiences of using
  Smalltalk on a small project, where re-use has been
  extremely cheap and effective. We need to be able to
  obtain these benefits in large production systems.

- The objects produced by OOD, can be used as a natural
  split of work between teams within a company and or
  other contractors.

- OOD objects can be used as a good basis for software
  size estimating

- Tools for OOD do not adequately support its use.

5.   CONCLUSIONS

In a sense the lessons learnt in Section 4 are
conclusions in themselves, although of a rather negative
nature stressing what should not be done rather than what
should be done.

Although the paper title mentions OOD and Ada,
much of our discussion above has related more to OOD than to
Ada. We make no apology for this since without the use of
OOD, we believe, the benefits of Ada cannot be achieved.

Our work to date has confirmed our belief that OOD
is a major advance in the design, management and maintenance
of large software systems. Although object oriented
programming and design have been around for many years, we
are still in the early stages of converting this research
work into a complete technology for use in industry. This
has management and technical aspects.

The conversion to OOD has many implication which
are still not fully understood or accepted by management.
These can be summarised as requirements for:

-   a new approach to requirements analysis

-   new standards

-   training of engineers, managers and quality engineers

-   development of a method with automation by CASE
    tools in mind.

On the technical side we need to harness the OO
concepts into guidelines and procedures for use by teams of
industrial software engineers. The work continues. Until an
adequate method is achieved we offer the following rules of
thumb for producing software systems in an OO way.

-   Structure requirements around entities rather than
    around functions.

- Each time a new concept or entity emerges during the design process, encapsulate it as an object and make it available to all other objects.

- Do not nest objects.

- Use class hierarchies and inheritance to express abstraction rather than using (functional) decomposition.

- Be prepared to experiment with several variants of the overall software architecture.

- Use a formal specification language to describe the semantics of objects at the architectural design stage.

- Build documentation into the software and avoid or minimize the amount of separate documentation.

- Avoid finalising design decisions until all necessary information is available.

These above rules seem to us to be the best that can be done at present, but as a final comment we would urge that suitable methods, supported by tools are developed in the near future so that the advantages of OOD and Ada can be realised. As an example of such a method see, for example Davis et al (2), which describes a OO method based on the experiences described in this paper.

REFERENCES

1.   HOOD Manual, 1988, ESTEC Publication, ESA, Issue 2.2.
2.   Davis N., Irving M. and Lee J., Object Oriented Design: Philosophy to Method, 1988, Proceedings of the International Symposium on Space Engineering: COLUMBUS and Space Infrasructures, Turin, Italy.

3.   Booch G., 1986, Software Engineering with Ada,
        Benjamin/Cummings, Second Edition.
4.   Boehm, B. W., 1981, Software Engineering Economics,
        Prentice Hall.

A PORTABLE COMMON EXECUTION ENVIRONMENT FOR ADA

A. Burns
Department of Computing, University of Bradford, UK.

C.W. McKay
Software Engineering Research Center, University of Houston, USA.

Abstract

This paper gives a top level description of the architecture of a Portable Common Execution Environment (PCEE) for distributed Ada programs. The motivations for such an environment are discussed. A user application can gain access to the underlying services by using the interfaces provided by the PCEE. These include a Distributed Operating System, Distributed Communication System and Distributed Information System. In addition an integration environment can access the Distributed Configuration and Control System. Each of these components is described. The motivation behind the design of the PCEE is the support of mission and safety critical systems.

INTRODUCTION

Perhaps the greatest challenge facing Ada is in the domain of the large distributed real-time system. Because of the long lead time associated with such complex applications no real experience of the use of Ada, in this type of domain, has yet been gained. Nevertheless there are projects of a large and complex nature that are committed to the use of Ada, even though the language has yet to fully prove itself.

One such project is the NASA Space Station. The work presented in this paper has used the Space Station as a focus for analysis and as a yardstick for assessing Ada. The analysis is not, however, limited to this one application.

The Space Station is due for commission in 1996 at which point it will consist of one station, two free flying platforms and one orbital transfer vehicle. There is, of course, also ground control. When first occupied the Space Station will probably support six people and will have a computer architecture based on a fiber-optic local area network with perhaps 11 clusters of processors. This number is projected to rise to over 20 as the station becomes fully operational. The different flying structures and ground control will be linked via a wide area network.

The primary function of the computer systems is mission and life support. Other activities include flight coordination (particularly of the orbital transfer vehicle), external monitoring, the control and coordination of experiments, and the management of the mission database.

It has been estimated that 10 million lines of application code (in Ada) will be needed for the Space Station. If one also considers systems code and host environment concerns then a figure closer to 100 million could be reached.

If we focus on the on-board execution environment the Space Station has the following pertinent characteristics:

- It is large and complex.

- It has non-stop execution.

- It has a long operational life.

- It will experience evolutionary software changes (ie dynamic reconfiguration).

- It consists of a mixture of safety and mission critical modules (ie high reliability requirements including fault tolerance).

- It will have components with hard real-time deadlines.

- It will make use of multiprogramming.

- It will have distributed processing.

- It will contain heterogeneous processors.

- It will support applications written in Ada.

It follows that the Ada programs must execute in an environment that combines features of redundancy, deadline scheduling, network operating systems and fault tolerant databases. The PCEE (Portable Common Execution Environment) is an attempt to specify an architecture that is applicable to the Space Station and similar large projects. Moreover, the PCEE is not just aimed at supporting Ada but is designed to be also implemented in Ada.

PCEE recognises three types of software environments, each with different functional and operational requirements. The three are:

(i)   *host*; primary concern: the development and maintenance of software;

(ii) *target*, primary concern: the deployment and operation of executing code;

(iii) *integration*; primary concern: managing changes in the target environment.

This paper focuses on the architecture of the target environment and those parts of the integration environment that interact with the target environment or execute on target hardware.

The primary aim of a PCEE is to provide a portable interface to a fault tolerant distributed real-time operating system. In doing so it inevitably prescribes certain properties for the underlying software and hardware. It therefore can perhaps best be seen as an interface specification plus the minimal architecture needed to build/implement the interface.

As application software will primarily be written in Ada, the interface that PCEE provides will take the form of package specifications. These library packages extend the view that an application has of the underlying functionality of the system. Different applications will need different views and therefore a number of distinct packages will be made available. Note that some PCEE interface packages will only be available to authorised host environment tools; for example the basic run-time library may only be used by appropriate compilers. Other libraries will be used directly by the application code; an example here would be an extended set of run-time features to control, say, scheduling.

It follows from the above point, and from the need to partition the software components of the operating system (for fault tolerant as well as good engineering reasons), that the services provided in a PCEE are built from distinct software modules arranged in layers and operating on top of a run-time system (RTS). A bare machine approach is taken, ie the RTS is supported by a kernel that interacts directly with the hardware. The following sections will look at each PCEE service, starting with a minimal view of the hardware configuration.

The PCEE uses an object oriented paradigm. An object may be an arbitrarily complex piece of data (know as a data object), a subprogram, a package, an individual thread of control or even a complete program. All objects are seen as instances of some abstraction; it follows that all operations that can be applied to any object type are visible and are declared with the object's abstraction. In essence the PCEE, together with the applications it supports, forms an object management system. Distribution is supported at the object level. This can accommodate both pre and post partitioning approaches, and coarse or fine grain granularity. The project that has the most influence on PCEE has been the Alpha Kernel[7].

HARDWARE ARCHITECTURE

The processing elements of the hardware are assumed to be grouped into clusters; the clusters themselves are linked via local area or even wide area networks (including gateway connections). At the basic level of communication between clusters a reliable service is not assumed. Clusters do not share memory with each other and have the following properties:

- They can fail completely
- They can experience faults that will lead to downgraded operation.
- They can be added at any time.
- They can be removed at any time.
- They can have their software changed (dynamically).
- They have access to memory subsystems including some stable storage.
- They may control access to system resources such as:

    (i) Large virtual memory capabilities.
    (ii) Floating point units.
    (iii) Specific external devices, eg ADCs

- They have the capability to be restarted after failure.
- They contain processors of the same type, ie they run the same instruction code and have identical data representation (different cluster need not use the same processor type).

The stable storage, which is used to construct a fault tolerant distributed information system, will exhibit high reliability but will nevertheless have a small probability of failure, ie it cannot be considered to be truly permanent memory. Within the long operational life of the Space Station this probability may become a liability and other techniques (such as redundant copies) will need to be provided by the appropriate system component.

KERNEL FEATURES

As processors are not required to be of the same type, a kernel layer is placed on top of the hardware. It hides features that are machine-dependent. This minimal kernel supports the basic run-time system and will typically include functions such as disc I/O services, memory management, process management, run-time error handling, basic interrupt handling and the primitives for constructing atomic actions.

Process management will consist of a policy free dispatcher. Schedulable objects (typically Ada tasks) that are eligible to execute will be held on an appropriate data structure. The implications being that they are queued in priority order. Measures must be taken to ensure that the kernel and its data structures are fault tolerant.

DISTRIBUTED OPERATING SYSTEM

The full run-time environment is implemented via extended kernel services and library modules. It will support functions such as:

- dynamic memory management including virtual memory services;

- object storage management;

- an execution environment for Ada tasking (eg task create etc);

- scheduling services for real-time control processing.

From this list the major interfaces by which the software system interacts with the kernel can be identified (these are collectively known as the DOS — Distributed Operating System):

(a) object system interface, including visibility of stable, non-volatile and volatile storage

(b) standard run-time library (RTL) available to the Ada compiler and to other components of the PCEE

(c) extended run-time library (XRTL) available to the applications programmer for real-time computations (ie ARTEWG CIFO)[1]. Provisions for deadline scheduling are included

(d) atomic action (transaction) system interface

Although the device driver for the stable storage device is considered part of the kernel facilities, other drivers are viewed as application utilities.

All RTL services (eg high level scheduler, transaction manager, etc) are provided as schedulable objects for the kernel; they will typically have higher priorities than application tasks and may additionally have kernel level privileges. This approach allows the kernel to be policy free, with the policy dependent modules running as "tasks" above the kernel.

One consequence of this architecture is that the functionality of the RTS can be changed during execution. To this end the highest priority "task" at any cluster will be one that has the capability to effect other RTS or application tasks. This *configuration* task can only be called by the DCCS (see below).

SOFTWARE COMPONENTS OF THE PCEE

For all software components it is possible to take three views of their functionality, structure and availability:

(a) definition of the objects that are exported from the component (together with the operations that can be applied to these objects). For many components the objects may need to be subdivided into classes, with the understanding that not all classes will be available to all "clients" and that under abnormal operation a component may have its functionality restricted.

(b) definition of the subcomponents from which the main component is built. This definition will include the relationships between the objects of the component itself and those of any hidden subcomponent.

(c) definition of the external clients (other PCEE components or application software) that can use (or are using) the objects (or classes) available.

There is a need to formally (or at least precisely) specify these views for each component of the PCEE. One approach would be to make use of semantics models of the EA/RA form.

To the application layer only view (a) is significant. This gives the interface to the component. The collection of all such interfaces is known as the *system interface set* (SIS). By contrast the integration environment will need to have access to all three views.

Each view has itself a static and a dynamic perspective. The static perspective encompass the complete interface, all subcomponent relations and all access rights to the interface (for security). The dynamic perspective gives the current usage of the interface and subcomponents.

The integration environment will obtain the static information from the host environment. The dynamic behaviour requires the monitoring of the target.

Three major software components have been recognised as necessary in any PCEE:

- **Distributed Communication System (DCS)**
- **Distributed Configuration and Control System (DCCS)**
- **Distributed Information System (DIS)**

Each of these will now be considered in turn.

Distributed Communication System

All low-level communications appropriate to network traffic are hidden within this component. It provides higher level message abstractions. In particular it must provide:

(a) asynchronous sends (including broadcasts) and associated buffers (mailboxes).

(b) remote procedure calls.

(c) remote rendezvous.

The semantics of asynchronous send is receive-once. However use of this primitive is limited as the receipt of any such message cannot be assumed by the sender within a predefined time period.

To implement the latter two it will be necessary for the DCS to create surrogates tasks in the RTS of the designated cluster.

A remote procedure call has many of the attributes of an atomic action; it is therefore defined to have *at-most-once* semantics[3].

This usually means that the call is made exactly once with a single reply being generated and received by the caller; if this fails to happen then the call is not made at all (in effect). Within a real-time context this definition has to be weakened somewhat. By use of stable storage and a commit protocol it is possible to ensure that a failed procedure's execution will leave the distributed (persistent) information system unchanged (see discussion on DIS). However an external event may have been triggered by a partial execution of the procedure (prior to cluster failure for example). The required semantics for a remote procedure call therefore cover the following three cases:

(a) procedure executes exactly once with any changes to persistent objects being committed.

(b) procedure's execution did not begin; an exception being raised (say, PROCEDURE_START_ERROR).

(c) procedure's execution did not complete. No persistent objects have been committed; a distinct exception being raised (say, PROCEDURE_TERMINATION_ERROR).

As a remote rendezvous will effect the thread of control of another (remote) object then the only semantics information returned to the caller will be either that the rendezvous was successful or:

(i) It failed because of language defined semantics (ie TASKING_ERROR or other application defined exception); or

(ii) It failed because of a failed cluster (ie CLUSTER_ERROR).

Note that there is an important difference between the raising of TASKING_ERROR and CLUSTER_ERROR. If a rendezvous request generated TASKING_ERROR then all subsequent calls must produce the same effect. This is not the case with CLUSTER_ERROR; a second rendezvous attempt may indeed succeed.

The necessary mechanism to implement a remote rendezvous are discussed by Burns, Lister and Wellings[4]. Experimental work with remote rendezvous has been undertaken by Honeywell[5] and as part of the Diadem projects[2].

The interface that DCS provides has two important classes. The actual objects for making use of remote procedure calls and remote rendezvous are only available to the application software via tools in the host environment. However the libraries that define the necessary exceptions may be made directly available to the application.

Within the PCEE other logical messages will need to be constructed and communicated (eg remote elaboration, two-phase commit, etc); these will be made available at a layer above the DCS and will use DCS facilities (only).

Within the DCS consideration must be taken of the processor types that the two partners in the communication are executing upon. If the processors are of the same type (ie they have the same data representation) then no internal data transformations are necessary or desirable. However it is possible that heterogeneous processors are involved; in this case a transformation protocol is needed. The protocol must be extensible as new processor types may be added to a running system.

Distributed Configuration and Control System

The primary function of the DCCS is to be the window on the target environment for the integration environment. Under normal operation the DCCS will monitor the behaviour of the clusters and report this (using the DCS) to where the functionality of the integration environment resides. Other normal facilities that it will control are:

- The introduction of a new object to a cluster.

- The movement of an object from one cluster to another (or the simple removal of an object).

- The loading of a subprogram (or task) object (load module) for subsequent usage.

- The start up of a program.

- The unloading of a program object (load module).

- The introduction of new RTS objects.

- The dynamic replacement of a program object by an equivalent (extended or modified) object.

Under abnormal conditions the integration environment may need to reduce activity in order to deal with a potentially hazardous situation. In this eventuality the DCCS may be called upon to:

- abort a program object.

- freeze a program object (ie give it no further processor time until the hazard has been dealt with).

- reduce the availability of software components by limiting access to their interfaces.

Distributed Information System

One of the consequences of multiprogramming is that there will be many objects that are shared between applications. The DIS component on each cluster gives access to a distributed object base and provides the operators by which these objects may be manipulated.

For a new application its use of existing DIS objects will first need to be sanctioned by the integration environment. Applications may also be allowed to add to the DIS object base.

To protect persistent objects from failures in particular applications (and from system failures) all operations on DIS objects are implemented as transactions. An application may group these transactions together thereby exploiting nested transactions[6].

All objects reside within the stable storage of some cluster. Each cluster's DIS knows what objects it has access to. It can also find out which cluster holds any specified object. The movement of objects is however under DCCS control. If the DIS gets a request (from an application) to access a non-local object then the appropriate (external) DIS will be sent a message via the DCS. This message will take the form of a remote procedure call and is thus itself a transaction. In general objects will remain static (stay at the same cluster) the DIS will therefore have been given knowledge of where all objects, an application uses, are located. Any change to the location of an object can only be done through the integration environment which knows which applications use it and therefore which DISs need to be informed.

An application executing a remote procedure call or remote rendezvous will interact with both the DIS and DCS. The destination of the cluster will be given by the DIS; the actual call being undertaken by the DCS.

To increase reliability an object may be duplicated on more than one cluster. The details of duplication are however transparent to the application (and to the transaction manager in the RTS). The DIS will give access to one site and will update shadow copies whenever any commit is done to update the main one.

In general an application will manipulate objects that are either: managed by the DIS, or held completely within the application space. An application may use any fault-tolerant technique it wishes to control its own objects (including programming its own shadow copies). It may however make use of the DIS even when the object is not shared. If it does this it can take advantage of:

(a)   transaction updates, and/or

(b)   duplication.

To summarise, the DIS interface must:

*   define the objects that are accessible to applications (under access control for security).

*   define the operations for manipulating these objects; these will be implemented as transactions (or at least atomic actions).

- allow transactions to be nested by defining top-level transaction "start" and "commit" operations.

- allow new objects (and operators) to be added to the DIS (under the control of the DCCS).

- allow objects to be deleted (under appropriate control).

A new object would have a number of characteristics; eg temporary or permanent, single-user or multi-program access, duplication needed or single site.

INTEGRATION ENVIRONMENT

As was stated earlier the integration environment (IE) controls changes in the target. The "static" behaviour of the target is said to represent a baseline. During execution of a baseline the IE has no direct function; it will however monitor cluster and network performance, via the DCCS.

The main operation of the IE is to extend the baseline by introducing new (possibly distributed) application programs. This will involve four distinct steps:

(a)   Verify that new application software is in an appropriate state to be transferred to the target. This stage is, essentially, an interaction between the host and integration environments. The IE may need behavioural measurements from the target to accomplish this verification.

(b)   Pass, via the DIS and DCS, load-module objects to the effected clusters. This may include redundant copies for fault tolerance (or for simple flexibility - see below).

(c)   Load the load-modules on the target clusters. At this point the DIS at each cluster will be given a static map for all external objects (including shadow copies if they exist).

(d)   If loading was successful then the application can be started by sending the appropriate main module a "start" message.

Note that some applications will run non-stop (having once started), others may be invoked (either automatically or under human control) periodically. For this latter class there may be some flexibility as to where a new execution (or part of it) is placed. However all allocations must have been verified by the IE. Typically the load modules will already be in place and a new execution will merely involve choosing a version and undertaking steps (c) and (d). For terminating programs the IE (DCCS) will also need to 'unload' modules.

The other main action of the IE is to reduce (or change) the baseline under abnormal conditions. This may include: symbolic debugging, dynamic reconfiguration of application software, reconfiguring object base, aborting transactions, aborting applications, changing priorities of application tasks, and reducing PCEE services. All of these activities will be affected by the DCCS.

CONCLUSION

This paper gives a top level description of the architecture of the PCEE. A user application can gain access to the underlying services by using the interfaces provided by the Distributed Operating System, Distributed Communication System and Distributed Information System. In addition the Integration Environment has access to the Distributed Configuration and Control System.

The motivation behind the design of the PCEE is the provision of mission and safety critical systems. To this end the following features are significant:

- An extended run-time library for real-time computation.

- Redundancy at the kernel level so that non-fatal processor failures can be trapped and corrected for.

- An interface at the kernel level to stable storage so that transaction commit protocols can be implemented.

- An information system that supports nested transactions and, separately, object replication.

- A communication system that hides communication failures (but will notify users of processor failure).

- An integration environment that controls changes to the baseline.

- An integration environment that can abort (or reduce) functionality so that critical systems can be executed more effectively.

Current work on the PCEE involves the building of a test-bed implementation.

References

1. ARTEWG, *A Catalog of Interface Features and Options for the Ada Runtime Environment*, p. ARTEWG, December 1987.

2. C. Atkinson, T. Moreton, and A. Natali, *Ada for Distributed Systems,* Ada Companion Series, Cambridge University Press, 1988.

3. A. D. Birrell and B. J. Nelson, "Implementing Remote Procedure Calls," *ACM Transactions on Computer Systems*, vol. 2, no. 1, pp. 39-59, 1984.

4. A. Burns, A.M. Lister, and A.J. Wellings, *A Review of Ada Tasking,* Lecture Notes in Computer Science, Volume 262, Springer-Verlag, 1987.

5. D. Cornhill, "A Survivable Distributed Computing System for Embedded Application Programs written in Ada," *Ada Letters*, vol. 3, no. 3, 1984.

6. J.E.B. Moss, *Nested Transactions: An Approach to Reliable Distributed Computing,* Massachusetts Institute of Technology, April 1981.

7. J.D. Northcutt, *Mechanisms for Reliable Distributed Real-Time Operating Systems: The Alpha Kernel,* Academic Press, 1987.

Promethee: Designing a Process Control System

G. Auxiette
TOTAL, Cedex 47, 92 069 Paris La Défense, France

J.F. Cabadi
CISI INGENIERIE, 3 rue Le Corbusier, SILIC 232, 94 528 Rungis, France

P. Rehbinder
CISI INGENIERIE, 3 rue Le Corbusier, SILIC 232, 94 528 Rungis, France

Abstract.
The general aim of the paper is to show the 'state of the art' of several activities related to Ada (design for Ada, integration in Unix, compatibility with software libraries or networks) as felt by the authors during the development of a process control system. For some of these activities, satisfactory solutions will be shown; for other activities, only costly or incomplete ones have been found, and the problem will be left open. The context of the study (specifications, hardware, ...) will first be stated. The main characteristics of the design process will be described. Some selected topics of the design work will then be discussed, especially those relevant to soft real-time systems.

THE PROMETHEE PROJECT

Oil recovery techniques

According to the domain experts, classical techniques allow the recovery of only a few part of the subsoil oil (much less than 50 %). More advanced techniques, known and used today (steam injection for instance), improve this efficiency in a significant way in the case of shallow fields only, typically 1000 meters deep. Beyond this depth, air injection should be a very promising way, always according to these same experts.

Badly controled up to now, this technique is experimentally studied in several laboratories in the world. These laboratories are nevertheless few in number, because of the high cost of a really significative implementation. TOTAL decided to develop such a laboratory. It looks like a small plant containing 'equipments' (fig. 1).

A process control system

Using such mechanics involves a process control system the software of which should help in solving different problems: automating for several weeks the command of the process without an operator present; managing process i/o (several thousands of sensors and actuators); real-time and offline analysis of measurement data; step by step installing and testing a complex system; ensuring that the equipment works properly; allowing a friendly operator interface (synoptics, telecommand, menus, messages, dialogs, hard-copy, parameters).

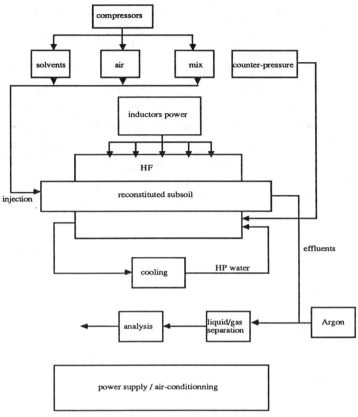

Fig. 1

Basic choices

Given some basic choices (or wishes), CISI INGENIERIE has been in charge of the process control system, and especially the software. These basic choices are the following ones:

Modularity of the system

Given the availability today of cheap and powerfull processors, the intelligence of the system has been distributed in so-called 'functionnal units', which are as much as possible independant. This choice rather than a hierarchical and layered organization or even a completely centralized one implies interesting characteristics: the installation and even specification of the system can be more easily repartitioned in time. Each node technology can be adapted to its functions. Cost savings are involved in hardware purchases and cabling works. The intelligence being near the sensors, the quality of measures can be much better than it is when using common industrial acquisition tools.

The main problem involved is the need of a communication network.

Development plan

One basic choice was a development plan including the validation of a subset. This subset has been chosen to be as representative as possible of the whole system, and this is actually the control system for a stand-alone module. Other features of the adopted development plan derive from CISI INGENIERIE's typical life-cycle for new software. Of course, the development was not absolutely planned as described at the early beginning of the project. This is thus a description of the typical life-cycle for new software ... given the experience of this project ! these features are:

1985:	Specs of whole system v1 (not complete); use of SADT
	Specs of validation system v1 (almost complete)
1986:	Design of validation system v1
1987:	Realization up to software integration of validation system v1
1988:	Specs of whole system v2 (not complete)
	Specs of validation system v2 (complete)
	Design of software v2
1989:	Realization of software v2

Network nodes

Another basic choice was to use the VME bus as key concept for the instrumentation computers. The VME bus is at once a *de facto* standard supported by numerous harware and software suppliers, and by competent subcontractors, and a technically adapted solution (modular, performant, mature). The VME bus has not been retained for the development computers and for the operator interface computers. Unix workstations have been retained while supporting higher quality tools.

Programming language

It was wished that Ada be the unique programming language for the whole project. It was definitely chosen at the begining of 1987. As for VME, Ada is both a standard with multiple users and suppliers, and a technically adapted solution (DoD requirements, performance, maturity). One of the reasons why this language has been chosen is perhaps that the project leader (not just the software leader) has been previously involved in software-only projects and thus appreciates more easily its advantages.

THE DESIGN PROCESS
Guidelines

In the context of the previously described development plan, we will insist on the design work of version 1 and on the experience we got in implementing this design and transforming it into the version 2 design.

Context

Most pieces of work of this project have been performed by people working during several years on different domains rather than by specialists in the sense: THE expert of Ada, or THE expert of numerical control, or THE expert of software design. In such a context, it was not possible to invest in very specialized CASE tools or methods, and we stood at the Unix, Ada and paper level. This sparsity of exotic concepts in the project allowed 5 different engineers and 2 students to work on the software without need for too many specific tools or education.

It was finally found important to standardize code and architecture. This can be done with the above-mentionned tools. Engineers must however in such a case follow project rules. When these rules are built upon the above-mentionned low level tools, we are sure they can be understood and eventually applied by everyone. Rules supported by higher level tools could be (we have no experience of it) harder to ensure. It is possible the software leader itself would not be able to fully understand them!

OOD

Before we began the design of the version 1 system, two possibilities have been evaluated:

- using one of the emerging OOD (Object Oriented Design) methods,
- using classical and not very formalized techniques.

OOD as described in [EVB, 85] and [Booch, 83] was finally found unsatisfactory on several grounds which are mainly:

We had users who approximately knew what they wanted for their process control system. We wanted to build an implementation of their wishes upon existing supports (Ada, 68020, electricity, that sort of existing things). The initial task of clarifying the demand without the help of the system version 1 (*Specifications*) was performed in a very classical way by using interviews and readers/writers cycles supported by text and SADT-like diagrams. The next task (*Design*), consists in evaluating, comparing and justifying the so-called 'design choices'. These design choices (or 'architecture') must be expressed in terms relevant to the domain of the solution, not the problem. In our case, the minimum contents of the architecture are:

- which environment (hardware configuration, development system, operating systems, reused components) should we use ?
- how will concurrency be organized (synchronization and communication between external world, Unix processes, Ada tasks and network nodes) ?

- what is the statiç architecture and development plan (modules, interfaces, tests) ?

Only the last question is partially answered by the OOD methods. Actually, even this point is unsufficiently covered by the method, the following areas having to be solved for each case outside the method: test and integration support, large-scale software, choice qualification or justification. Finally we did not find it useful to devote specific education time and documentation to OOD during our design work.

As OOD methods consist in working on the problem domain only, without taking into account the target environment, they should not be named *design* methods. An area in which they could perhaps be of some help is the *specifications* one, when the problem is to work, detail, formalize, understand or organize the problem. Perhaps a promising trend in this area is that of the methods used to implement an informal specification in an object oriented environment (see KOD in [Vogel, 88]), or in a database environment (see [Shlaer et al., 88]). It is interesting to notice that OOD uses in a more simple and less professional way the same elementary techniques as the two above-mentionned methods (analysis of the natural language).

HOOD

The design of this system being carried out by CISI INGENIERIE members, one could ask why not use HOOD (Hierarchical Object Oriented Design, see [Heitz, 87]) ? HOOD was not widly used for the simple reason it was not entirely defined at this time; it was only available as preliminary versions. However, a discussion of HOOD can be attempted in the Promethee context.

The standard HOOD documentation and typical life-cycle contain 'hooks' but little formalism to be used in order to specify the environment. These hooks are the chapter 1.2.Analysis and structuration of givens filled during the phase 1-Problem definition.

The standard HOOD documentation contains hooks for the dynamic architecture; these are the fields Object Control Structure of the ODS (Object Description Skeleton). The formalism however is limited to the design of Ada concurrency and is not directly applicable to other concurrency supports like Unix and network as in the Promethee case.

The static architecture is well taken into account for our middle-sized Ada software. The adequacy for large-scale software or non-Ada software is to be studied. Other aspects of design like development plan or tests are not prohibited but not directly taken into account.

The more formal parts of the method were found needlessly constraining: Formalization-of-the-strategy rules can not be used formally. Architecture qualification criteria (passive object cycles, coupling/cohesion definition) are too simply stated in the basic HOOD manual. To get the detailed criteria, we must have a look into the references of HOOD (Buhr, Yourdon, Parnas).

Chosen principles

An architecture was finally elaborated in roughly one year. This design work was essentially based on HOOD for the formalism added with older general principles. These general principles are those of classical software engineering books and articles published in the seventies ([Yourdon et al., 79], [Parnas, 72], [Parnas, 79]). Most of them are referenced in the HOOD reference manual.

The architecture finally consists of an Hardware architecture documentation, a Dynamic architecture documentation (concurrency management), and a Static architecture documentation. The Static architecture documentation itself consists of a hierarchy of documents similar to that of HOOD.

Our temporary conclusion is that the architecture documentation (including formalisms such as structure charts, dataflow diagrams, data models, state-transition diagrams), as well as the design rules should be tailored to the domain, or even to the project. We didn't need for instance data models, and few state-transition diagrams, but specific concurrency languages. We are rather client of a toolbox than of a close self-contained method. For instance, we find valuable the heuristics contained in [Buhr, 84] (unfortunately, we fully understood them only after the system has been integrated!).

System architecture

The final architecture can be described in two parts: system architecture and software architecture. The system architecture itself consists of a target system and a development system. The software architecture will be described latter.

The target consists of instrumentation computers and operator interface computer(s) linked through a communication network (Fig. 2).

The development system manages the project database (source files, libraries, executable generation scripts, documentation editing, library products), and provides tools to test and run a distributed application including hardware. The two keywords of the chosen development system are Unix and Ada (Fig. 3). Unix is used in a standard almost raw mode which is found to be perfectly sufficient and powerful. The Ada tools are those of Alsys and their basic capabilities were found sufficient too.

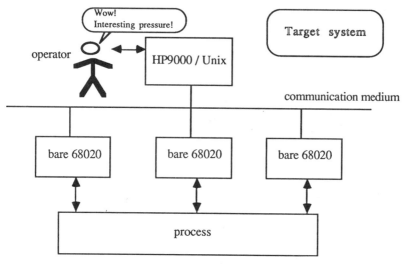

Fig. 2

The limits of the Ada tools are found when problems arise at the lowest and highest levels. There is generally no problem at the lowest level in the native environment, but there can be in the cross one (hardware faults, unexpected interrupts or traps, memory conflicts or limits ...). When the tests reach the final integration steps, the debugging tools are generally no longer usable, because of limits like time management, multiple io's, multi-processor execution, addition of localized debugger limits, ... in these two cases (analysis of lowest and highest level problems), debugging tools specific to the hardware and the application must be prepared apart from the standard Ada facilities.

The source files are managed the same way are they intended to be executed on Unix or on a bare 68020. The physical organization of the source files on the development file system is tightly linked to the static architecture of the application (modules) and not at all to its dynamic architecture (which partially takes into account native / cross subtle differences). Some modules must be included both in Unix and bare 68020 programs. Actually, every module intended to be included in a bare 68020 program is tested on Unix before being tested on a bare machine, except for the ones directly interfaced with hardware, which are rare. It is clear that development and especially testing is easier in a native context (Unix, VMS, AOS/VS, ...) than in a cross one. Although preliminary native tests greatly speed up final cross tests, the latter must always be performed. In a cross development targeted to a bare machine, enough months (eventually weeks, depending on experience) must be spent on installing and testing the development tool before trying to use it for the application. This is not the case in the native case where the marketed tools can be immediately downloaded and used. The quantity of work implied by using a cross development toolset is due to several reasons. The main reason we identified is that installing such a toolset is dependent on two opposite work methods: large-scale software and small-scale electronic. The first one must be precise and not neglect a single detail, the second one allows approximations and incomplete definition of components.

The C language remains used as little as possible, and today in only 2 cases: interface with Unix packages (graphics, io, signals, ipc) and bodies of two bit manipulation packages. Hardware interfacing and time-critical modules are written in Ada.

All 'real-time' problems are managed around the 68020 Ada kernels. We did not use bare processors with a sequential language or another real-time kernel, or the real-time features of our Unix.

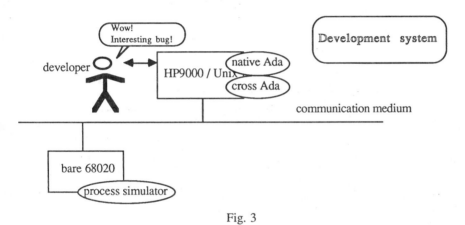

Fig. 3

Software architecture

From the static point of view, the software architecture (Fig. 4) consists of several modules in the classical sense of software engineering (or objects in the OOD or HOOD terminologies).

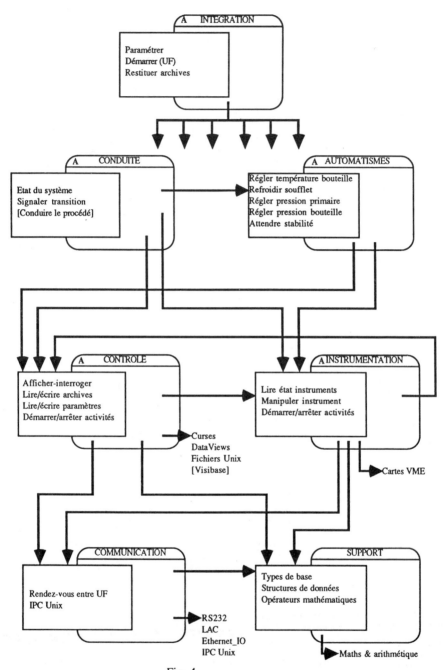

Fig. 4

These modules can also be classified in respect to the adequacy of Ada as a support to build them. From this point of view, we have 'parameters', 'application modules' and 'basic modules'.

Parameters

The process parameters are managed by the users. They are often numerical values like equipment tuning, software regulator setting, effluent analysis results. These parameters have a short life-cycle. Bare Ada is not a particularly suitable tool for them, but the designer must look for a solution in technologies like papers, menus and screen forms, graphical packages or user interface toolboxes. The programming language is not the main design choice is this area.

There are other parameters which must be considered apart. These are the control system parameters like communication time-outs or process IO configuration (VME-boards list, with name, address, node name, board type). For these parameters, bare Ada is perfectly suitable. We did not use however the Ada features which seem at first glance to address this problem: *constants* and *generics*. Ada constants used as parameters do not allow easily the tuning of an application and other constructs must be used. Concerning large-scale generics, we have always had problems with the tools, in this project as well as in others. Perhaps this last problem will disappear in the future?

Application modules

The application modules are closer to the developpers, they are dedicated to a particular use of equipment. For instance, they contain the algorithms used to fill a bottle at a given pressure and volume, or the description of coherency tests to be periodically performed on a sensors set, or the high level process control rules. These modules are generally written in such applications by using specific languages like Grafcet associated to lower level operations (control of sensors / actuators, delays, elementary synchronization / communication between automata, computation black boxes). The same situation can be found in robotic, where the application programming language is not a general-purpose one. We have tried to let these modules be written by the computer people under control of the process people, by using standard Ada associated to lower level operations. Standard Ada is used to express delays, synchronization / communication between automata which actually are Ada tasks, and computation. The lower level operations are Ada library units among those described above.

Integration with the process and maintenance of these modules will show if Ada is suitable for the long-dated life of these modules. For the design and first implementation of these modules, it is clear that Ada is a well-suited tool.

Basic modules

The basic modules are entirely managed by the developpers, from specification to implementation. Their life-cycle is independant of that of the process, and they perform tasks like user interface, archive storage and analysis, process parameters management, synoptic animation and telecommand, VME-boards control, single sensor / actuator control for each sensor / actuator type, communication. Ada is here used as a low-level system programming language and as an integrating tool; such modules include reused software (Ada source and commercially available binary products). The language is a good solution for the low-level system programming problems. Concerning the integrating tool problem, it is a good solution when the problem is to reuse already existing sources (mathematical libraries, data structures, format management, ...). When the problem is to integrate a commercially available binary product into the application , the language itself is of no particular help. The problem must then be analysed in each case: which product, which compiler, which operating system.

SELECTED TOPICS

Concurrency design

After the specification step, we dispose of specification documents and knowledge describing a hardware/software system along with usual quality criteria. The different points of view of the architecture must then be studied simultaneously : selection of the support environment, dynamic architecture and static architecture in our case. In the very first design steps, each of these three points of view interacts with the others. After the main choices are outlined, these different points of view can be almost independantly refined, because they have then well identified and localized interfaces. We will now describe the dynamic architecture design process, without interest in its effects upon the other design processes, and assuming the other architectures are known from the beginning.

Objectives of the dynamic architecture

As previously introduced, the dynamic architecture is aimed at defining synchronization and communication between external world, Unix processes, Ada tasks and network. Actually, we want to decide in our case:

- what should we buy or declare among hardware processors, Ada tasks, and Unix processes ?

- how will these components share ressources (priorities) ?

- how will these tasks be synchronized and how will they communicate? we can use Ada rendez-vous, Ada shared memory, hardware networking, Unix files, and Unix inter-process-communication facilities (mainly semaphors, messages and shared memories). We will not use VME-bus facilities while only one of the processor boards of each bus supports a part of the application.

- how will these tasks be synchronized and how will they communicate with the environment (Text_IO, Unix system call, register polling, interrupt) ?

Classical support for concurrency design

The general rules we can find in methods or research papers which address this problem generally try to reduce the hardware costs or to implement severe timing requirements (Rate monotonic scheduling, cyclic executives, [Softech, 86], ...). These systems are generally named 'hard real-time systems'. In our case, hardware costs depend mainly on the sensors / actuators number and localization, or on user interface requirements, but little on software architecture. Given our 'cool real-time system' problem and no applicable rules, we did not use hardware costs or timing requirements as decision criteria. We just discovered during version 1 development which rules were valuable and we checked during version 1 integration that the timing requirements were reached.

Initial dynamic architecture

The first task identification criteria are:

- tasks must be in charge of the management of external events: operator input, clock. We do not use for the moment input VME-boards interrupts.

- tasks must be used in the solution to express the parallelism of specifications (e.g. fill simultaneously two bottles). This rule eventually wastes CPU time, but certainly saves design and maintenance time.

In the case of the validation system, these rules let us define 16 tasks, consisting of 6 operator interface tasks and 10 specifications tasks.

Improvement of the dynamic architecture

This initial architecture is unsatisfactory on several grounds. We will gradually modify it by analysing and solving problems one by one. Actually, we will see that these problems are mostly independent, and this is the reason why we can solve them one by one.

Each hardware processor is identified by the needs of remaining near a localized sensors / actuators set or near user interface media. Each processor needs a task which starts at processor reset, initializes the environment, starts other tasks,... in the case of the two-nodes validation system, we thus need 2 new tasks.

Several tasks (exactly 4) are dedicated to off-line file management. They should than be Unix processes rather than Ada tasks. Our architecture now contains 18 tasks, which are 12 named Ada tasks plus 6 anonymous Ada tasks or 6 Ada programs, 5 of which are Unix process.

A development method called 'distributed rendez-vous' has already been studied by CISI INGENIERIE for the European Space Agency [Farail et al., 87]. A similar approach targeting the available concurrency support has been used. It implies 'sender' tasks to transform remote subprogram calls into network messages and 'server' tasks to transform network messages into local subprogram calls. The list of server tasks is a compromise between only one task for all remotely callable subprograms and one task for each remotely callable subprogram. The first choice does not preserve the Ada semantic, but the second one would not be acceptable in certain cases (when numerous remotely callable subprograms are actually mapped to a single underlying task). In the validation system, 17 more Ada tasks are thus created (current count: 35 tasks).

User interface echoes should be made available to the output devices (screens) less than tenthes of second after the input event (keybord and mouse events). The native Ada executive we use forbids task periods lower than 1 second in multi-tasking programs. Unix allows process periods lower than 1 second. Our current architecture contains two Ada tasks dedicated to input event management, including echo generation. To satisfy the above-mentionned requirement, we must transform these two Ada tasks into two Unix processes (or Ada programs). Communication between these two new programs and the Ada tasks remaining in the main program can no more be performed through rendez-vous and shared variables. We need 'server' tasks of the kind of those already described. Instead of distributing upon a send/receive network, we just distribute upon Unix IPC (Inter Process Communication). Of course, using concurrent Unix processes involves several problems to be solved by using local Unix concepts (parent-child relationships, fixed or changing priorities, which priorities) and no more Ada concepts only. In the validation system, 2 Ada tasks are changed to Unix processes and 3 more Ada tasks are created (current count: 38 tasks).

Mutual exclusion between concurrent access to shared ressources involves 5 new tasks. Current and final count: 43 tasks.

Conclusion

Most of the concurrency design choices have been determined by using rules highly dependent on the particular Promethee context. We have even not detailed dynamic architecture choices related to communication/synchronization between the concurrent tasks. We have tried to generalize the above applied rules. Several of them depend on minor specification or support environment features, but have major development consequences. The actual value of the acceptable user interface speed was for instance one of these specifications. The 'one-second' feature of our version of the compiler is one of these support environment features. Using Unix IPC is one of these major development consequences. Most of the rules are largely arguable. However, we think they will be applicable to the fully-specified system. An interesting job would be to try to generalize these rules to other domains (specifications and support environment).

Performance characteristics

As described above concerning the dynamic architecture design, we generally tried to chose simple and general solutions against locally acceptable but sophisticated ones. We only checked selected performances during the version 1 integration and took these results into account during the version 2 design. This attitude can already be justified. Firstly, we didn't get performance problems other than the user echo one during the version 1 integration. Secondly, simple and general choices allowed us evolutions we couldn't afford otherwise. For instance, we designed the application with 68000 processors in mind, but actually implemented it on 68020 and we could profit of 68030 if necessary. We can even execute the bare-machine program on different boards. Another example is the change from VRTX to ARTK (profit on simplicity and performance), which has been transparent for the application. Another example is the ability to easily move a high level task from one node to another (in order to improve performance, perform most of the tests under Unix, execute the process simulators under Unix as well as on a bare machine, ...).

Let's look at performances measured on a particular module. This module is included in every VME-hosted program and manages all input/output signals of the bus. Its function is to export subprograms such as 'set the digital output #17', or 'clear the digital output #17', or 'get the digital input #1', or 'set the analog output #12 to 0.4 Volt', or 'move 1_230 steps forward the stepper motor #3'. Each such module is parametrized (without recompilation) by the actual configuration of its bus. By configuration, we mean boards list, including name, address and type, and analog input filtering options. For the validation system configuration (20 analog input, 2 analog output, 92 digital input, 20 digital output, 3 stepper motors), the module periodically consumes 6 ms. For an acquisition bus driving 200 thermocouples, the same module consumes periodically 15 ms. These numbers allow us to set all bus periods to 100 ms without bothering about optimization or unreliable situation.

CONCLUSION

This application project uses multiple techniques. The first point of this conclusion will be that we found valuable and less valuable supports:

- valuable formal support: Ada, Unix
- not valuable formal support: OOD, networking
- valuable yet not formal support: classical software development life-cycle and associated heuristics, with cycles as short and numerous as the problem is new.

The second point is that it would be interesting to try to generalize selected topics of the described approach outside of the Promethee context . The limit is to be defined: process control, robotics, embedded system, Ada software? The topics to be generalized are to be defined as well: design, concurrency design, architecture documentation, simulation, life-cycle?

BIBLIOGRAPHY

Booch G.
Software Engineering with Ada, Benjamin Cumings, Menlo Park, California, 1983

Buhr R.J.A.
System Design with Ada, Prentice-Hall Inc, Englewood Cliffs, NJ, 1984

EVB
Object Oriented Design Handbook, EVB Software Engineering Inc., 1985

Farail P., Labreuille B.
"Application du langage Ada aux systèmes temps-réel distribués", *Journées Ada-AFCET*, 1987

Heitz M.
"Hood, une méthode de conception hiérarchisée orientée objets pour le développement des logiciels techniques et temps-réel", *Journées Ada-AFCET*, 1987

Parnas D.L.
"On the criteria to be used in decomposing systems into modules", *Commun. ACM 15*, 12 (dec. 1972), 1053-1058

Parnas D.L.
"Designing software for ease of extension and contraction", *IEEE transactions on software engineering*, vol SE5, N°2, march 79, 128-137

Shlaer S., Mellor S.J.
Object-Oriented Systems Analysis, Prentice-Hall Inc, Englewood Cliffs, NJ, 1988

Softech Inc
Designing Real-Time Systems in Ada, Waltham, MA, 1986

Vogel C.
Génie Cognitif, Masson, Paris, 1988

Yourdon E., Constantine L.
Structured Design, Prentice-Hall Inc, Englewood Cliffs, NJ, 1979

Ada Tools for Rapid Prototyping of Real-Time Systems.

A. Crespo(*), J. A. de la Puente(**), A. Espinosa(*), A. Garcia-Fornés(*).

(*) Grupo de Informática Industrial, Universidad Politécnica de Valencia,
PO Box 22012, E-46071 Valencia, Spain.

(**) Facultad de Informática, Universidad Politécnica de Madrid,
E-28660 Boadilla del Monte, Madrid, Spain.

Abstract. The QUISAP language, based on the event-action model developed by Jahanian and Mok, is taken as a basis for the specification and rapid prototyping of real-time systems. The approach focuses on the formal description of the reactive behaviour of a system subject to timing constraints, showing how an Ada prototype of such a real-time system can be derived from its specification in an automatic manner.

INTRODUCTION.

Real-time systems are recognized to be especially hard to specify, design, implement and test (Glass, 1984; Stankovic, 1988). The main reason for it is their reactive behaviour and the time dependency caused by the need to respond to external events within specifiable delays, which makes most of the methods used for developing sequential and even concurrent programs unapplicable (Wirth 1977).

A promising approach is the use of rapid prototyping techniques based on a high-level description of the system (Ince & Hekmatpour, 1987). A prototype is an incomplete realization of the system, used to assess requirements specification or system design. The execution of the prototype provides a foreview of the behaviour of the final system, and can thus be used to validate the specification against the user requirements until an agreement is reached. In this way, errors and misconceptions can be located at an early stage of the software production process, when they can be corrected without incurring in unreasonable costs.

Prototypes may be derived from a formal description of the intended system. A number of formal techniques have been proposed to describe reactive behaviour, including Petri nets (Peterson, 1977), temporal logic (Pnueli, 1986), CSP (Hoare, 1985), and CCS (Milner, 1980). All of these, however, are asynchronous in nature and thus fail in capturing the time dependencies which appear in real-time systems. A better support is provided by models with some kind of built-in time representation. Examples of this approach were first provided by SREM (Alford 1977, 1987), followed by other developments, such as PAISLey (Zave, 1982), PSDL (Luqi and others, 1988), and the work by Henninger (1980). A more formal treatment was introduced by synchronous models, such as the Esterel language model (Berry, 1984) and the event-action model (Jahanian and Mok, 1986, 1987). The latter provides a formal framework for real-time systems specification based on a real-time logic (RTL) .

In addition to a formal model, rapid prototyping needs a set of adequate software tools. The rest of the paper introduces a set of such tools, centered around the

---

This work has been partially supported by the Comisión de Investigación Científica y Técnica (CICYT), project no. PA85-0286-C02-02.

QUISAP language which is, in turn, based on the event-action model. First, a brief description of the event-action model is made. Then, the QUISAP language is introduced. The paper continues with a functional description of the tools which have been developed and the techniques used for their implementation. An example of a simple real-time system is also presented in the paper, including its specification in QUISAP and the most relevant parts of the generated prototype Ada code.

DESCRIPTION OF THE MODEL.

The computational model that forms the basis of the QUISAP language is a variant of the event-action model introduced by Jahanian and Mok (1986). It includes four types of elements: events, actions, conditions and real-time requirements.

Events

Events are instantaneous and occur at definite points in time. Four kinds of events will be considered:

- External events, caused by an agent outside the real-time system.
- Start and stop events, which mark the initiation and completion of actions.
- Transition events, which mark changes in the system operating conditions.
- Internal events, which are caused or emitted within the real-time system.

External and internal events are identified by unique names. All the events are supposed to be simultaneously visible to all the components of the system. In this way, the occurrence of an event activates at the same time all the actions in the system that depend on it.

Actions

Actions represent the reactions of the system to events. Actions can be simple or composite. Simple actions are of three kinds:

- Named actions, identified by a unique name.
- Transitions, which are changes in the state of the system, represented by the value of some condition.
- Emissions of internal events.

The execution of a named action takes a finite time. Transitions and signal emissions are assumed to be instantaneous.

Composite actions establish a partial order for other actions. Sequence, alternative, and parallel operators can be used to form composite actions. The operators should be viewed as a means to express time ordering constraints between actions, and not as an implementation scheme.

Conditions

Conditions are predicates that represent sets of states of the system. Conditions are changed by the execution of transition actions, which results in the occurrence of a transition event.

Real-time requirements

A real-time requirement specifies the response of the system to a single event, represented by some simple or composite action, and the time interval in which the response must be produced. Two kinds of real-time requirements are considered:

- Periodic requirements specify that some action is to be performed at regular time intervals. In this case, the action is assumed to be produced in response to some implicit event that occurs at the specified intervals.
- Sporadic requirements specificy that some action is to be performed each time that some event occurs.

Both kinds of requirements may be guarded by some condition. In this case, the action is performed only when the condition is true. Boolean expressions involving two or more conditions can also be used in guards.

Real-time logic.

The event-action model has a direct relationship with the real-time logic (RTL) introduced by Jahanian and Mok (1986). RTL is an extension of first-order logic with a so called occurrence function which assigns a time value to each occurrence of an event. RTL formulae may be used to express real-time requirements in a formal way or to set up additional safety constraints that the system must comply with. Mechanical methods have been devised to translate real-time requirements into RTL formulae and to validate a class of safety assertions against a specification (Jahanian & Mok, 1986, 1987).

THE QUISAP LANGUAGE.

QUISAP is a specification language for real-time systems based on the event-action model described above. The language is intended to formally describe the real-time behaviour of the system. Other aspects of the system, such as the definition of data types, are left aside, as they can be dealt with using other formalisms.

The syntax of QUISAP (see Appendix) has been made close to Ada in order to simplify its use in the real-time systems framework. Figure 1 shows an example specification written in QUISAP.

A specification consists of three parts:

- A context clause, which describes the dependence of the specification with respect to other Ada components.This kind of clause is written in the same way, and has the same semantics, as in Ada.
- A declarative part, where events and conditions are declared. Conditions are supposed to be derived from the Ada BOOLEAN type, and can be assigned an initial value. Other data types may be specified in separate packages, possibly with the help of some data specification language as exemplified in (Goguen, 1986) or (Luckham and Henke, 1985).

```
with INTERFACE; use INTERFACE;     -- context clause
specification SIMPLE_SYSTEM is
-- declarative part
   CHANGE_MODE  : EVENT;
   RUNNING         : CONDITION := FALSE;
-- real-time requirements
   requirement MONITOR is
      when RUNNING =>
         every 10.0*SEC do                        -- periodic requirement
            SENSOR_READ;  CHECK_LIMITS;
         with deadline = 2.0*SEC
   end MONITOR;
   requirement RUN is
      when not RUNNING =>
         on CHANGE_MODE do                         -- sporadic requirement
            RUNNING := TRUE;
         with deadline = 0.5*SEC;  separation = 1.0*SEC;
   end RUN;
   requirement STOP is
      when RUNNING =>
         on CHANGE_MODE do                         -- sporadic requirement
            RUNNING := FALSE;
         with deadline = 0.2*SEC;
         exception
            when DEADLINE_FAILURE => RED_LIGHT;
   end STOP;
end SIMPLE_SYSTEM;
```

Figure 1. Example of QUISAP specification.

- A requirements list, where the behaviour of the system is defined. Requirements can be periodic or sporadic. Periodic requirements are characterized by the period and deadline of the requested action. Sporadic requirements, in turn, are characterized by a starting event and the deadline of the requested action. In addition, a minimum separation between consecutive occurrences of the same event and a timeout (maximum interval between occurences) can be defined in sporadic requirements. In both kind of requirements, the actions to be performed when a time constraint is violated can be specified in an exception section.

PROTOTYPING TOOLS.

General description

One of the main goals of the QUISAP project was to build an environment for rapid prototyping of real-time systems. The next step after defining the language was to define a set of tools for requirements analysis, validation and prototyping. The tools already in use are a parser, a prototype generator, and an environment simulator. Figure 2 shows the data flow of the prototype generation process. Other tools, such as translators to Petri Net or Real-Time Logic notations, have been envisaged in order to provide further help in validating the specification in a more formal manner. Existing packages can be used for this purpose once the specification has been translated into the appropriate notation.

A QUISAP specification is first analysed and transformed into an internal representation by the parser. This representation is used as an input for the rest of the tools to perform different kinds of analysis on the specification.

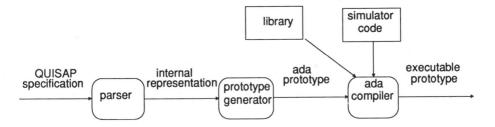

Figure 2. Prototyping tools.

The prototype generator produces a prototype Ada program from the internal representation. The source code is compiled together with the environment simulator and some library packages to produce an executable prototype. The prototype can then be executed with a simulated process and human interface, which is provided by the simulator. The execution is performed in simulated time, related to real time by a time scale factor. In this way, the behaviour of a rapid system can be exercised in a convenient way.

The main functions made available to the operator by the simulated interface are:

- Automatic and manual generation of external events.
- Setting of the time scale factor.
- Examination and modification of the internal state of the system (condition values).
- Trace of the actions attached to a requirement when it is started.

All these functions are accessed through a graphical interface which includes icons for buttons, clocks, dials, etc.

Prototype generation.

Since rapid prototyping often involves many design modifications, a prototype structure with a high degree of module independence is desirable. Moreover, this low degree of module coupling should be preserved across modifications.

In order to achieve this goal, a prototype structure as the one depicted in figure 3 has been devised. A prototype consists of a clock task, a scheduler task, a state task, and a number of application tasks that perform the actions specified in real-time requirements. Some predefined packages are also used by the tasks.

The clock task, whose specification is shown in figure 4, implements the simulated time clock functions. It ticks the scheduler at regular intervals to signal the advance of time.

The scheduler starts the execution of application tasks whenever their activating events occur or their periodic activation times are reached, provided the corresponding requirement guards hold. The scheduler task definition is shown in figure 5. When the scheduler gets a tick signal from the clock, it examines a periodic tasks scheduling table, and starts those tasks whose activation time has come. The scheduler works in a similar

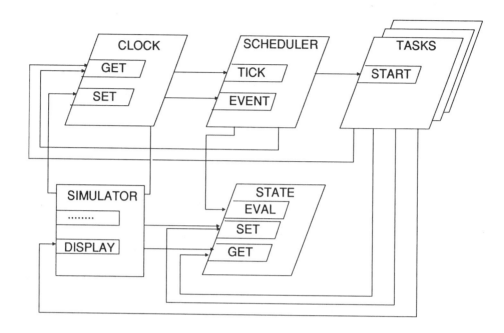

Figure 3. Structure of a prototype.

way for sporadic task scheduling, but in this case the occurrence of an external event is signalled by the simulator. All the tasks reacting to the same event are started by the scheduler each time the event occurs.

The state task keeps track of the system conditions, and performs the evaluation of requirement guards for the scheduler. Its specification is shown in figure 6.The state must be implemented within a task to prevent race conditions, as it is updated and read by several other tasks.

The prototype and simulator tasks use a DATA package, in which the pointers and data structures used to implement events, conditions, and requirements, are declared. There is no risk of race conditions in keeping these data in a shared package, as all these items remain constant for each specification. There is also a TYPES package, where the basic types EVENT, CONDITION, and REQUIREMENT are defined.

Requirements are translated into application tasks. There are a number of ways of decomposing real-time requirements into tasks (Mok, 1984; Luqi, 1988). The one we have chosen to implement the prototype generator assigns a task to each real-time requirement. This strategy ensures a high degree of independence between tasks and a minimum of adjustment in response to specification changes (Mok, 1984). Its main drawback is a possible lack of efficiency when compared to other decomposition methods. This,

```
with TYPES; use TYPES;
task CLOCK Is
    entry SET_TIME_SCALE(FACTOR : In NATURAL);
    entry GET_TIME(T : out SIMUL_TIME);
end CLOCK;
```

Figure 4. Specification of the clock task.

```
with DATA; use DATA;
with TYPES; use TYPES;
task SCHEDULER Is
    entry TICK;
    entry EVENT(ID: In EVENT_ID);
end SCHEDULER;
```

Figure 5. Specification of the scheduler task.

```
with DATA; use DATA;
with TYPES; use TYPES;
task STATE Is
    entry SET_CONDITION(ID: In CONDITION_ID; VALUE: In BOOLEAN);
    entry GET_CONDITION(ID: In CONDITION_ID; VALUE: out BOOLEAN);
    entry EVAL_GUARD(ID: In REQ_ID; VALUE: out BOOLEAN);
end STATE;
```

Figure 6. Specification of the state task.

however, is not of prime importance in rapid prototyping, where design can proceed further using a different task structure. There are two kinds of application tasks, which correspond to the two kinds of requirements, periodic and sporadic. Code for application tasks is produced by the prototype generator using a predefined scheme. Figure 7 shows an example of application task code for the example in figure1.

Named actions are implemented as calls to simulator procedures which display the name of the actions. This simple scheme can be further enriched by manual editing of the code. A straightforward modification is to implement actions as procedures defined in separately coded packages.

Timing constraints are checked as follows:

- Deadlines are checked in application tasks after the execution of the required actions.
- Separation between events is checked in application tasks before the execution of the required actions.
- Timeouts are checked within the scheduler task.

Violation of a timing constraint results in raising an exception (fig. 7). Exception handlers are automatically generated. When no exception actions are specified for some requirement, a default handler is included in the protoype.

Environment simulation.

The simulator is implemented as an Ada package which interacts with the prototype and with the graphical interface. The interface is implemented with the help of a standard X-Windows system, and consists of a number of windows where state information is displayed, parameters can be set, and events can be triggered. The simulator is internally divided into a set of tasks which perform different input, output, and control functions.

```
task STOP is
    entry START(T: In SIMULATED_TIME);
end STOP;

task body STOP is
    START_TIME: SIMULATED_TIME;
begin
    loop
        begin
            accept START(T: In SIMULATED_TIME) do
                START_TIME := T;
            end START;
            DISPLAY_ACTION("RESET RUNNING CONDITION");
            SET_CONDITION(RUNNING_ID,FALSE);
            GET_TIME(COMPLETION_TIME);
            If (COMPLETION_TIME-START_TIME) > DEADLINE(STOP_ID)
            then
                raise (DEADLINE_FAILURE);
            end If;
        exception
            when DEADLINE_FAILURE => DISPLAY_ACTION("RED_LIGHT");
        end;
    end loop;
end STOP;
```

Figure 7. Example of application task.

Implementation status.

A first version of the prototyping system is operational. The parser and prototype generator have been coded in C using *lex* and *yacc*. The system runs on workstations supporting Unix (TM) and X-Windows. An HP-UX Ada compiler has been used to produce the executable prototype code.

CONCLUDING REMARKS.

The first version of the system has been used to specify a number of existing real-time systems, including an operational industrial control system, in order to check the validity of the approach (Espinosa, 1988; García-Fornés, 1988). The prototypes generated from the QUISAP specifications have been obtained in all the cases in a straightforward way. In the particular case of the industrial control system, prototypes have proven to be very helpful in analysing the requirements with the plant engineers, who have used the QUISAP tools to test several modifications to the original control system.

The main point where research is to be continued is time simulation and real-time constraints checking. At present, checking deadline violations in simulated time does not make much sense, as the computation of each task is performed in the host system real time. Some of the techniques currently used in simulation languages to manage simulated time in computations could possibly be incorporated in order to improve this aspect of the prototyping system. Of course, this would require appropriate scheduling of application tasks. Other improvements to be done refer to the language modularity and expandibility, as well as the graphical interface.

REFERENCES.

M.W. Alford (1977): *A requirements engineering methodology for real-time processing requirements.* IEEE Tr. on Software Engineering, vol. SE-3, no. 1.

G. Berry and L. Cosserat (1984): *The ESTEREL synchronous programming language and its mathematical semantics.* Logics and models for concurrent systems, NATO ASI Series, Springer-Verlag.

A. Espinosa (1988): *QUISAP: un lenguaje para la especificación de sistemas de tiempo real.* Universidad Politécnica de Valencia.

A. García-Fornés (1988): Diseño de herramientas para el análisis y ejecución de especificaciones realizadas en el lenguaje QUISAP.Universidad Politécnica de Valencia.

R.L. Glass (1984): *Real-time: the 'lost world' of software debugging and testing.*Comm. ACM, vol. 23, no. 5.

J.A. Goguen (1986): *Reusing and interconnecting software components.* IEEE Computer, feb. 1986.

K.L. Henninger (1980): *Specifying software requirements for complex systems: new techniques and their application.* IEEE Tr. on Software Engineering, vol. SE-6, no. 1.

C.A.R. Hoare (1985): Communicating sequential processes. Prentice-Hall.

D.C. Ince and S. Hekmatpour (1987): *Software prototyping - progress and prospects.* Information and Software Technology vol. 29, no. 1

F. Jahanian and A.K. Mok (1986): *Safety analysis of timing properties in real-time systems,* IEEE Tr. on Software Engineering, vol. SE-12, no. 9.

F. Jahanian and A.K. Mok (1987): *A graph-theoretic approach for timing analysis and its implementation,* IEEE Tr. on Computers, vol.C-36, no.8.

D.C. Luckham and F.W. von Henke (1985): *An overview of Anna, a specification language for Ada.* IEEE Software, march 1985.

Luqi, V. Berzins and R. T. Yeh (1988): *A prototyping language for real-time software.* IEEE Tr. on Software Engineering, vol. SE-14, no. 10.

R. Milner (1980): A calculus of communicating systems. Springer-Verlag, LNCS, no. 92.

A.K. Mok (1984): *The decomposition of real-time system requirements into process modes.* IEEE Real-Time Systems Symp., 1984.

J.L. Peterson (1977): *Petri nets.* ACM Comput. Surveys, vol. 9, pp. 223-252.

A. Pnueli (1986): *Specification and development of reactive systems.* Information Processing 86, North-Holland.

J. Stankovic (1988): *Misconceptions about real-time computing.* IEEE Computer, oct. 1988.

N.Wirth(1977): *Toward a discipline of real-time programming.* Comm. ACM, vol. 20, no. 8.

P. Zave (1982): *An operational approach to requirements specification for embedded systems.*IEEE Tr. on Software Engineering, vol. SE-8, no. 5.

ۤۤۤۤ

Appendix. Syntax of QUISAP.

```
specification ::=
    [context_clause]
    specification spec_name is
        [declarative_part]
        requirements_list
    end spec_name;
context_clause ::= {with_clause {use-clause}}
with_clause ::= with unit_name {,unit_name};
use_clause ::= use package_name {,package_name};
declarative_part ::= {basic_declaration}
basic_declaration ::= event_declaration | condition_declaration
event_declaraction ::= identifier_list : EVENT;
condition_declaraction ::= identifier_list : CONDITION [:= expression];
requirements_list ::= simple_requirement {,simple_requirement}
simple_requirement ::= periodic_requirement | sporadic_requirement
periodic_requirement ::=
    requirement req_name is
        [guard]
            every time_expression do
                action
            [with deadline = time_expression;]
            [exception
                exception_handler
                {exception_handler}]
    end req_name;
sporadic_requirement ::=
    requirement req_name is

        [guard]
        on event_name do
            action
        [with [deadline = time_expression;]
               [separation =time_expression;]
               [timeout = time_expression;]]
        [exception
            exception_handler
            {exception_handler}]
    end req_name;
guard ::= when condition_expression =>
action ::= simple_action | composite action
simple_action ::=procedure_name | transition | event_emission
transition ::= condition_name := condition_expression;
event_emission ::= cause event_name;
composite action ::= sequence | alternative | parallel
sequence ::= action {action}
alternative ::=
    If condition_expression
    then action
    [else action
    end If;
parallel ::=
    par
        action {|| action}
    end par;
exception_handler ::= when exception_name => action;
```

Part 3 Real-Time Scheduling

Hard Real Time Systems and Ada

Juan L. Freniche, Construcciones Aeronáuticas S. A., Projects Div., I.D.S. Dept., Madrid

Abstract.

Hard Real Time Systems (HRTS) are Real Time Systems with stringent time constraints. Their implementation with Ada should include a co-operative or a pre-emptive scheduler, which may be built as an actor or server scheduler for the first case or as a scheduler using the Ada RunTime capabilities for the second case. Despite the required determinism, the introduction of event-driven issues is supported in some HRTS. Current Ada implementations are suitable for HRTS but specific tests should be carried out to assess the impact of certain features of Ada such as task creation and abortion, scheduling points, and the latency time for the delay statement. Even with some drawbacks, Ada and its priority-based pre-emptive scheduling is one of the better solutions for the HRTS implementation.

Hard Real Time Systems.

HRTS are a class of Real Time Systems with additional constraints concerning time intervals where information is valid. In some Real Time Systems, information produced by some processes may be used by other processes even if this information arrives before or after required. In HRTS, if information does not arrive within a strict time interval, not only is it neither useful nor valid but it can also produce an abnormal behaviour of the system. Frequently HRTS are systems in which a failure can be hazardous to human life, prevent fulfilment of a mission or lead to severe economic loss. They can be found in several fields as manufacturing control, patient care, flight control, nuclear plant control, space missions, simulators, and military systems (missiles, avionics, antisubmarine warfare, etc.).

HRTS often consist of a set of cyclic processes performing independent but cooperative functions, e.g. an avionic system with navigation, target tracking and radar display. Process independency means that their execution needs not to be fully synchronized. Synchronization is not used in the interprocess communication, instead they will run independently but communicating by means of Global Data Areas (GDA). Logic protection of GDA may be achieved by classical mechanisms of synchronization such as semaphores, monitors or rendezvous, but also a scheduling policy may control the process progression and supervise their access to GDA. This approach makes the synchronization easier and justifies the spreading of the cyclic executive.

The GDA will contain information used and deposited by the processes, and also global information about the system state. Obviously, the consistency of the information contained within the GDA must be guaranteed. Firstly, application processes accessing GDA must maintain it in a consistent state. Secondly, the activation and deactivation of the processes must be made in a smooth way. The cyclic processes are serialized, their progression are recorded in the GDA and timeouts are set up to control erroneous behaviours.

Cooperative cyclic scheduling has been the traditional approach to HRTS. Full preemptive scheduling has been used less in spite of its advantages: automatic priority based time slicing avoiding the need of manually dividing the processes into segments which will fit into the cycle time slots. For this purpose, Ada provides a priority-driven pre-emptive scheduling that should be favourably considered when selecting the scheduling policy for these systems.

HRTS are not event-driven but time-driven: the system functions are distributed in time in ordered Producer-Consumer relationships. HRTS using a time-driven approach are appropriate for flight or manufacturing control systems, where the behaviour is rather constant in the time. For other HRTS this approach also is effective however a change in the environment where the HRTS is running could need a fast reconfiguration to respond to the new situation. Therefore the event-driven approach should be considered, at least at system reconfiguration level.

A full event-driven HRTS would have a complicated internal logic in order to guarantee that the information arrives at the required time. Producer-Consumer relationships would have to be complemented with timeouts over the information exchange, and reversionary actions would have to be taken by the Consumer in case the Producer fails to provide the information. Constructions such as Ada timed entry call will help to implement these systems.

Even with an event-driven approach to HRTS there are some basic characteristics which still maintain cyclic scheduling (cooperative or pre-emptive) as an effective solution. This is because the cyclic and independent functions are inherent properties of the system that do not disappear with the selected design approach. Thus it seems more rational to keep the deterministic cyclic scheduling and to add the necessary event-driven issues (event signalling, process activation/deactivation, etc.) but always taking into account the deadlines for all the activities.

Using Ada as the implementation language also has positive or negative influences in the construction of HRTS. Two aspects should be considered: the performance of the target code obtained with current Ada development systems and the suitability of the features offered by Ada for Concurrence and Real Time, in particular the tasking model and the priority-driven pre-emptive scheduling.

With the continuous improvements to Ada implementations, the solution to the first aspect is just a matter of time. Particularly, for some compilers current performance of Ada target code is not only acceptable, but even good. Finally, the Ada high-level features for Concurrence and Real Time were justified to improve aspects such as homogeneity, readability, security, testability, portability and understandability [ICH86]. The next sections will examine the use of these Ada facilities in HRTS.

Scheduling in HRTS.

Embedded computers have not a developed operating system which offers sophisticated services to the application software. Instead they have a small (from 3K to 20K) multitasking Runtime System (RTS) which schedules the processes and to some extent provides Device and Interrupt handling, Process creation, activation, deactivation, abortion and removal, Process synchronization and communication, Memory management (not virtual memory) and Time handling (including real time clock set and reset, future event handling and timeouts) [ARTEWG87a].

For event-driven issues, the above services seem sufficient. The critical applications where the HRTS are used claim for an additional and essential requirement: *predictability*, both in response time to RTS operations and behaviour under heavy loads.

Ada Runtime Systems should provide to the Ada application these services as described in the Ada Language Reference Manual (ALRM) [AJPO83]. The evolution of RTS for Ada has gone through the following steps:

- The first Ada RTS "prototypes", implementing ALRM but not the whole Chapter 13.
- RTS for Ada obtained as an adaptation or interfacing to commercial preexisting general Runtime Systems (as VRTX).
- New generation of RTS specific for Ada, incorporating the previous experiences.

Performance has been increased in each step. For example, for a simple rendezvous, the figures are in the order of 500, 125 and 80 microseconds respectively, tested on Motorola MC68020 boards. This last figures indicate that Ada overheads are now at an acceptable level [ROA88].

For HRTS, a cyclic scheduling policy must be implemented, whether relying on the RTS or by means of a separate module. In particular, with Ada, the implementor has the possibility to include in the application its own separate cooperative Scheduler (also written in Ada) or to use directly the pre-emptive scheduling features of Ada RTS. For both cases, the scheduler may be defined as a general periodic activity which activates the processes in sequence. Its period is called the major cycle period. It is divided in a number of equal minor cycles. Each process is forced to have a period multiple of the minor cycle duration. The scheme of the system behaviour is always repetitive across major cycles.

In each minor cycle several processes may be executed. For cooperative scheduling the code of each process should be manually divided into sections whose execution time along with the other processes is less than the minor cycle duration. Every modification to the HRTS software requires to repeat the above division. This operation is automatically performed using pre-emptive scheduling but, which is more important, the process logic is not artificially divided to deal with the minor cycle time constraints.

The execution order within the minor cycle will be indicated by the process scheduling priority. Conceptually it is convenient to distinguish between system priority (the priority of the ALRM) and scheduling priority of the process in a minor cycle. The system priority is used to order the system tasks of the HRTS (clock driver, scheduler if it is a separate module, main program and perhaps others), while scheduling priority is used to schedule the processes in each minor cycle. Using the scheduling features provided by Ada RTS, these priorities will also be Ada priorities. Alternatively, using a separate cooperative scheduler, they can be a parameter of each process. With this last approach, the explicit scheduling priorities can even be completely removed, sorting by hand the processes in each minor cycle in a strict way.

The application processes can be unrelated in which case their execution order is irrelevant, or they can be related on a Producer-Consumer basis. The Producers will generate several items and deposit them in the GDA, the Consumer will use these items, pulling them out of the GDA. Producers should therefore run in the minor cycles before the Consumer, or if they run in the same minor cycle, Producers should have a higher relative priority than the Consumer in these minor cycles.

The parameters of the HRTS scheduling are:

1. Duration of the minor cycle. For some demanding systems, it may be even less than 10 milliseconds (in Aerospace industry).

2. The different rates allowed to the processes. Usually it is 2^n times the minor cycle duration $(0 \leq n \leq 7)$, being the maximum rate the major cycle period.

3. For each process, its rate.

4. For each process, its scheduling priority. Again, the priority can be explicit (as Ada priority or as a parameter) or implicit into the activation order within the minor cycle. For the cooperative scheduler, in each minor cycle the sum of duration of all processes to be executed must sensibly be less than the minor cycle duration, due to overheads in task switching. This restriction is not applicable to the pre-emptive scheduling, where a process execution can overlap consecutive minor cycles. In particular, the *rate monotonic algorithm* shows that if priorities are assigned according to the frequencies, the processes can meet their deadlines if and only if an easily checkable bound is fulfilled [LIU73].

5. For each execution of an application process, the maximum duration of this execution, after which a timeout error should be raised. The subsequent actions to be taken in this case should be specified too. The deadline is measured in CPU time dedicated to the process.

The execution time of each process must be strictly controlled. If a timeout is raised, the execution must be cancelled. Subsequent actions will depend on the particular system: the timed out process can be aborted and removed, a reversionary process may start, or simply the timed out process may return the current approximate results. Task Synchronization is solved by the cyclic scheduling while Task Communication is made by global data areas. When a process modifies global data, it is responsible for preserving the consistency. If a process is pre-empted or a timeout is raised, some global data area could not to be fully updated. Excluding blocking solutions (semaphores, monitors, rendezvous, etc.) because blocking can interfere with the fulfilment of the deadlines, each process should monitor its own progress, setting up appropriate global flags to indicate how much it progressed before a timeout or preemption. The subsequent processes know about the progress by reading these global flags. Obviously, change to global flags must be atomic operations. If critical regions were allowed, it should be pointed out that using the *priority ceiling protocol* for assigning priorities in the pre-emptive scheduling approach, it can be guaranteed that high priority processes could be blocked at most once by lower priority processes [GOO88].

Depending on the system, parameters included in 1 to 5 could change dynamically. Small changes are expected in order to accommodate the HRTS to the events of their current working scenarios. Big changes, also called system reconfigurations, could be necessary for responding to new situations on the environment. For example, small changes would be necessary if a supplementary threat to a combat aircraft has been detected, but big changes would be necessary in case of mission change from normal navigation to defensive actions in the same avionic system. Big or small changes should always maintain the deterministic behaviour.

Handling interrupting devices is not a trivial problem for HRTS. In many cases, all interrupts are disabled, except the real time clock interrupt used to produce timeouts. The processes poll the devices taking samples or sending results. An example of polling with system reconfiguration is the case of a mission change for an antisubmarine helicopter, from rescue to submarine detection. Being in rescue, some sensors (relative to sonobuoy) will be polled at low rate or not polled, but when performing submarine detection mission, they will be polled more frequently.

The determinism should not be lost by the introduction of event-driven issues. Several kinds of events can be identified: internal and external events, and input and output events between the external ones. Obviously, internal event-driven behaviour is subordinated to external input/output events and does not seem to add new difficulties.

Output events consist of data sent by processes governing external devices such as displays, valves, actuators, etc. The event triggering the process is the completion of data to be sent. However one extra difficulty can be present when external devices require a rate of data sent different to that provided by the event-driven output process.

Input events are interrupts of devices providing data to the processes. Incoming data may be classified as critical and non-critical. Critical input data must be processed without delay while non-critical can be buffered by high priority system tasks (drivers) to make it available later to Consumers when their turn arrive. That is the case of keystrokes of a human operator, that may be buffered until completion of the command, and then processed by the command interpreter. The case of control messages travelling by the interconnecting bus of a multiprocessor avionic system is different. These messages could require immediate response and cannot be buffered until the consumer process has the go-ahead. Global synchronous approach (the cyclic scheduling) may help to solve the problem. In particular, if incoming data arrive with known frequencies, service can be provided to them in the framework of a priority-driven pre-emptive scheduler. The servers will encapsulate the corresponding interrupt routines for the input data, representing an essential improvement in response time to events over the polling or buffering solutions [LEH87].

In conclusion, incoming non-critical data is handled by buffering techniques and it seems compatible with the required predictable behaviour of HRTS. For the pre-emptive scheduling approach, input critical data with known frequencies can be handled by the *Deferrable Server* or other algorithms [LEH87]. However, for the general case, input critical data should not be provided by interrupts because it would be impossible to schedule processes on a regular basis, losing the determinism. For particular HRTS some solutions such as skipping minor cycles or optimization of the activity in case of minor cycle overflow due to intensive incoming critical data have been explored [MAC80].

Ada in Hard Real Time Systems.

Ada is mandatory for military applications but its use is not restricted to the military field. Civil aviation, air and ground traffic control, simulators, nuclear, hospital and banking applications, manufacturing control and telecommunications are areas where Ada can find its application. For the kind of problems concerning the HRTS world, Ada provides some effective solutions and introduces some particular difficulties. The implementors, as with any other programming language, should take advantage of the solutions offered by Ada and deal with the problems which its use introduces.

Event-driven approach to Real Time Systems is widely reported in Ada literature [BUH84; NIE85]. Process representation, events, interrupt handlers, device handlers, synchronization, decoupling, communication and resource acquisition are some aspects of this method. By contrast less experience exists for Ada implementation of HRTS using the cyclic approach with cooperative or pre-emptive scheduling. The previous section stated the Ada topics to be analysed.

Application Process Representation.

Two choices are possible: to implement processes as subroutines of the main program or as Ada tasks. The first choice avoids the Ada tasking overhead and it is recommended for safety critical applications [HOL88]. However, when a process is out of order (for example, when a timeout occurs), it must be aborted. It does not seem easy to abort an uncontrolled subroutine of a program without also aborting the program as well. The real fact is that separate control flows are necessary for the scheduler and for each application process. Using subroutines would require extensive modifications to the RTS and it is strictly against the official definition of Ada [AJPO83]. Therefore, the second solution should be preferred since it is closer to the Ada tasking model and appears to be more compatible with future introduction of event-driven issues.

Task Control.

All task interactions in Ada are cooperative (excepting abortion). However, in HRTS it is only necessary to control the readiness of each task for scheduling. The pre-emptive approach solves it by a combined use of priorities for the main program and the remaining tasks: the main program enables the other tasks making rendezvous with them in turn, then the pre-emption by priorities will do the rest.

For the cooperative scheduling, controlling tasks by rendezvous is the natural choice. But now the controller must know the identity of each one of the controlled tasks. Possible solutions are:

- The implementor provides a routine with an **in** numeric parameter. The controller calls the routine which in turn makes the rendezvous or any other operation with the appropriate task identified by the parameter. Lack of flexibility in case of major reconfiguration of the scheduling policy could be the main drawback.
- Each task identifies itself to the controller by a pointer. This solution implies to define each task as an access to task type or to use the **ADDRESS** attribute to get the address of the task. Tasks obtain their own identities (the pointer value) and provide it to the controller task. The exact behaviour is highly dependent on the particular Ada Compiler [AJPO83] and should be tested in advance.
- The last alternative is to use special Ada Runtime features, as proposed by [ARTEWG87b].

Task Abortion.

When a task runs improperly, it should be stopped. A controller task should detect the anomaly when a timeout is raised. Tasks can stop themselves by checking the status of a flag set up by the controller in case of timeout, although this is not effective if the task is engaged, in case of local hardware malfunctioning or if no polling is made within the uncontrolled loop.

The most powerful solution is abortion. A controller task should abort the anomalous task, examine its progress and repair the GDA. A drawback is the abortion overhead. Moreover, the ALRM allows that an abortion occurs only at some places in the Ada program, placing the aborted task in an abnormal state but not releasing its resources. It has been proposed to include strategic **delay 0.0** statements in the task body but this adds problems in positioning these statements and also time overhead due the polling of the RTS. Again, the behaviour is implementation dependent and should be properly tested.

In some cases, polling the flags allows repairing and restart the activity of an anomalous process while the abortion solution needs, in order to restart, an Ada task creation which also is a time consuming operation. The usual situation is to have a reversionary task waiting on an **accept** statement for the go-ahead until the main task is aborted. However this is a memory consuming option because the stack of each reversionary task is allocated even if never used.

Communication and Synchronization.

While task communication is performed by means of GDA, task synchronization in HRTS is necessary only when updating global flags indicating the task progression. These updating operations must be atomic. If a task is updating a global flag, task drivers of devices or high priority processes (for the case of pre-emptive scheduling) could interrupt the updating operation. In particular, the real time clock may interrupt signalling a timeout on a task updating a global flag. The next action of the controller would be to abort the timed out task. Therefore, global flags must be represented in Ada in such a way that only a single machine operation is required for updating. The pragma **SHARED** for this kind of variables should be used, with special application to tightly coupled multiprocessor systems.

GDA, including global flags, would be represented as Ada Abstract Data Types or State Machines, encapsulating the data structures and exporting the allowed operations. This makes testing easier.

Resource Acquisition.

Only three resources can be identified in HRTS: CPU time, data buffers for buffered non critical input or output data, and global flags. Global flags have been examined before. Data buffers can tolerate the classical Ada protection of data structures by semaphore or monitor tasks [BUH84]. Finally, CPU time is acquired by the tasks depending of the scheduling information and timeouts. If a cooperative scheduler is selected, it should then distribute itself the CPU time among the tasks, according to minor cycles and scheduling priorities. Relying on Ada RTS for scheduling, a careful scheme of application tasks, timeout-guard tasks and reversionary tasks should be designed.

Timeouts can be set up, cancelled and raised by a selective wait. The drawbacks of the Ada delay statement have been indicated in the literature, in particular the lack of a bound for the wait time. The latency time when a delay has concluded and the task is resumed should be taken into account. The current figures are too coarse to allow fine scheduling. The alternative way is to build up a specific real time clock driver using standard features of Ada (interrupt entry) but in this case, the time queue should be also handled by the implementor.

Event Handling.

The cooperative approach only disposes of the polling solution to deal with external events: interrupts are disabled and server tasks are introduced which poll the hardware interface. The response time will depend of the server priority, and polling represents a waste of time if there are no data to send or receive.

Scheduling with Ada RTS may use the polling alternative, either polling the hardware interface (with interrupts disabled) or polling software buffers for incoming data provided by interrupts. But the response time to this events can be improved, still maintaining the determinism, using the for example the *Deferrable Server algorithm* for interrupts with known frequencies. This allows the event servers to pre-empt the cyclic tasks, therefore enabling/disabling interrupt operations should be included into the servers code to control frequent arrivals. The slice of code corresponding to the interrupt handler (the accept interrupt bodies) are executed with Ada priority higher than any user defined task. The remaining code must have an Ada priority that allow a fast recovery for the next interrupts but compatible with the deadline requirements for the other tasks.

Priorities.

With the current definition of the language, Ada priorities should only be used to indicate the priority of the system tasks, not for scheduling purposes, because more flexibility and control than is provided by Ada is necessary. System reconfiguration would be impossible because Ada priorities are static. Obviously, relying on the Ada RTS capabilities, the scheduling priorities will be Ada priorities. A package with additional flexibility has been proposed in [ARTEWG87b].

The typical software in Ada for a HRTS consists of:

- Main Program, with maximum priority m.
- Driver task for real time clock, with high priority p.
- Some other driver tasks for devices, with priority q.
- If cooperative scheduling has been selected, scheduler task, with priority r.
- Some other server tasks, with priority s. According to the priority ceiling protocol, the priority of a server encapsulating a critical region must be strictly greater than the priority of its clients. This applies for servers that are interrupt handler tasks for external events.
- Application processes, whose priorities lie within the low range t.
- Low priority tasks as the background task, to perform built-in-test or other residual activity, with priority u.

The relation among these Ada priorities should be $u < t < s < r < q < p < m$. This choice allows the Main Program to activate all the tasks in the software system in an ordered manner, however the *priority inversion phenomenon* is not avoided due to possible priority conflicts among server and client tasks [COR87].

For the separate scheduler approach, scheduling priorities should be just another parameter varying in an appropriate range. Also a strict serialization of tasks to be executed on each minor cycle makes explicit scheduling priority unnecessary. To avoid the interference with the Ada scheduling, all the application processes should have the same Ada priority t_0.

Scheduling Information.

This has been listed in a previous section. There are two forms of implementation in Ada. The first form is to keep the scheduling information as a global table, providing operations to access it. The main advantages of this approach are easy system reconfiguration and testing. The second form is to distribute scheduling information over each process. This last option follows information localization principles, as addressed by modern Object Oriented Methods [BOO87].

Scheduling Control.

As previously stated, there are several alternative choices: a separate cooperative scheduler (actor or server) or the implicit Ada RTS scheduling. Nearly all HRTS have been built with an *actor scheduler* giving control to the application processes. This action is implemented in Ada by means of a main loop in the task bodies which contains an **accept** statement. The scheduler calls the task determined by the scheduling information.

Another way is a *server scheduler*. The processes, according to scheduling parameters, call the server to acquire the resource *execution time*. The server uses a double rendezvous with family entries to give control [BUR87].

The last choice, *Ada RTS*, has been used less. For each application process, there exists a timer task which controls the timeouts of the first one. Both tasks may be encapsulated in a package. Ada demands static expressions for priorities, therefore a complete generic package cannot be used.

In terms of rendezvous, the actor scheduler needs about 4 rendezvous for each execution of a process, while the server scheduler needs about 6 and the Ada RTS scheduling needs only 2. In each case, 2 rendezvous (or equivalent code) are required for setting and cancelling timeouts. It must be pointed out that the **delay** statement measures elapsed time, not CPU time dedicated to a task. Therefore, in case of pre-emption, a timeout could be raised because a correct task has been pre-empted before cancelling its timeout. The solution is to increase the deadline for low priority tasks to deal with possible pre-emption. The inclusion in Ada of a statement similar to the delay but for CPU task time would represent a valuable improvement.

Ada Features for Real Time.

Ada provides a high level tasking model that should be used in HRTS development. Otherwise, the implementor would have to use an old generation process model, with complex interrelations with Ada, possibly introducing reliability problems. Today, the Ada model seems robust and efficient enough for HRTS.

However, some aspects have to be carefully considered. The first one is the latency time of the **delay** statement, already mentioned. Second aspect is the Ada handling of task entry queues. The discipline is First In, First Out. For other disciplines, family entries should be used. HRTS with cooperative scheduling will use family entries for scheduling the application processes by relative priority, causing an overhead that should be compared to the overhead caused by priority queues in other systems (as

VRTX) [BUR87]. It is also necessary to investigate the aspects left by ALRM to the criteria of the Ada Compiler implementor, as the selection of coincident calls to several alternative of a **select** statement, and the activation order of several task with concluding delays at very near instants. These issues will affect the scheduler behaviour and must be determined for the project Ada Compiler.

The complete set of dependencies may be studied in [ARTEWG87c]. Experience shows that these Ada features should be examined and tested and the influence in timing and memory overhead under different conditions should be evaluated. A predictable behaviour must be the essential requirement for its use in HRTS.

Acknowledgements.

I gratefully acknowledge J. Castellano and C. Fernández-Hoz for the contributions to the ideas stated in this paper. I also wish to thanks to C. Dobson for the support and useful discussions during the preparation of the paper.

Motorola and VRTX are registered trademarks of Motorola Inc. and Ready Systems respectively.

References.

[AJPO83] Ada Joint Program Office: *Ada Programming Language*, ANSI/MIL-STD-1815A, U.S. Dept. of Defense, Washington D. C., Jan. 1983.

[ARTEWG87a] Ada RunTime Environment Working Group (ARTEWG): "A Framework for Describing Ada Runtime Environments", Oct. 1987.

[ARTEWG87b] ARTEWG: "A Catalogue of Interface Features and Options for the Ada Runtime Environment", Release 2.0, Dec. 1987.

[ARTEWG87c] ARTEWG: "Catalogue of Ada Runtime Implementation Dependencies", Dec. 1987.

[BOO87] G. Booch: *Software Components with Ada*, Benjamin/Cummings, Menlo Park, California 1987.

[BUH84] R. Buhr: *System Design with Ada*, Prentice Hall, Englewood Cliffs, New Jersey 1984.

[BUR87] A. Burns, A. Lister, A. Wellings: *A Review of Ada Tasking*, Lecture Notes in Computer Science no. 262, Springer-Verlag, 1987.

[COR87] D. Cornhill, L. Sha and others: "Limitations of Ada for Real-Time Scheduling", Proceedings of the 1st ACM International Workshop on Real-Time Ada Issues, Ada Letters VOL. VII, no. 6, Special Edition, 1987.

[GOO88] J. Goodenough, L. Sha: "The Priority Ceiling Protocol: A Method for Minimizing the Blocking of High Priority Ada Tasks", Proceedings of the 2nd ACM International Workshop on Real Time, 1988 (To appear in a special issue of Ada Letters).

[HOL88] R. Holzapfel, G. Winterstein: "Ada in Safety Critical Applications", Proceedings of the 1988 Ada-Europe International Conference, Cambridge University Press, 1988.

[ICH86] J. Ichbiah, J. Barnes, R. Firth, M. Woodger: *Rationale for the Design of the Ada Programming Language*, Honeywell-Alsys, 1986.

[LEH87] J. Lehoczky, J. Sha, J. Strosnider: "Enhanced Aperiodic Responsiveness in A Hard Real Time Environment". IEEE Real-Time System Symposium, 1987.

[LIU73] C. Liu, J. Layland: "Scheduling Algorithms for Multiprogramming in a Hard Real Time Environment". Journal of the ACM, VOL. 20, no. 1, 1973.

[MAC80] L. MacLaren: "Evolving Towards Ada in Real Time Systems", Proceedings of the ACM SIGPLAN Symposium on the Ada Language, Boston 1980 (SIGPLAN NOTICES VOL. 15, no. 11, Nov. 1980).

[NIE85] K. Nielsen, K. Shumate: "Designing Large Real-Time Systems with Ada", Communications of the ACM, VOL. 30, no. 8, August 1985.

[ROA88] C. Roark, R. McAfee: "The Applicability of Ada to MIL-STD-1750A", Ada Letters VOL. VIII, no. 3, May/June 1988.

[SEI87] Software Engineering Institute: "Ada Performance Benchmarks on the Motorola MC68020: Summary and Results", version 1.0. CMU/SEI-87-TR-40, Dec. 1987.

COMPREHENSIVE RACE CONTROLS: A VERSATILE SCHEDULING MECHANISM FOR REAL-TIME APPLICATIONS

TZILLA ELRAD[*]

Department Of Computer Science
Illinois Institute Of Technology
IIT Center Chicago IL 60616
BITNET: CSELRAD@IITVAX

ABSTRACT

Of the issues submitted to the JIAWG, four were deemed significant to the scheduling category and worthy of being revisited at a later date. JIAWG plans to submit these issues for consideration in Ada 9X. The issues of dynamic priority, as well as the issue of Ada task scheduling are discussed in this paper. Two propositions to solve the problem, the priority inheritance scheduler [GS], and the comprehensive set of race controls [E1], are evaluated and compared.

CLASSIFICATION

In order to present and discuss these issues, we need a set of general definitions for scheduling controls. Evaluating Ada against these control capacities will provide us with a scientific approach to the task of forming an integrated design of comprehensive scheduling controls for Ada [EM1].

Comprehensive Scheduling Controls - the set of all possible decision making controls and scheduling controls used by a language. These break down into Availability Controls and Race Controls.

> Availability Controls - can enable or disable nondeterministic choices; are used to hold back events for which the decision making unit is not ready.

> These can be further broken down into four categories:

>> Private Control - The capacity to enable/disable a Nondeterministic choice based on an expression over the local state of the task.

---

* This work supported in part by grant from U.S. Army CECOM Army Research Office, and Battelle under Scientific Services Program #1263

Consensus Control ~~~ - The capacity to enable/disable a nondeterministic choice based on pending communication requests.
Mutual Control - The capacity to enable/disable a nondeterministic choice based on an expression over both the caller state and the server state.
Hybrid Control - The capacity to enable/disable a nondeterministic choice based on any combination of the above controls.

Figure #1 is an example which uses Ada style notation (but not Ada syntax) to elucidate these controls:

```
task body EXAMPLE is

X: integer; --X is local to the task EXAMPLE

begin
 loop
  select

    when X=0; --any list of commands
  or
    accept E1( ... ) do...end E1;
  or
    only-when  X=Y
    => accept E2 (Y: in integer) do...end E2;
  or
    when X>0 only-when X>y
    => accept E3 (Y: in integer) do...end E3;

  end select;
 end loop;
end EXAMPLE;
```

Figure #1   Availability Controls

Figure #1 shows a select command with four different availability controls. The first alternative is controled by a private control; the second by a consensus control; the third by a consensus control and a mutual control; and the forth by a hybrid of private, mutual, and consensus controls.

CHARACTERISTICS OF AVAILABILITY CONTROLS IN ADA:

Ada does not permit pure private control (e.g. the first alternative in the example above). Pure private control can be simulated in Ada by using a "delay alternative". The "else" part might be used to partially simulate pure private control, but is well known to cause unnecessary polling. Ada's selective-wait has an asymmetric consensus control. Therefore, only an "accept" may be part of a consensus control; a "call" is not allowed. Conditional Entry Call and Timed Entry Call allow restricted use of asymmetric consensus control by using calls only.

Ada does not allow for mutual control. A complete discussion on possible alternatives to simulate mutual control in Ada can be found in [E2]. Evaluation of availability controls is not within the scope of this presentation.

Race Controls - can select an event among available choices, and are thus used to prioritize events. The expressive capacity of race controls is crucial for real-time applications. as the latter rely heavily on prioritization of events.

These can be further broken down into three categories according to the level on which they function; Program level, task level, and entry level.

Priority control - prioritize tasks within a unit.
Preference control - prioritize entries within a task.
Forerunner control -prioritize pending calls within an entry.

CHARACTERISTICS OF RACE CONTROLS IN ADA:
Using the above terminology, we can state the following:
I. Ada has an explicit static priority control, but one which may be not powerful enough.
II. Ada does not have a preference control; an arbitrary selection is made among available entries.
III. Ada has an implicit forerunner control, which uses FIFO queues to service pending calls to an entry.

The above characterization shows that the three different races in Ada are not treated consistently. An integrated approach is needed. For real-time applications Ada's capacity to control these races is not versatile enough. Systems programed in the language are unpredictable; thus it is very difficult to program intelligent and efficient decision controls. Also, software is not portable, and so reuse and maintainence are relatively difficult. The nature of race controls in Ada does not give the user the capacity to avoid priority inversion.
Priority inversion has been defined by Lui Sha [C] as phenomenon whereby low priority tasks are served before high priority tasks.

Two viable solutions to Ada's lack of an integrated approach to race controls are:
1. THE PRIORITY INHERITANCE SCHEDULER
2. THE E & D COMPREHENSIVE SET OF RACE CONTROLS

THE PRIORITY INHERITANCE SCHEDULER

The priority inheritance scheduler implicitly controls all three types of races (e.g. priority race, preference race and forerunner race) according to the priority of the task involved. This suggests the following:

(i) implicit priority control - a high priority task calling a low priority server would lead to the server's priority being modified to that of the caller.

(ii) implicit preference control - a task choosing an alternative within a select statement bases its decision on the priority of the calling tasks. The winner of a preference race is the entry for which the calling task has the highest priority.

(iii) implicit forerunner control - a task accepting pending calls for a specific entry bases its decision on the priority of the calling task to this entry, rather than taking calls in a FIFO order. Thus the winner of a forerunner race would be the waiting task with the highest priority.

The priority inheritance scheduler exhibits an integrated approach to race controls, and so it solves the problem of priority inversion. Systems which use this scheduler are more predicable, portable, and allow for reuse and easier maintenance.

THE E & D COMPREHENSIVE SET OF RACE CONTROLS

The E & D set is the most versatile integrated set of race controls It is characterized by an explicit dynamic priority control, an explicit dynamic preference control, and an explicit dynamic forerunner control.

Resolutions to all occurrences of a race are made explicitly. The language itself permits controls over all types of races. For real-time applications race controls are critical to meet the specifications. The E & D set proposes the most powerful and unified set of controls to implement these requirements.

The following possible Ada Language constructs express dynamic preference and dynamic forerunner controls:

type PREFERENCES is (LOW, MEDIUM, HIGH);

task REAL_TIME is
   prefer HIGH: entry ATTACK (.....) by (-DISTANCE);
   prefer MEDIUM : entry OFFENSE (.....);
   prefer LOW: entry DANGER (.....) by (priority);
end REAL_TIME;

Figure #2
Preference and forerunner controls

In this example the key words "prefer" and "by" are used to implement preference control and forerunner control respectively; preference and forerunner are part of task specification.

Also, an attack message is accepted before any

other messages regardless of the priority of callers to the entries OFFENSE and DANGER.

Of all pending calls to entry ATTACK, the call reporting an attack from the shortest distance is accepted first. (DISTANCE might be a parameter passed by the callers).

Calls to the entry DANGER are accepted according to the priority of the callers, and calls to the entry OFFENSE are accepted on a FIFO basis.

This example shows how Comprehensive Scheduling Controls can simulate an intelligent decision making process, and thus control Ada's high degree of nondeterminism. The use of this explicit and dynamic comprehensive set of race controls provides an integrated approach which is powerful enough to avoid the problem of priority inversion but is not limited to priority inheritance only; the set of comprehensive race controls is a versatile capacity which can be used to realized any scheduling algorithm. Systems programed in a language equipped with comprehensive race controls are as predictable as the external environment. A user may choose not to control a specific occurrence of a race, or he might choose to control the race. The control can be tailored to the specification of the problem. The versatility of the comprehensive set of race controls make the software written for it more portable, reusable, and simpler to maintain.

EVALUATION OF THE TWO PROPOSALS

The advantage of the priority inheritance scheduler is that the user does not have to know its internal implementation. It is a simple tool to use. The programmer has to decide only whether to turn the scheduler on or off. When the scheduler is on, race controls are resolved implicitly, and when the scheduler is off preference control is left unspecified and forerunner control is observed by the FIFO rule.

There are, however, restrictions to the use of the priority inheritance scheduler. First, it is tailored to a very specific algorithm and thus is not general enough or versatile enough to deal with other scheduling algorithms [EM2, EM3].

Secondly, priority inheritance can be successfully implemented on a uni-processor system. Hence programs written under the assumption of the use of uni-processor are not portable.

Still another restriction of Priority Inheritance is that it can be imposed only when the calling task has higher priority than the task accepting the call. Therefore, priority inheritance could not be enforced when a high priority task is waiting on an accept for which there are no waiting calls, as it would be impossible to determine the identity of a potential caller due to the asymmetric naming convention in Ada. Ada does not have the adequate capability to express and enforce good system design.

By comparison, the set of comprehensive scheduling controls allows the user to define the race conditions explicitly for each occurrence of a conflict. Thus it is not restricted to a specific algorithm, but provides the necessary controls to define one. (Figure #3, for example, simulates priority inheritance).

To preserve priority inheritance the following procedures should be followed:

(i). A high priority task waiting for a rendezvous should explicitly request that a potential partner inherit its priority. This is a stronger command than the priority inheritance scheduler, as a high priority task waiting on an accept may explicitly assign its priority to a potential caller (this information is available to the programmer; it should be possible to pass it to the system)

The capacity of explicit and dynamic priority controls enables the inheritance of priority within program level.

(ii). The preference of an entry must correlate to the pending call with the highest priority. As a result, the entry selected will be the one on which the waiting caller has the highest priority.

The capacity for explicit and dynamic preference controls enables the inheritance of priority on the task level.

(iii). The forerunner control must be used to select from the entry queue the task with the highest priority.

The capacity for explicit and dynamic forerunner control enables the inheritance of priority on the entry level.

The following example is a simulation of priority inheritance on the task level and on the entry level (procedures ii, and iii).

Assume a program with a set of prioritized tasks in three different categories and a task called REAL_TIME_SERVER with the highest possible priority. REAL_TIME_SERVER has three entries denoted by A, B, and C. The specifications of the problem are such that tasks calling on entry A are known to have higher priorities than tasks calling on entry B. Entry C might be called by any one of the tasks.

Specifications of REAL_TIME_SERVER might be the following:

```
type PREFERENCES is ( LOW, MEDIUM, HIGH );
task REAL_TIME is
   prefer HIGH: entry A (..... );
   prefer MEDIUM: entry C (..... ) by (priority);
   prefer LOW : entry B (..... );
end REAL_TIME;
```

Figure #3 Simulation of priority inheritance

THE NEED FOR VERSATILE SCHEDULING CONTROLS

For some real time applications, it is not the priority
of a specific task, but rather the urgency of a service
or a communication request which poses the primary time
constraint. Thus an entry to accept a call reporting of
a major event should be served first regardless of the
priority of the called task. When a decision control
task in a distributed system is ready to accept
messages from several sensors it might becomes swamped
with calls. In these situations, the need to
prioritize calls becomes all the more important (more
examples of the need for dynamic preference control can
be found in [EM2] and [EM3]). The need for a
forerunner control is best demonstrated thorough the
implementation of a server which has to accept calls to
entry ATTACK from the caller which reports on the
closest attack, regardless of the priority of the
caller. Without forerunner control, the number of
communications needed would be doubled [GR].
Although in most applications it is necessary to avoid
priority inversion, in some real-time applications
priority inversion is necessary to meet deadline
constraints. Priority inheritance can be considered a
greedy algorithm which tries to do the next best action
for the moment; thus its results are not necessarily
optimal. In many cases, real-time applications depend
on the optimization of these results.
The following language principles are recommended to
support good system design capacity of a language:

Preservation of Timing Information:
The language should allow the representation of
information that the user might know and that the
compiler might need concerning time constraints and
relative urgency of alternatives.
Preservation of Control:
The language should allow the representation of
complete control over all possible decision choices
that the system might face.

CONCLUSION

Two propositions to solve the lack of race controls in
Ada were presented. For an application where the user
consistently need to avoid priority inversion with no
exception, the priority inheritance scheduler is the
best solution. It observes the principle of automation
and the principle of information hiding and hence
consistent with Ada's "culture". It is a realization
of a specific scheduling algorithm.
The set of explicit and dynamic race controls does not
realize any specific scheduling algorithm, but rather
serves as a versatile vehicle to construct one. As
such, the set of comprehensive race controls
complements the priority inheritance scheduler. The

comprehensive set of race controls satisfies the principle of preservation of timing information and preservation of control; thus it is necessary for good system design. Ada should be adequete as a programming language for the problem domain of real-time applications in distributed systems. Thus the need for a versatile mechanism to realize large arrays of scheduling algorithms is apparent. There are still many problems to confront. Further study and more experience is needed in order to arrive at the best solution for Ada 9X.

References

[C]   D. Cornhil, "Tasking Session Summary" Proceeding of the 1st International Workshop on Real Time Ada Issues Moretonhampstead, Devon, UK. 1987 Ada Letters Vol. VII, Num. 6, Fall 1987.

[E1]   T. Elrad, "Comprehensive Scheduling Controls for Ada Tasking", Proceedings of the International Workshop on Real-Time Ada Issues, Devon, UK, June 1-3 1988.

[E2]   T. Elrad, "The Issue of Mutual Control: Synchronization and Decision Making Control for Embedded Systems", Department of Computer Science, Illinois Institute of Technology, January 1989.

[EM1]   T. Elrad, F. Maymir-Ducharme "Introducing the Preference Control Primitive: "Experience with Controlling Nondeterminism in Ada", Proceedings of the 1986 Washington Ada Symposium in Lurel, Maryland, March 24 -26, 1986.

[EM2]   T. Elrad, F. Maymir-Ducharme, "Efficiently Controlling Communication in Ada Using Preference Control", Proceedings of the IEEE 1986 Military Communications Conference in Monterey, California, October 5-9, 1986.

[EM3]   T. Elrad, F. Maymir " Satisfying Emergency Communication Requirements With Dynamic Preference Control" Proceeding of the Sixth Annual National Conference on Ada Technology , Mach 14-17 1988.

[GR]   N. Gehani, W. Roome "Concurrent-C*" AT&T Bell Lab. Murray Hill, New Jersy. 07974, 1985.

[GS]   J. Goodenough, L. Sha, "The priority Ceiling Protocol: A Method for Minimizing The Blocking of High Priority Ada Tasks", Proceedings of the International Workshop on Real-Time Ada Issues, Devon, UK, June 1-3 1988.

A Review of Analytic Real-Time Scheduling Theory and its Application to Ada

Lui Sha
John B. Goodenough

Software Engineering Institute,[1] Carnegie-Mellon University, Pittsburgh, PA 15238, USA

Abstract: The Ada tasking model was intended to support the management of concurrency in a priority-driven real-time scheduling environment. In this paper, we will review some important results of a priority-based scheduling theory, illustrate its applications with examples, discuss its implications for the Ada tasking model, and suggest workarounds that permit us to implement analytical scheduling algorithms within the existing framework of Ada.

1. Introduction

Background

The Real-Time Scheduling in Ada Project at the Software Engineering Institute is a cooperative effort between the SEI, Carnegie-Mellon University, system developers in industry, Ada vendors, and DoD agencies. It aims at applying the scheduling theory reviewed in this paper to the design and implementation of hard real-time systems in Ada. The scheduling algorithms and theories developed under this project and at Carnegie-Mellon University provide an analytical basis for understanding the timing behavior of real-time systems. The project is implementing these scheduling algorithms in an Ada runtime system, and is coding examples of real-time systems to evaluate the suitability of the whole approach. This paper summarizes some of the scheduling approaches being studied and shows how they can be applied in an Ada context.

Traditionally, many real-time systems use cyclical executives to schedule concurrent threads of execution. Under this approach, a programmer lays out an execution timeline by hand to serialize the execution of critical sections and to meet task deadlines. While such an approach is adequate for simple systems, it quickly becomes unmanageable for large systems. It is a painful process to develop application code so the compiled segments fit into the time slots of a cyclical executive and to ensure that the critical sections of different tasks do not interleave. Forcing programmers to schedule tasks by fitting code segments on a timeline is no better than the outdated approach of managing memory by manual memory overlay. Such an approach often destroys program structure and results in real-time programs that are difficult to understand and maintain.

The Ada tasking model represents a fundamental departure from the cyclical executive model. Indeed, the dynamic preemption of tasks at runtime generates non-deterministic timelines that are at odds with the very idea of a fixed execution timeline.

---

[1]The Software Engineering Instituted is sponsored by the U. S. Department of Defense. This work was supported in part by the Office of Naval Research under contract F19628-85-C-003.

This non-determinism seems to make it impossible to decide whether real-time deadlines will be met. However, Ada's tasking concepts are well-suited to the analytic scheduling theories being considered in our project. In essence, these theories ensure that as long as the CPU utilization of all tasks lies below a certain bound and appropriate scheduling algorithms are used for the CPU and I/O processing, all tasks will meet their deadlines without knowing exactly when any given task will be running. Even if there is a transient overload, a fixed subset of *critical* tasks will still meet their deadlines as long as their CPU utilizations lie within the appropriate bound. The theories also deal with aperiodic processing requirements, mode changes, and jitter requirements. Applying these theories to Ada makes Ada tasking truly useful for real-time applications while also putting the development and maintenance of real-time systems on an analytic, engineering basis, making these systems easier to develop and maintain.

In the next section, we review some of the important results in real-time scheduling theory. We begin with the problem of scheduling independent periodic tasks. We then review the problems of real-time synchronization. (In an extended version of this paper [Sha & Goodenough 88], we also address how to deal with transient overload and aperiodic tasks.) In Section 3, we review the rules for scheduling Ada tasks and suggest some approaches that permit the use of the scheduling theory within the framework of these rules. Section 4 concludes the paper.

2.   Scheduling Real-Time Tasks

In this section, we provide an overview of the basis for an analytic scheduling theory, starting with the problem of ensuring that independent periodic tasks meet their deadlines. We then address the problem of ensuring deadlines are met when tasks must synchronize or communicate with each other.

Scheduling Periodic Tasks

Tasks are *independent* if their executions need not be synchronized. Given a set of independent periodic tasks, the *rate monotonic scheduling algorithm* gives each task a fixed priority and assigns higher priorities to tasks with shorter periods. A task set is said to be *schedulable* if all its deadlines are met, i.e., if every periodic task finishes its execution before the end of its period. Any set of independent periodic tasks is schedulable by the rate monotonic algorithm if the condition of Theorem 1 is met [Liu & Layland 73].

> **Theorem 1:** A set of n independent periodic tasks scheduled by the rate monotonic algorithm will always meet its deadlines, for all task phasings, if
>
> $$\frac{C_1}{T_1} + \cdots + \frac{C_n}{T_n} \leq n(2^{1/n}-1) = U(n)$$
>
> where C_i and T_i are the execution time and period of task τ_i respectively.

Theorem 1 offers a sufficient (worst-case) condition that characterizes the schedulability of the rate monotonic algorithm. This bound converges to 69% (*ln* 2) as the number of tasks approaches infinity. Table 1 shows values of the bound for one to nine tasks.

The bound of Theorem 1 is very pessimistic because the worst-case task set is contrived and unlikely to be encountered in practice. For a randomly chosen task set, the likely bound is 88% [Lehoczky et al. 87]. To know if a set of given tasks with utilization greater than the bound of Theorem 1 can meet its deadlines, the conditions of Theorem 2

U(1) = 1.0	U(4) = 0.756	U(7) = 0.728
U(2) = 0.828	U(5) = 0.743	U(8) = 0.724
U(3) = 0.779	U(6) = 0.734	U(9) = 0.720

Table 1:   Scheduling Bounds for One to Nine Independent Tasks

must be checked [Lehoczky et al. 87]:

Theorem 2: A set of n independent periodic tasks scheduled by the rate monotonic algorithm will always meet its deadlines, for all task phasings, if and only if

$$\forall\, i,\ 1 \le i \le n, \qquad min \sum_{j=1}^{i} C_j \frac{1}{l\,T_k} \left\lceil \frac{l\,T_k}{T_j} \right\rceil \le 1$$
$$(k, l) \,\varepsilon\, R_i$$

where C_j and T_j are the execution time and period of task τ_j respectively and $R_i = \{(k, l) \mid 1 \le k \le i, l = 1, \cdots, \lfloor T_i/T_k \rfloor \}$.

This theorem provides the exact schedulability criterion for independent periodic task sets under the rate monotonic algorithm. In effect, the theorem checks if each task can complete its execution before its first deadline by checking all the scheduling points. (It was shown in [Liu & Layland 73] that when all the tasks are initiated at the same time (the worst-case phasing), if a task completes its execution before the end of its first period, it will never miss a deadline.) The *scheduling points* for task τ are τ's first deadline and the ends of periods of higher priority tasks within τ's first deadline. In the formula, i denotes the task to be checked and k denotes each of the tasks that affects the completion time of task i, i.e., task i and the higher priority tasks. The application of these theorems is illustrated by Examples 1 and 2 below.

Example 1: Consider the case of three periodic tasks, where $U_i = C_i/T_i$.
- Task τ_1: $C_1 = 20$; $T_1 = 100$; $U_1 = 0.2$
- Task τ_2: $C_2 = 40$; $T_2 = 150$; $U_2 = 0.267$
- Task τ_3: $C_3 = 100$; $T_3 = 350$; $U_3 = 0.286$

The total utilization of these three tasks is 0.753, which is below Theorem 1's bound for three tasks: $3(2^{1/3} - 1) = 0.779$. Hence, we know these three tasks are schedulable, i.e., they will meet their deadlines if τ_1 is given the highest priority, τ_2 the next highest, and τ_3 the lowest. The remaining 24.7% processor capacity can be used for low priority background processing. However, we can also use it for additional hard real-time computation.

Example 2: Suppose we replace τ_1's algorithm with one that is more accurate and computationally intensive. Suppose the new algorithm doubles τ_1's computation time from 20 to 40, so the total processor utilization increases from 0.753 to 0.953. Since the utilization of the first two tasks is 0.667, which is below Theorem 1's bound for two tasks, $2(2^{1/2} - 1) = 0.828$, the first two tasks cannot miss their deadlines. For task τ_3, we use Theorem 2 to check whether the task set is schedulable, i.e., we set $i = n = 3$, and check whether one of the following equations holds:

$$\forall\ k, l,\ 1 \le k,l \le 3,\quad \sum_{j=1}^{3} \left\lceil \frac{l\,T_k}{T_j} \right\rceil C_j \le l\,T_k$$

To check if task τ_3 can meet its deadline, it is only necessary to check the equation for values of l and k such that $l\,T_k \le T_3 = 350$. If one of the equations is satisfied, the task set is schedulable.

$$C_1 + C_2 + C_3 \le T_1 \qquad 40 + 40 + 100 > 100 \qquad l = 1, k = 1$$

or $\quad 2C_1 + C_2 + C_3 \le T_2 \qquad 80 + 40 + 100 > 150 \qquad l = 1, k = 2$

or $\quad 2C_1 + 2C_2 + C_3 \le 2T_1 \qquad 80 + 80 + 100 > 200 \qquad l = 2, k = 1$

or $\quad 3C_1 + 2C_2 + C_3 \le 2T_2 \qquad 120 + 80 + 100 = 300 \qquad l = 2, k = 2,\ \text{or}\ l = 3, k = 1$

or $\quad 4C_1 + 3C_2 + C_3 \le T_3 \qquad 160 + 120 + 100 > 350 \qquad l = 1, k = 3$

The analysis shows that after 300 units of time, τ_1 will have run three times, τ_2 will have run twice, and τ_3 will have run once. The required amount of computation just fits within the allowed time, so each task meets its deadline. [Liu & Layland 73] showed that since the tasks meet their deadlines at least once within the period T_3, they will always meet their deadlines. The analysis therefore shows that task τ_3 is also schedulable and in the worst-case phasing will meet its deadline exactly at time 300. Hence, we can double the utilization of the first task from 20% to 40% and still meet all the deadlines. The remaining 4.7% processor capacity can be used for either background processing or a fourth hard deadline task, which has a period longer than that of τ_3 and which satisfies the condition of Theorem 2. (The period of the fourth task must be longer than τ_3's period since task τ_3 just meets its deadline at 300 and hence we cannot add a task with a priority higher than that of task τ_3.)

A major advantage of using the rate monotonic algorithm is that it allows us to separate logical correctness concerns from timing correctness concerns. Suppose that a cyclical executive is used for this example. The major cycle must be the least common multiple of the task periods. In this example, the task periods are in the ratio 100:150:350 = 2:3:7. A minor cycle of 50 units would induce a major cycle of 42 minor cycles, which is an overly complex design. To reduce the number of minor cycles, we can try to modify the periods. For example, it might be possible to reduce the period of the longest task, from 350 to 300. The total utilization is then exactly 100%, and the period ratios are 2:3:6; the major cycle can then be 6 minor cycles of 50 units. To implement this approach and minimize the splitting of computations belonging to a single task, we could split task τ_1 into two parts of 20 units computation each. The computation of task τ_2 similarly could be split into at least two parts such that task τ_3 need only be split into four parts. A possible timeline indicating the amount of computation for each task in each minor cycle is shown in the following table, where 20_1 on the first line indicates the first part of task τ_1's computation, which takes 20 units of time.

When processor utilization level is high and there are many tasks, fitting code segments into time slots can be a time-consuming iterative process. In addition, a later modification of any task may overflow a particular minor cycle and require the entire timeline to be redone. But more important, the cyclic executive approach has required us to modify the period of one of the tasks, increasing the utilization to 100% *without in fact*

Cyclic Timeline for Example 3						
	1	2	3	4	5	6
τ_1	20_1	20_2	20_1	20_2	20_1	20_2
τ_2	30_1	10_2			30_1	10_2
τ_3		20_1	30_2		20_3	30_4

Table 2: Minor Cycle Timeline: Each minor cycle is 50.

doing more useful work. Under the rate monotonic approach for this example, all deadlines are met, but total machine utilization must be 95.3% or less instead of 100% or less. This doesn't mean the rate monotonic approach is less efficient. The capacity that isn't needed to service real-time tasks in the rate monotonic approach can be used by background tasks, e.g., for built-in-test purposes. With the cyclic executive approach, no such additional work can be done in this example. Of course, the scheduling overhead for task preemption needs to be taken into account. If S is the amount of time needed for a single scheduling action, then since there are two scheduling actions per task, the total utilization devoted to scheduling is $2S/T_1 + 2S/T_2 + 2S/T_3$. In the cyclic case, the scheduling overhead is partly in the (very small) time needed to dispatch each task's code segment in each minor cycle and partly in the utilization wasted by decreasing the period for task 3. For this example, the scheduling overhead for the cyclic approach is at least 4.7%:

$Actual\_Utilization - Required\_Utilization$, i.e.,
$100/300 - 100/350 = .333 - .\overline{286} = .047$

Thus, although the rate monotonic approach may seem to yield a lower maximum utilization than the cyclic approach, in practice, the cyclic approach may simply be consuming more machine time because the periods have been artificially shortened. In addition, cyclic executives get complicated when they have to deal with aperiodic events. The rate monotonic approach, as shown in [Sha & Goodenough 88], readily accommodates aperiodic processing. Finally, the rate monotonic utilization bound as computed by Theorem 2 is a function of the periods and computation times of the task set. The utilization bound can always be increased by transforming task periods, i.e., by splitting a task's work over several short periods. This kind of transformation should be familiar to users of cyclic executives. The difference here is that we don't need to adjust the code segment sizes so different code segments fit into time slots. Instead, a task simply requests suspension after performing $C/2$ amount of work. Alternatively, the runtime scheduler can be instructed to suspend the task after a certain amount of computation has been done, without affecting the application code. An important use of period transformation is to give critical long-period tasks a higher priority while keeping priority assignments consistent with rate monotonic rules. This is the approach used to ensure critical tasks meet their deadlines in transient overload situations. (See [Sha & Goodenough 88] for further discussion of this point.)

Task Synchronization

In the previous sections we have discussed the scheduling of independent tasks. Tasks, however, do interact. In this section, we discuss how the rate monotonic scheduling theory can be applied to real-time tasks that must interact. The discussion is limited in this paper to scheduling within a uniprocessor. Readers who are interested in the multiprocessor synchronization problem should see [Rajkumar et al. 88].

Common synchronization primitives include semaphores, locks, monitors, and Ada rendezvous. Although the use of these or equivalent methods is necessary to protect the consistency of shared data or to guarantee the proper use of non-preemptable resources, their use may jeopardize the ability of the system to meet its timing requirements. In fact, a direct application of these synchronization mechanisms may lead to an indefinite period of priority inversion and low schedulability. (*Priority inversion* occurs when the use of a resource by a low priority task delays the execution of a high priority task. Priority inversion occurs either when task priorities are incorrectly assigned or when they are not used correctly when allocating resources. Although priority inversion is undesirable, it cannot be completely eliminated. Instead, programmers and system designers must be aware of its existence and attempt to minimize it.)

The *priority ceiling protocol* is a real-time synchronization protocol with two important properties: 1) freedom from mutual deadlock, and 2) bounded blocking: at most one lower priority task can block a higher priority task [Goodenough & Sha 88, Sha et al. 87]. There are two ideas in the design of this protocol. First is the concept of priority inheritance: when a task τ blocks the execution of higher priority tasks, task τ executes at the highest priority level of all the tasks it blocks. Second, a critical section is allowed to start execution only if the section will always execute at a priority level that is higher than the (inherited) priority levels of any preempted critical sections. It was shown in [Sha et al. 87] that such a prioritized total ordering in the execution of critical sections leads to the two desired properties. To achieve such a prioritized total ordering, we define the *priority ceiling* of a binary semaphore S to be the highest priority of all tasks that may lock S. When a task τ attempts to execute one of its critical sections, it will be suspended unless its priority is higher than the priority ceilings of all semaphores currently locked by tasks other than τ. If task τ is unable to enter its critical section for this reason, the task that holds the lock on the semaphore with the highest priority ceiling is said to be blocking τ and hence inherits the priority of τ. As long as a task τ is not attempting to enter one of its critical sections, it will preempt every task that has a lower priority. See [Goodenough & Sha 88] for a detailed example. Theorems 1 and 2 are readily extended to account for the effects of the priority ceiling protocol on schedulability (see [Sha & Goodenough 88]).

Example Application of the Theory

When all the theory, including the results for aperiodic task scheduling and task synchronization, is combined, examples like the following are readily addressed:

Example 3: Consider the following task set.

1. Emergency handling task: execution time = 5 msec; worst case interarrival time = 50 msec; deadline is 6 msec after arrival.

2. Aperiodic event handling tasks: average execution time = 2 msec; average inter-arrival time = 40 msec; fast response time is desirable but there are no hard deadlines.

3. Periodic task τ_1: execution time = 20 msec; period = 100 msec; deadline is at the end of each period. In addition, τ_3 may block τ_1 for 10 msec by using a shared communication server, and task τ_2 may block τ_1 for 20 msec by using a shared data object.

4. Periodic task τ_2: execution time = 40 msec; period = 150 msec; deadline is 20 msec before the end of each period.

5. Periodic task τ_3: execution time = 100 msec; period = 350 msec; deadline is

at the end of each period.

The theory can be readily applied to this example to show that all required deadlines can be met and that the expected response time for the aperiodic tasks is 4 msec. Although the worst-case workload in this example is 95%, we can still do quite a bit of background processing, since the soft deadline aperiodics and the emergency task are unlikely to fully utilize the servers. A detailed analysis of this example is given in [Sha & Goodenough 88]. The results derived for this example show how the scheduling theory puts real-time programming on an analytic *engineering* basis.

3.   Real-Time Scheduling in Ada

Although Ada was intended for use in building real-time systems, its suitability for real-time programming has been widely questioned. Many of these questions concern practical issues, such as the cost of performing a rendezvous, minimizing the duration of interrupt masking in the runtime system, efficient support for interrupt handling, etc. These problems are being addressed by compiler vendors who are aiming at the real-time market. More important are concerns about the suitability of Ada's conceptual model for dealing with real-time programming. For example, tasks in Ada run non-deterministically, making it hard for traditional real-time programmers to decide whether any tasks will meet their deadlines. In addition, the scheduling rules of Ada don't seem to support prioritized scheduling well. Prioritized tasks are queued in FIFO order rather than by priority, high priority tasks can be delayed indefinitely when calling low priority tasks (due to priority inversion; see [Goodenough & Sha 88] for an example), and task priorities cannot be changed when application demands change at runtime. Fortunately, it appears that none of these problems present insurmountable difficulties; solutions exist within the current language framework, although some language changes would be helpful to ensure uniform implementation support. The Real-Time Scheduling in Ada project at the SEI is specifying coding guidelines and runtime system support needed to use analytic scheduling theory in Ada programs. The rest of this section summarizes the approach being taken by the project, and then shows how Ada's scheduling rules can be interpreted to support the requirements of rate monotonic scheduling algorithms.

Ada Real-Time Design Guidelines

The coding and design guidelines being developed by the SEI real-time scheduling project reflect a basic principle of real-time programming — write systems in a way that minimizes priority inversion, i.e., minimize the time a high priority task has to wait for the execution of lower priority tasks.

For example, consider a set of periodic tasks, called *clients*, that must exchange data among themselves. They do not call each other to exchange data. Instead, whenever they must read or write shared data, they call a *server* task. Each server task has a simple structure — an endless loop with a single select statement with no guards. This structure models the notion of critical regions guarded by a semaphore; each entry is a critical region for the task calling the entry. The prohibition against guards simplifies the schedulability analysis and the runtime system implementation, but otherwise is not essential.

Client tasks are assigned priorities according to rate monotonic principles, i.e., tasks with the shortest periods are given the highest priorities. There are two options when assigning a priority to a server. If the Ada runtime system supports the priority ceiling protocol directly (the next section explains why the runtime system is allowed to support the protocol), then give the server a low or an undefined priority. In addition, tell the runtime system the priority ceiling of the server, i.e., the highest priority of all its clients. Then, when a server is executing on behalf of a client task, no other client task will be allowed to call any server unless the client's priority is higher than the executing server's priority ceiling. If the client does not have a sufficiently high priority, its call will be blocked (i.e., the caller will be preempted just before the call would be placed on an entry's queue), and the server's priority will be raised to the priority of the blocked caller. This treatment of competing calls will ensure that a high priority task is blocked at most once by a server [Goodenough & Sha 88]. Moreover, because calls are preempted *before* they are queued, when the executing server completes its rendezvous, the highest priority blocked task will be able to execute. In effect, calls will be processed in priority order and mutual deadlock caused by nested server calls will be impossible.

    If the priority ceiling protocol is not directly supported by an Ada runtime system, its effect can often nonetheless be achieved. Suppose a server is used to synchronize access to data shared by several tasks. The ceiling protocol requires that while a server is in rendezvous with a client, no other server be called by any client unless the client has a priority higher than the server's priority ceiling. This effect can be easily achieved using existing Ada runtime systems by assigning the server task a ceiling priority, i.e., a priority that is one greater than the priority of its highest priority caller. In this case, the server will either be waiting for a client or it will be serving a client at a priority that prevents other clients from from executing and calling any server with an equal or lower priority ceiling. This approach avoids the prioritized queueing problem because there will never be more than one queued client task. It is also not hard to see why mutual deadlock will be impossible.

    This simple approximation to the ceiling protocol will not work, however, if the server task suspends itself while in rendezvous. Such a suspension will allow client tasks with priorities lower than that of the suspended server to rendezvous with other servers and this violates the principle of the ceiling protocol. Such a suspension can be caused by either the server's need to synchronize with external I/O events in a uni-processor or the server's need to rendezvous with another task in other processor in a multi-processor. When a server task can suspend itself while in a rendezvous, care must be taken to ensure that no calls are accepted by other servers having the same or a lower ceiling priority. In addition, since queues can now develop, it is important that queued calls be serviced in priority order. Preventing inappropriate server calls and ensuring priority queueing can require quite complex code involving entry families, so this method of implementing the ceiling protocol is probably unsuitable when server tasks are allowed to suspend themselves.

    From a schedulability viewpoint, the execution time spent in each rendezvous with a server that does not suspend itself is counted as part of the computing time, C_i, for the client task τ_i. Since the use of servers is a synchronization problem, an extension of Theorems 1 and 2 must be used to account for blocking time (see [Sha & Goodenough 88]). Under the priority ceiling protocol, the maximal blocking time for a non-server task at priority level i is the longest entry call by a lower level client task to a server whose priority ceiling is equal to or higher than the priority of i. (Note that this definition of blocking time means that even if a task, τ, makes no server calls, the schedulability analysis for τ must include blocking time for lower priority client tasks; see [Sha & Goodenough 88] for an example.) If a server can suspend itself, it is sufficient to treat the suspension time as server execution time in the schedulability analysis; work is underway to see when less pessimistic treatment may be possible.

The worst-case blocking time for a client task is the same whether the ceiling protocol is supported directly by the runtime system or is approximated by giving the server an appropriately high priority. The essential difference between the direct implementation and the approximation method is that the server priority will be raised only when necessary when the direct implementation is used. This tends to generate less blocking on average and hence better response time when aperiodic tasks have a priority below that of a server's ceiling; in addition, in transient overload situations, non-critical periodic tasks having a priority lower than a server's ceiling are less likely to miss their deadlines. In short, the direct implementation gives better average case behavior, especially when the entry calls are relatively long. When the entry calls are short compared with client task execution times, the performance difference is insignificant.

Despite the complications that arise when server tasks can suspend themselves, our point is that the schedulability theory can be readily applied to Ada programs, ensuring that deadlines are met even when timelines are nondeterministic. In the next section we discuss how to interpret Ada's scheduling rules so Ada runtime systems can support rate monotonic scheduling algorithms directly.

On Ada Scheduling Rules

First of all, the Ada tasking model is well-suited, in principle, to the use of the analytic scheduling theories presented in this paper. When using these theories, a programmer doesn't need to know when tasks are running to be sure that deadlines will be met. That is, both Ada and the theory abstract away the details of an execution timeline. Although Ada tasks fit well with the theory at the conceptual level, Ada and the theory differ on the rules for determining when a task is eligible to run and its execution priority. For example, if a high priority task calls a server task that is already in rendezvous with a low priority task, the rendezvous can continue at the priority of the task being served instead of being increased because a high priority task is waiting. Under these circumstances, the high priority task can be blocked as long as there are medium priority jobs able to run. But there are a variety of solutions to this problem. The most general solution within the constraints of the language is to simply not use pragma PRIORITY at all. If all tasks in a program have no assigned priority, then the scheduler is free to use any convenient algorithm for deciding which eligible task to run. An implementation-dependent pragma could be used to give "scheduling priorities" to tasks, i.e., indications of scheduling importance that would be used in accordance with rate monotonic scheduling algorithms. This approach would even allow "priorities" to be changed dynamically by the programmer because such changes only affect the scheduling of tasks that, in a legalistic sense, have no Ada priorities at all. The only problem with this approach is that tasks are still queued in FIFO order rather than by priority. However, this problem can often be solved by using a coding style that prevents queues from having more than one task, making the FIFO issue irrelevant or by suspending calling tasks just before they are queued. Of course, telling programmers to assign "scheduling priorities" to tasks but not to use pragma PRIORITY, surely says we are fighting the language rather than taking advantage of it. *But the important point is that no official revisions to the language are needed to take advantage of the scheduling theories and algorithms described in this paper and being developed by our project.* Here are the relevant Ada rules and appropriate ways of interpreting them:

- CPU allocation: priorities must be observed. Ada requires that the highest priority task eligible to run be given the CPU when this is "sensible." "Sensible" for a uniprocessor is usually interpreted to mean that if an entry call by an executing task can be accepted, the call *must* be accepted and no lower priority task can be allowed to execute. Although this interpretation may seem to be obviously the best, it is in fact not correct for the priority ceiling protocol, which gives better service to high priority tasks and avoids deadlock by blocking calls from medium priority tasks when certain low priority entry calls are already in progress. This protocol sometimes requires that an entry call be blocked even though the called task is able to accept it (see [Goodenough & Sha 88] for a detailed example.)

Solution: There are several solutions to this problem. First of all, the priority ceiling protocol need not be applied to all called Ada tasks; it need only be applied to those tasks that are servers in the sense defined in the previous section. The simplest approach (in terms of living within the current interpretations of Ada rules) is to give each server task a unique priority that is higher than the priority of any task calling the server.

Another approach is to implement the priority ceiling protocol directly for server tasks. This approach is clearly allowed by Ada's scheduling rules as long as the server task is given no assigned priority. A server task with no assigned priority can preempt any other task at any time, since Ada's scheduling rules, in essence, do not specify how tasks with no priority are scheduled. Moreover, when a server with no assigned priority is in a rendezvous with a client task, the Ada rules say the server is executed with "at least" the priority of the client task. Since the priority ceiling rules require that the server task be executed with the priority of the calling task or of any blocked task, whichever is higher, the Ada rule allows the server to be executed with the (higher) priority of the blocked task. Hence, the priority ceiling protocol can certainly be implemented directly when server tasks have no assigned priority.

A more aggressive interpretation of Ada rules is to note that that a high priority task must preempt a lower priority task only when it is "sensible" to do so. Surely it is not "sensible" for a medium priority task to preempt a low priority task if the effect of the preemption is to potentially delay the execution of a high priority task unnecessarily. In short, the priority ceiling protocol provides a set of rules saying when it is "sensible" to allow a higher priority task to run, and hence, these rules can be followed directly by the runtime system even when a server task has an assigned priority.

In short, there are several ways to argue that it is possible to support the priority ceiling protocol's view of priorities within the current Ada rules.

• Hardware task priority: always higher than software task priorities. This Ada rule reflects current hardware designs, but hardware interrupts should not always have the highest priority from the viewpoint of the rate monotonic theory.

Solution: When handling an interrupt that, in terms of the rate monotonic theory, should have a lower priority than the priority of some application task, keep the interrupt handling actions short (which is already a common practice) and include the interrupt handling duration as blocking time in the rate monotonic analysis. In other words, use the scheduling theory to take into account the effect of this source of priority inversion.

• Priority rules for task rendezvous:

  • Selective wait: priority can be ignored. That is, the scheduler is allowed, but not required, to take priorities into account when tasks of different priorities are waiting at open select alternatives.

Solution: Since Ada allows, but does not require taking these priorities into account, ensure that the runtime system *does* use these priorities to decide which call to accept. Alternatively, if the priority ceiling protocol is used, there is never more than one waiting task to select.

• Called task priority: only increased during rendezvous.

Solution: Use the solutions discussed under "CPU allocation" above, i.e., increase the priority of a rendezvous when the ceiling protocol says this is "sensible," or give the called task no priority at all and use priority ceiling rules to say when the called task is allowed to execute, or give servers a priority higher than that of their callers.

FIFO entry queues: Ada requires that the priority of calling tasks must be ignored; calls must be serviced in their order of arrival, not in order of priority. Using FIFO queues rather than priorized queues usually has a serious negative effect on real-time schedulability. FIFO queues must be avoided.

Solution: As noted earlier, often it is possible to avoid FIFO queuing by preventing queues from being formed at all. If the runtime system does not prevent queues from forming, then entry families can, of course, be used to get the effect of prioritized queueing.

• Task priorities: fixed. This rule is inappropriate when task priorities need to be changed at runtime. For example, when a new mode is initiated, the frequency of a task and/or its criticality may change, implying its priority must change. In addition, the scheduling rules for a certain class of aperiodic servers demands that the priority of such a server be lowered when it is about to exceed the maximum execution time allowed for a certain interval of time, and be raised when its service capacity has been restored ([Sprunt et al. 89]).

Solution: When an application needs to adjust the priority of a task at runtime, this task should be declared as having no Ada priority. The runtime system can then be given a way of scheduling the task appropriately by, in effect, changing its priority.

From what our project has learned so far, it seems to be possible in practice to support analytic scheduling algorithms in Ada by using an enlightened interpretation of Ada's scheduling rules together with a combination of runtime system modifications and appropriate coding guidelines. Of course, it would be better if the language did not get in the way of priority scheduling principles. The future revision of Ada should probably reword some of these rules so priority-based scheduling is more clearly and uniformly supported.

4.   Conclusion

Ada tasking was intended to be used for real-time programming. However, the Ada tasking model represents a fundamental departure from the traditional cyclical executive model. Indeed, the dynamic preemption of tasks at runtime generates non-deterministic timelines that are at odds with the very idea of a fixed execution timeline required by a cyclical executive.

In this paper, we have reviewed some important results of priority scheduling theory. Together with Ada tasking, they allow programmers to reason with confidence about timing correctness at the tasking level of abstraction. As long as analytic scheduling algorithms are supported by the runtime system and resource utilization bounds on CPU, I/O drivers, and communication media are observed, the timing constraints will be guaranteed. Even if there is a transient overload, the tasks missing deadlines will be in a predefined order.

Although the treatment of priorities by the current Ada tasking model can and should be improved, it seems that the scheduling algorithms can be used today within the existing Ada rules if an appropriate coding and design approach is taken, and if schedulers are written to take full advantage of certain coding styles and the existing flexibility in the scheduling rules. Additional reports on how this can be done are in preparation at the Software Engineering Institute.

Acknowledgements

The authors would like to thank Mark Klein and Mark Borger for pointing out why the priority ceiling protocol cannot be correctly simulated simply by giving a server task a high priority when the server can suspend itself during a rendezvous. In addition, we would like to thank Anthony Gargaro for catching an error in an early draft of Example 2.

References

[Goodenough & Sha 88]   Goodenough, J. B., and Sha, L.
The Priority Ceiling Protocol: A Method for Minimizing the Blocking of High Priority Ada Tasks.
Ada Letters, Special Issue: Proceedings of the Second International Workshop on Real-Time Ada Issues VIII(7), Fall, 1988.

[Lehoczky et al. 87]   Lehoczky, J. P., Sha, L. and Ding, Y.
The Rate Monotonic Scheduling Algorithm — Exact Characterization and Average Case Behavior.
Technical Report, Department of Statistics, Carnegie-Mellon University, 1987.

[Liu & Layland 73]   Liu, C. L. and Layland J. W.
Scheduling Algorithms for Multiprogramming in a Hard Real Time Environment.
JACM 20 (1):46-61, 1973.

[Rajkumar et al. 88]   Rajkumar, R., Sha, L., and Lehockzy J.P.
Real-Time Synchronization Protocols for Multiprocessors.
In *Proceedings of the IEEE Real-Time Systems Symposium.* 1988.

[Sha & Goodenough 88]   Sha, L. and Goodenough, John B.
Real-Time Scheduling Theory and Ada.
Technical Report CMU/SEI-88-TR-33, Software Engineering Institute, Carnegie-Mellon University, November, 1988.

[Sha et al. 87]   Sha, L., Rajkumar, R. and Lehoczky, J. P.
Priority Inheritance Protocols: An Approach to Real-Time Synchronization.
Technical Report, Department of Computer Science, Carnegie-Mellon University, 1987.
To appear in IEEE Transactions on Computers.

[Sprunt et al. 89]   Sprunt, B., Sha, L. and Lehoczky, J. P.
Scheduling Sporadic and Aperiodic Events in a Hard Real-Time System.
Technical Report, Software Engineering Institute, Carnegie-Mellon University (in preparation), 1989.

Part 4 Design Languages

ADADL AND AISLE - AN ADA-BASED PDL AND SUPPORTING TOOLSET
WHICH ENCOURAGE THE USE OF ADA DURING DESIGN

ROBINSON, J.

PALMER, M.R.

KBSL, Campus Road, Listerhills Technology Park,
Bradford, West Yorkshire BD7 1HR, UK

ABSTRACT

ADADL, an Ada-based Design and Documentation Language, is
described together with its supporting toolset, AISLE.   A
simple example of an ADADL design is given.   The requirements
for an Ada-based Program Design Language (PDL) toolset are
examined and the functionality of the AISLE tools is described.   The means by which this toolset encourages the use of
Ada/PDL is discussed and integration with other tools and
methods is explored.

INTRODUCTION

The concept of using Ada or an Ada-based PDL during the design
phase has gained much support.   For example the United States Department
of Defense (DoD), in directive 3405.2, have stated that:

"An Ada-based PDL shall be used during the design of software."

Using ADADL and the AISLE toolset as an example,   this   paper
discusses the type of software tool support which helps make Ada/PDL
attractive for design.

The concept of integrating this textual representation of
design with a diagrammatic method and toolset is also examined.

REQUIREMENTS FOR AN ADA/PDL TOOLSET

The   authors   define   the   following   characteristics   as   the
minimum requirements for an Ada/PDL and its toolset:

* They should have a "smoothing" effect on the lifecycle, helping to
  blur the distinction between lifecycle phases.

* They should be capable of supporting many job functions by providing
  features for design, coding, testing, documentation, maintenance,
  quality assurance and technical management.

* They should readily interface to other methods,   toolsets and
  environments.

* They should be available in a standard form across a wide range of popular hosts.

THE ADADL Ada/PDL

ADADL embodies the full Ada language. To ease learning, Ada constructs are used wherever appropriate with simple ADADL extensions provided via structured comments, as proposed in [Morrison et al 1984].

ADADL designs are compilable by a validated Ada compiler, and hence can be combined with Ada source code. This is an important component of the lifecycle smoothing process highlighted above.

Four kinds of ADADL comment are provided:

--*   denotes project management information

--| denotes pseudo-code statements describing algorithmic design

--%   denotes descriptions of Ada declarations (associated with standard Ada declarations)

--#   denotes instructions to the ADADL processor, used to customise the processor or its interface to the documentation generator.

WHAT CONSTITUTES AN ADADL DESIGN

A system design expressed in ADADL consists of:

* an expression of system structure, using standard Ada syntax plus descriptive information provided by ADADL comments.

* an expression of algorithmic design, using ADADL pseudo-code. This pseudo-code is based on appropriate Ada constructs and provides an easy to learn, high level medium for the abstraction of algorithmic design.

* project management information, using ADADL comments to provide management information such as requirements tracing, identifying responsible personnel and monitoring current status of units (i.e. designed/coded/tested).

* documentation information, using ADADL comments to include documentation items in the design. These are extracted by the ADADL processor along with other design information in preparation for automatic documentation generation.

A SIMPLE EXAMPLE

A simple example of an ADADL design, taken from a small radar system, is included as Appendix 1.

It should be noted that the example design and implementation does not include the documentation items and project management information which would be present in a real system. This is to simplify the example by showing only those aspects of ADADL which are relevant to this paper.

A more complete example [Robinson & Palmer 1989] is available from the authors in which the different phases involved in creating such a design are highlighted and demonstrated.

FUNCTIONALITY OF THE SUPPORTING TOOLSET
Design analysis

The analytical capability of the toolset includes reporting on entities which have yet to be defined, highlighting Ada declared entities in the ADADL pseudo-code, identifying and cross referencing subprogram calls and highlighting premature exits from loops via return or exit statements.

The complexity of designs is measured and reported using McCabe and ADADL complexity measures [McCabe 1976, SSD 1988], with specific warnings being generated for any units which exceed defined complexity levels.

The toolset also maintains a library of design components in a compiler independent database. Reference reports include cross referencing for Ada entities, identifying relationships between types/ subtypes/derived types and referencing generic units together with their instantiations.

However, the major contribution to design is provided by a software tool called the "Design Review Expert Assistant". This prepares a design review document for each unit which identifies every possible set of design conditions and shows the expected result for each set of conditions.

This improves productivity in the design phase by allowing design reviews to be carried out on this document rather than directly on the design code.

An "Effort Estimator" is also provided to help estimate the effort required during design review by showing the number of design cases present for each unit.

An extract from a design review document is provided in Appendix 2. An example test case effort report is provided in Appendix 3.

Coding, testing and documentation

During coding the AISLE tools highlight any inconsistencies between design and code, for example entities used in the design but not in the code or vice versa.

In addition, reports similar to those produced for the design are created to help the engineer analyse and understand the implementation code whilst during the test phase the "Test Effort Estimator" and "Unit Test Strategy Generator" help to plan the test phase and design test cases.

Once testing has been planned and test cases developed, the "Test Coverage Monitor" can be used to monitor the test case execution and verify that the test cases have been designed correctly.

A more detailed description of testing support provided by AISLE is given in [Radi 1988].

Documentation can be generated directly from ADADL designs and/or Ada source code. Documentation content is extracted both from the ADADL/Ada source and user defined "extract" sections which can be used to extend the documentation content to suit user defined documentation standards.

The format of documentation is dictated by either predefined or user defined templates. Predefined templates are provided in common formats such as DoD-Std-2167.

It should be noted that the documentation generated does not consist simply of templates. Rather, the system analyses the pseudo-code design and Ada implementation to extract appropriate information. For examples of these capabilities see [Robinson & Palmer 1989].

Quality assurance

Quality assurance activities are supported at all stages of the lifecycle via quality reports generated from ADADL designs and/or Ada source code.

These quality reports help to monitor the status of the project and the quality of design and code. A full list of reports can be found in [Robinson & Palmer 1989].

Reports can be added to support specific quality standards or guidelines, eg Safe Ada.

Automated documentation facilities combine with the above reports to help ensure that design, code and documentation remains consistent throughout the lifecycle.

Maintenance

During maintenance the cross reference and descriptive reports make the system easier to understand. In addition, the close integration of design and code together with the cross checking between them reduces the possibility of inconsistencies being introduced by maintenance activity.

INTEGRATION WITH OTHER METHODS AND TOOLSETS

Integration of AISLE with diagrammatic methods and tools leads to an important "seamless interface" between graphical architectural design and textual algorithmic design, vital in achieving the lifecycle smoothing effect which Ada/PDL users find attractive [NAC 1988].

This integration is reasonably simple to implement, particularly in Ada oriented systems such as Adagen [Mark V Systems 1988]. For graphical methods such as HOOD in which partial or complete Ada code may be generated, the tool can be customised to generate ADADL source, ensuring that a tight integration is achieved.

This is particularly beneficial where design or documentation information can be included in the graphical design and "fed through" into ADADL and hence subsequent stages. This "enter once" policy brings significant benefits.

HOW ADADL AND AISLE ENCOURAGE THE USE OF ADA IN DESIGN

The AISLE toolset provides many automated features which take much of the drudgery out of activities such as design review preparation, test case design and documentation production. Clearly, the ADADL Ada/PDL is central to the success of the toolset. Indeed, the earlier that ADADL can be applied in the lifecycle the sooner the toolset can be employed. This is particularly true when the toolset may be integrated with front end design tools allowing an early ADADL representation of design to be produced. By applying ADADL correctly in design, the engineer can significantly reduce his/her workload later in the lifecycle.

Once engineers have seen this work in practice, experience with the toolset has shown that they are keen to take advantage of the benefits gained through the use of ADADL. Similarly, the toolset brings increased visibility across a project for personnel such as quality assurance staff and project management. A wide range of staff therefore

are keen to ensure that the benefits of the toolset are maximised. Hence,
all staff are encouraged to apply an Ada/PDL during the design phase.

CONCLUSION

The application of appropriate software tools can encourage
use of Ada and an Ada-based PDL during design. However, the supported PDL
and supporting toolset must satisfy certain requirements in order to be
successful. In particular they must act to smooth the lifecycle via tight
integration across the toolset and with other tools and methods. In order
to attract widespread acceptance they must also support a broad range of
job functions.

REFERENCES

Mark V Systems Ltd. (1988). Adagen User's Manual.
McCabe, T. (1976) A Complexity Measure. IEEE Transactions SE-2 (4), pp.
        308-320.
Morrison, I.W. Robinson, J. & Burns, A. (1984). Rationale for Comments:
        the effects on Programming Languages and Implementation.
        Symposium on Empirical Foundations of Information and Software
        Science, Atlanta, pp. 197-207. New York: Plenum Press.
Naval Avionics Center Ada-based Design Languages Workshop - Summary of
        Events. (1988) Ada Letters. Vol VIII No 4. pp. 104-118.
Radi, T.S. (1988) TestGen - Testing Tool for Ada Designs and Ada Code.
        Aerospace Technology Conference and Exposition, Anaheim, USA.
Robinson, J. & Palmer, M. (1989) An Overview of the AISLE Toolset. under
        preparation.
Software Systems Design Inc. (1988). AISLE User's Manual.

Appendix 1

The Detailed Design

Note that due to space restrictions this procedure has been
extracted from a package body containing further declarations.

```
procedure Associate_Tracks_And_Plots
 (Track_Sector : in Radar_Direction.Sector_ID_Type) is

  -- Documentation items and project management information,
  -- normally inserted at this point, have been removed for clarity
  -- Note also that, during coding, Ada implementation code would be
  -- inserted into the gaps left in the detailed pseudo-code design

  type Plot_Status_Type is (Associated, Unassociated);
  --%
  --% A single plot can have one of these states

  type Plot_Record is
  record
    Plot_Status : Plot_Status_Type;
    Plot_Position : Plots.Plot_Type;
    Track         : Track_Type;
  end record;
  --%
  --% An abstraction of each plot within the system

  type Plot_List_Type is array (1 .. 100) of Plot_Record;

  Plot_List       : Plot_List_Type;
  --%
  --% All plots within the system, up to a maximum of 100.

  Track_ID         : Track_ID_Type;
  Current_Sector   : Radar_Direction.Sector_ID_Type;
  Number_Of_Plots  : Natural range 0 .. 100;
  Plot_Queue_Empty : Boolean := False;

begin
  --| loop

  --|    while the plot queue for this sector is not empty
  --|    loop
  --|      get a plot from the queue
  --|      save the plot in the plot list
  --|    end loop
```

```
--|  for all tracks in the track list
--|  loop
--|    if the track is in the current radar sector and &
--|        it has its position predicted then
--|          for all the plots in this sector
--|          loop
--|            if the plot is inside a gate then
--|              case of the tracks status
--|                when its normal set the track's status to faded
--|                when its position is predicted | its initiated
--|                              set the track's status to normal
--|              end case
--|              set the plot to associated
--|            end if
--|          end loop
--|      end if
--|    end loop
--|  end loop;

end Associate_Tracks_And_Plots;
```

Appendix 2

Extracts From a Design Review Document and Effort Report

The Design conditions examined for design case 1 are:

238:   (the Track is in the current radar sector and it has
        its position predicted) is False

Expected results for design case 1 are:

184:   Procedure Associate_Tracks_And_Plots' is
219:   Begin
222:   While the plot queue for this sector is not empty loop
224:     get a plot from the queue
225:     save the plot in the plot list
226:   End Loop
*** Exit loop at 222 when
            (the plot queue for this sector is not empty) is false.
236:   For all tracks in the Track list loop
238:   If the Track is in the current radar sector and
          it has its position predicted then
          *** Condition is False
252:   End if   — for 238
253:   End Loop
*** Exit loop at 236 after (all tracks in the Track list) iterations.
279:   End

Appendix 3

Test Case Effort Report

Number of Test Cases Required for Module Name	Basis Testing	Branch Testing	Full Path Testing
Radar_Direction	1	1	1
World	1	1	1
Plots	1	1	1
Plot_Association_Queue	1	1	1
Track_Picture	1	1	1
Plot_In_Gate	1	1	1
Associate_Tracks_And_Plots	5	5	5
Rate_Aid_Or_Cancel_Tracks	1	1	1
Predict_Position	1	1	1
Polar_Position	1	1	1
Construct_A_Plot	1	1	1

Formalising the Design of Ada Systems using LOTOS

D.W. Bustard
Department Of Computer Science, The Queen's University of Belfast, Belfast, BT7 1NN, Northern Ireland

M.T. Norris & R.A. Orr
British Telecom Research Laboratories, System and Software Engineering Division, Martlesham Heath, Ipswich, IP5 7RE, England

Abstract.
LOTOS is a formal description language developed within ISO (International Standards Organisation) to support the precise definition of open distributed systems (OSI). Despite this rather narrow field of application the facilities of LOTOS have been defined in a sufficiently general way to enable it to be used for the description of many types of concurrent and sequential system. The main purpose of this paper is to evaluate the use of LOTOS as an Ada design language. The paper also contributes to the debate on whether Ada needs such support and raises, once again, the thorny issue of the role of formality in software engineering.

The paper tends to evaluate both sides of a discussion rather than draw any firm conclusions. The main summary point is that LOTOS promises to be a useful aid to the construction of Ada systems assuming that adequate tools become available to support both the production of LOTOS definitions, and their subsequent refinement into Ada implementations.

Introduction.
Software design is essentially the process of dividing a piece of software into a set of relatively self-contained modules, each of which is defined to a level where it can be implemented independently. The main module constructs in Ada are the *package* and the *task*. The declaration part of either Ada module serves to identify the operations which that module must support and also to define the data manipulated by those operations. The meaning of each operation, however, cannot be expressed precisely in Ada, short of an actual implementation. In practice, meaning is usually attributed informally in natural language. Since natural language definitions are open to misinterpretation it follows that there is a need for a more precise method for defining Ada modules and their interaction. This need could be met in one of three ways:

1. enhance the Ada language with suitable facilities to support the formal (algebraic or axiomatic) specification of its components,

2. use a specification/design language based on Ada (like Anna as described by Krieg-Bruckner & Luckham 1980) which can be converted into Ada in a systematic manner, or

3. use a higher level specification/design language that supports greater abstraction.

The third approach has the advantage that it deals with a distinctly separate step in software development but has the disadvantage that it yields a representation from which it may be difficult to derive an implementation. The purpose of this paper is to discuss the third approach with respect to the recently defined language LOTOS (Language of Temporal Ordering Specification) (Brinksma 1988). LOTOS has been developed to support a formal description of the behaviour of concurrent systems, especially OSI (Open Systems Interconnection) systems (e.g. Carchiolo et al. 1986). Its concurrency features are based on CCS (Milner 1980) and CSP (Hoare 1985). The language also includes an algebraic data typing facility, based on ACT ONE (Erhig & Mahr 1985). The main structural features of LOTOS and Ada are similar. In particular, there is a recognised correspondence between LOTOS data types and the Ada package (Sommerville & Morrison 1987) and both languages have a concurrency model based on synchronised process (task) communication. This similarity suggests that LOTOS might serve as an appropriate higher level description language for Ada systems.

There is nothing new in the idea of using separate (but related) languages for specification and implementation. For example, this has been shown to be a useful way of staging the design of systems specified in SDL (Franco 1987; Karlsson 1987). The main difference between that work and the work reported here is the level of formality in the specification language: in addition to clarifying the outline design, LOTOS can, by virtue of its mathematical basis, be used for analysis at an early stage in development.

The remainder of this paper discusses the main features of LOTOS, their relationship with Ada constructs and the advantages and disadvantages of using LOTOS as an Ada design language. The discussion is illustrated using parts of a LOTOS definition for the well-known children's game of pass-the-parcel (Bustard et al. 1988 a, c). This game is simple to describe in broad terms but its precise definition in LOTOS and its implementation in Ada (as a simulation model) are less obvious.

Acknowledgements.

The authors of this paper would like to thank the director of British Telecom Research Laboratories for permission to publish this paper. Thanks are also due to Adam Winstanley who commented on an earlier draft.

1.   LOTOS Features.

In general, a LOTOS specification is made up of a hierarchy of process and data type definitions which together describe the intended system behaviour. For example, consider a LOTOS description for the children's game of pass-the-parcel whose main rules, expressed informally, are as follows:

"Children seated in a circle pass a present, wrapped in several layers of paper, from one to another as music is played. The music stops from time to time. When this occurs the child with the parcel removes its outermost wrapper. If the present is uncovered the game terminates; otherwise the music is restarted and the parcel is circulated once again. The game is begun by an adult who passes the parcel to one of the children. The game may be interrupted at any time by an adult calling everyone to tea."

In a LOTOS description for this game, processes might be used to define the behaviour of each identifiable component (entity) in the system and a data type used to define the parcel and the operations that are performed on it. Processes and data types are discussed separately in the two sub-sections that follow.

1.1.   Processes.

The processes in the pass-the-parcel game are shown graphically in Figure 1. The diagram represents a version of the game with four children, where the two adults involved have been identified (arbitrarily!) as a *father* and a *mother*. The father passes the parcel to the children initially and the mother may interrupt the game to call everyone to tea. The *Child* processes interact with each other and with a *Music* process, modelling the starting and stopping of music.

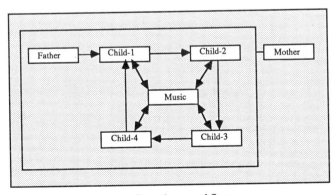

Figure 1: Pass-the-parcel System

LOTOS processes, like Ada tasks, define entities which operate concurrently and which communicate synchronously. As an example of the representation of a LOTOS process consider the following (simplified) definition of the Music process:

```
1   process  Music [MusicPlaying, MusicStopped, ParcelCirculating, PresentFound]: exit:=
2     (MusicPlaying; Music [MusicPlaying, MusicStopped, ParcelCirculating, PresentFound])
3     []
4     (MusicStopped;
5       ((ParcelCirculating; Music [MusicPlaying, MusicStopped, ParcelCirculating, PresentFound])
6       []
7       (PresentFound; exit)))
8   endproc (* Music *)
```

The following observations can be made:

- The LOTOS notation has been designed to facilitate the same type of analysis that is performed on programs. In particular, a LOTOS definition can be checked for syntactic accuracy and semantic consistency; it can also be executed, known as *animation* (Bustard et al. 1988b), to investigate the behaviour specified.
- In LOTOS, looping behaviour is defined in a recursive fashion. For example, in the *Music* process, recursive instantiation occurs (lines 2 and 5) when the subsequent behaviour of the process is equivalent to returning to its initial state.
- LOTOS processes are used for structuring purposes as well as indicating concurrent activity and so are often equivalent to Ada procedures or functions.

Process behaviour is defined in terms of *event* sequences, where an event is the synchronisation of two or more processes. LOTOS processes synchronise on *event gates* of which four are defined in the *Music* process. The meaning of the events involved is largely explained by the gate names: the *Music* process is required to report that music is either playing (*MusicPlaying*) or has stopped (*MusicStopped*); when the music stops a layer of paper is removed from the parcel by a *Child* process, which then indicates whether the present has been uncovered (*PresentFound*) or the the parcel is back in circulation (*ParcelCirculating*). If the present has been found the *Music* process terminates otherwise it returns to its initial state.

Event gates roughly correspond to Ada entries. Thus, for example, an Ada task implementing the *Music* process might have a definition part of the form:

```
task Music is
  entry MusicPlaying;
  entry MusicStopped;
  entry ParcelCirculating;
  entry PresentFound;
end Music;
```

In general, process interaction may involve the communication of data values. In Ada, this is handled by defining the names and types of the values concerned in a formal parameter list for each entry affected. LOTOS event gates are more flexible in that they permit the number and type of the communicated values to be defined implicitly at the point where an event gate is used - the *event offer*.

The LOTOS model of communication is one of processes *agreeing* values; a synchronisation occurs if two or more processes make event offers that are *compatible*. More specifically, synchronisation occurs if the values offered by one process intersect with values offered by another process, naming the same event gate. (Space precludes a more detailed discussion here but further details may be found in Brinksma (1988))

In LOTOS a selection is made from among a set of possible events using a *choice* expression. This roughly corresponds to the *select* statement in Ada. For example, the body of a *Music* task implementing the LOTOS *Music* process might be expressed as follows:

```
task body Music is
    Finished: Boolean := False;
begin
    while not Finished loop
      select
        accept  MusicPlaying;
      or
        accept  MusicStopped;
        select
          accept  ParcelCirculating;
        or
          accept  PresentFound do Finished := True;
        end select;
      end select ;
    end loop;
end Music;
```

In the LOTOS specification, it is sufficient to indicate a non-deterministic choice between music playing and music stopped. In a corresponding simulation program, however, the relative frequency of the events must also be controlled. This is generally achieved with the aid of a random number generator and guards on the limbs of the select statement, as suggested in the following pseudo-code:

```
determine Playing or Stopped by sampling from a defined frequency distribution;
select
   when Playing -> accept MusicPlaying;
or
   when Stopped -> accept MusicStopped;
```

Thus, in practice only one limb of the select statement is open at any time.

One important difference to note between the LOTOS and Ada communication mechanisms is that in LOTOS the partners in an event have equal status whereas in Ada the interaction is asymmetric - one task instigates an interaction, by making an entry call, and the receiving task accepts the interaction. A consequence of this asymmetry is that there are types of communication that can occur in LOTOS definitions which cannot be expressed directly in Ada. The interaction between the *Music* process and each *Child* process is one example! In LOTOS a *Child* process offers synchronisation on either the *MusicPlaying* or *MusicStopped* events to match the offer made in the *Music* process (lines 2 and 4). However, this behaviour cannot be captured in Ada using the select statement because the rules for conditional entry calls are not equivalent to those for conditional acceptance. In this case the problem can be readily avoided with a little restructuring; one possibility, for example, is to combine the playing and stopped task entries into a single state inquiry which then returns a value indicating whether music is playing or not. In general, however, because of the variety of situations that may occur, there is no systematic method of dealing with structural clashes of this type; it is thus part of the refinement process to replace LOTOS generalities with Ada specifics.

Another potential problem area is multi-way synchronisation. LOTOS permits three or more processes to synchronise on the same event whereas Ada process communication is always two-way. In this instance, however, there is a general strategy for translating into an equivalent Ada form. The technique is to introduce an auxiliary task through which the processes then synchronise. This task waits until all of the main tasks arrive and then allows each to proceed, connecting communicated values as required.

One facility of LOTOS which maps directly onto Ada is the *disable* operator. This allows one process to terminate the execution of others as, for example, in the pass-the-parcel example where the *Mother* process terminates the game when tea is ready by disabling all of the other processes in the system. In Ada, the same effect can be achieved with the **abort** operation.

The majority of LOTOS process behaviour specifications can be refined into Ada programs in a straightforward manner.

1.2   Data Types.

LOTOS has an algebraic data type facility for describing data and the operations that are performed on it. Like processes, Ada has a counterpart for the data type: the *package*. A consideration of the relationship between algebraic data types and Ada packages appears in (Sommerville & Morrison 1987). As an illustration of this relationship, consider the LOTOS definition of the parcel used in the pass-the-parcel game:

```
1    type ParcelType is NaturalNumber, Boolean
2      sorts Parcel
3      opns (* operations *)
4        NewParcel:        Nat        -> Parcel
5        WrappersRemain:   Parcel     -> Bool
6        Unwrap:           Parcel     -> Parcel
7      eqns (* equations *)
8        forall  n: Nat
9        ofsort Bool
10         WrappersRemain (NewParcel(0))          = false;
11         WrappersRemain ((NewParcel(succ(n)))   = true;
12       ofsort Parcel
13         Unwrap (NewParcel(0))        = NewParcel (0);
14         Unwrap (NewParcel(succ(n)))  = NewParcel (n);
15     endtype (* ParcelType *)
```

The first line of the definition indicates that *ParcelType* is based on the definitions of natural numbers and Booleans. The remainder of the definition has three parts:

- line 2: the identification of a new *sort - Parcel*, a name for the values taken by the type,

- lines 3-6: a set of *operations* (or *functions*) and their parameters (inputs to the left of the arrow, outputs to the right), identifying what can be done with a parcel, and

- lines 7-14: a set of *equations* defining, in effect, what the operations mean.

A parcel is manipulated by three operations: *NewParcel*, which creates a parcel, *WrappersRemain*, which reports whether or not the present has been uncovered and *Unwrap*, which removes a layer of paper from the parcel. The properties of the parcel operations are defined by accompanying equations. For example, one equation (line 14) defines the *Unwrap* operation as equivalent to the inverse of the successor operation (*succ*) for natural numbers and two others (lines 10 and 11) indicate that *WrappersRemain* is true if and only if the number of wrappers is non-zero. Note that the parcel type definition makes no statement about the implementation of a parcel, restricting itself entirely to a set of abstract operations for its manipulation.

An Ada package corresponding to the *ParcelType* definition might be expressed as follows:

```
package ParcelType is
  type Parcel is limited private;
  subtype ParcelRange is Integer range 0..Integer'Last;
  function NewParcel (Size: ParcelRange) return Parcel;
  function WrappersRemain (P: Parcel) return Boolean;
  function UnWrap (P: Parcel) return Parcel;
private
  Parcel is ParcelRange;
```

```
--|  eqns  (* equations *)
--|     forall  n: Nat
--|     ofsort Bool
--|        WrappersRemain (NewParcel(0))       = false;
--|        WrappersRemain ((NewParcel(succ(n)))) = true;
--|     ofsort  Parcel
--|        Unwrap (NewParcel(0))        = NewParcel (0);
--|        Unwrap (NewParcel(succ(n)))  = NewParcel (n);
end ParcelType;
```

The main points to note here are:

- the operations in the LOTOS *PracelType* definition have been realised by Ada functions; in general it may be necessary to use procedures in cases where error values need to be returned (Sommerville & Morrison 1987);

- the sort of the *ParcelType* is defined as an Ada *limited private type* which imposes the required restrictions on the use of variables of this type, namely that they can only be manipulated within the *ParcelType* package;

- in Ada the representation of the parcel must be defined before implementation - albeit in a **private** section; the representation used here is simply the positive integer subrange;

- the equations of the LOTOS data type definition serve as documentation for the *ParcelType* package and provide information on which to base an implementation;

- the equations have a special introductory character 'l' which allows for the possibility of corresponding assertion code to be added during compilation.

Further details, and many more examples of the use of algebraic data types definitions as specifications for Ada packages may be found in (Sommerville & Morrison 1987).

2.   LOTOS as an Ada Design Language.

This section highlights some of the main points brought out in the preceding sections. In essence, LOTOS offers some advantages to the Ada system developer but there are costs involved.

The advantages that LOTOS offers are:

- In common with other higher level languages, LOTOS yields abstract system designs that should be easier to understand and so easier to modify than more detailed designs expressed in Ada.

- LOTOS has been designed as an executable language, thereby enabling designs to be evaluated before implementation; tools might also be developed to support the transition from LOTOS to Ada. Some examples have been given of constructs that either map directly onto Ada (*disable* operator) or can be translated systematically from one notation to another (multi-way synchronisation).

- At a more pragmatic level, the fact that LOTOS has an ISO standard for its definition means that it is better supported that other similar design languages.

On the debit side:

- Some LOTOS constructs cannot be translated directly into Ada as illustrated with the communication problem discussed earlier. If it is known that the specification is for an Ada system then the problematic constructs could be avoided but this tends to defeat the purpose of using a higher level definition; also Ada implementations may be required for existing LOTOS specifications, such as those of standard communication protocols and services, which have been constructed without regard to implementation language.

- LOTOS is sufficiently different from Ada to require a significant investment in time and effort to learn the language thoroughly. Many remain to be convinced that this effort is worthwhile.

- LOTOS is sufficiently *similar* to Ada to be frustrating to Ada experts who might feel that LOTOS is an unnecessary step in their progress towards an implementation. Indeed, realistically, many will find it easier to express their ideas in Ada than in LOTOS because of their greater experience with Ada and because specification and design are inherently difficult activities.

- LOTOS, being a new language, has few high quality tools to support its application. This is the usual chicken-and-egg situation: many are reluctant to adopt a new language until tools are available to support its use but such tools are only likely to be produced if the language is already heavily used.

- LOTOS can serve as a either a specification or a design language. In the latter case descriptions tend to be close to an implementation and so are easily developed into programs. In the former case, descriptions tend to be more abstract and their relationship to the final program may not be obvious. If LOTOS is to be applied effectively its role, or roles with respect to Ada must be more clearly defined.

The reader is left to draw a conclusion from this discussion! For those that feel that designs expressed as a combination of Ada interfaces and natural language annotation are adequate, then the list of problems associated with using LOTOS for expressing design will be enough to damn this approach. For those that consider additional formality to be highly desirable and find LOTOS appealing, then the problems with its use are simply minor drawbacks that will be sorted out in due course. Most people will have a view that lies somewhere in the middle: many accept the need for some formality but are not convinced that the LOTOS approach is necessarily the best. LOTOS promises to be a useful aid to the construction of Ada systems when adequate development tools become available - tools to support both the production of LOTOS definitions and their subsequent refinement into Ada implementations.

Conclusion

Ada system developers would seem to require a more formal means of specifying the semantics of the modules identified during system design. This paper has discussed the use of LOTOS for this purpose. LOTOS is well supported in the sense that it has an ISO definition but its acceptance as a higher level design language for Ada will probably depend on the quality of the tools that emerge to aid its use. Tools to support the development and analysis of LOTOS specifications are already available in prototype form and the viability of the partial automatic translation from LOTOS into Ada promises to enable this increased level of rigour in design to be carried through to implementation.

References

Brinksma, E. (Ed.) (1988) *Information processing systems - Open systems interconnection - LOTOS - A Formal Technique Based on the Temporal Ordering of Observational Behaviour*, ISO 8807.

Bustard, D.W., Elder, J.W.G. & Welsh, J. (1988a) *Concurrent Program Structures*: Prentice Hall International.

Bustard, D.W., Norris M.T. & Orr R.A. (1988b) *A Pictorial Approach to the Animation of Process-Oriented Formal Specifications*, IEE Software Engineering Journal, 3(4), pp114-118.

Bustard, D.W., Winstanley, A.C., Norris, M.T., Orr, R.A. & Patel, S. (1988c) *Graphical Views of Process-Oriented Specifications*, Proc. FORTE '88: North Holland.

Carchiolo, V., et al. (1986) *A LOTOS Specification of the PROWAY Highway Service*, IEEE Transactions on Computers, Vol. C-35, No. 11.

Erhig, H. & Mahr, B. (1985) *Fundamentals of Algebraic Specification 1*: Springer-Verlag.

Franco, J.H.A., Haim, J. & Lima, H.M. (1987) *Going from SDL to CHILL: the TROPICO approach*, in SDL '87: state of the art and future trends, eds R Saracco and P Tilanus: North Holland.

Hoare, C.A.R. (1985) *Communicating Sequential Processes*: Prentice Hall International.

Karlsson, J. & Mansson, L. (1987) *Using SDL as a specificatioand design language, and Ada as an implementation language*, in SDL '87: state of the art and future trends, eds R Saracco and P Tilanus: North Holland.

Kreig-Bruckner, B. & Luckham, D.C. (1980) *Anna: Towards a language for annotating Ada programs*, ACM Sigplan Notices, 15 (11), pp128-138.

Milner, R. (1980) *A Calculus of Communicating Systems*, in Lecture Notes in Computer Science: Springer-Verlag.

Sommerville, I. & Morrison R. (1987) *Software Development with Ada*: Addison Wesley.

From Algebraic Specifications to Correct Ada Programs: the Esprit Project PROSPECTRA

P. De la Cruz
Alcatel SESA Research Center, Ramirez de Prado 5, E 2804 Madrid, Spain
B. Krieg-Brückner
FB3, Universität Bremen, Postfach 330440, D 2800 Bremen 33,Germany
A. Perez Riesco
Alcatel SESA Research Center, Ramirez de Prado 5, E 2804 Madrid, Spain

Abstract
The ESPRIT project PROSPECTRA is developing a methodology and an integrated support system for transforming axiomatic specifications into efficient Ada programs in a stepwise, reliable and reusable way.

1. Introduction

PROSPECTRA (PROgram Development by SPECification and TRAnsformation) is a multinational project under ESPRIT (the European Strategic Programme for Research and development in Information Technology). The PROSPECTRA Consortium consist of the Universities of Bremen (D) (Prime Contractor), Dortmund (D), Passau (D), Saarbrücken (D) and Strathclyde (UK), and the companies Computer Resources International A/S (DK), Syseca Logiciel (F) and Alcatel Standard Eléctrica S.A. (E).

The PROSPECTRA project [Krieg-Brückner et al. 87, Krieg-Brückner 87, 88b, 89] is developing a methodology and an integrated support system for developing formal, high level requirements specifications into efficient Ada programs in a stepwise, reliable and reusable way. It is based on previous work in the Munich CIP Project [Bauer 79, Bauer et al. 85, 87, Bauer & Wössner 82]. The underlying assumption is that it is hopeless to try to understand, analyze or prove the detailed code suitable for efficient execution on the current Von Neumann machines. The only way to build a correct program is to ensure by construction that it conforms to an "obviously good" abstract specification.

The PROSPECTRA methodology integrates program construction and verification during the development process. An initial requirements specification is gradually transformed into an executable program by stepwise application of transformation rules. The final version is correct by construction; only the applicability of transformation rules must be ensured at each step. Transformation rules are proved correct once and for all. Specifications, programs, transformations and development histories are recorded, providing a basis for knowledge accumulation and reuse, not only at the level of the product, but also at the level of the development process.

Any activity in the system can be viewed as a transformation of an object at some system level. This provides system uniformity, reduces complexity and allows generative construction of system components.

The PROSPECTRA system is built making extensive use of language processing metatools (syntax driven program generators) around a common representation of all the objects in the system as attributed syntax trees. The system includes interactive, syntax driven editors for both the object and transformation languages, verification components to assist both in proving transformation correctness and applicability, storage and retrieval support and a extendible set of transformation operations.

2.   The PROSPECTRA Development Cycle

The PROSPECTRA methodology integrates program construction and verification during the program development process. The development cycle (see fig. 1) starts with a loose formal requirements specification that is then gradually transformed into an a priori correct executable program. The development steps are formally defined transformations that preserve program correctness. Transformations are carried out by the system, with interactive guidance by the programmer. Developments are sequences of transformations that can be "replayed", under certain conditions, after change of specifications.

Prior to the formal development process, an informal requirements engineering phase is needed to establish the informal requirements of the system to be developed (by "informal" we mean that it is outside the PROSPECTRA formal methodology).

The PROSPECTRA formal development starts whith the formal *requirements specification*. This specification is typically a high-level, non-constructive, loose specification of a set of abstract data types and (mutually recursive) functions. It is basically a set of first order equational logic formulae with universal and existential quantifiers. As such, it is typically far from executable, at least in an efficient way.

The requirements specification is an implicit specification in general. It describes abstract properties, that is *what* is to be achieved rather than *how*. This yields more compact specifications at a higher level of abstraction and, more importantly, avoids specification in terms of a particular implementation model (say, sets or sequences) that might be difficult to get away from later on. It is important to stress here the possibility to make *loose* specifications, in other words to intentionally delay design decisions to a later stage of the development process. This avoids overspecification, gives the implementor a greater degree of freedom and thus decreases cost and increases efficiency potential.

The formal requirements specification must be validated in some way against the informal specification in order to increase confidence about its "correctness". This validation cannot be carried out formally, because of the informality of the initial requirements specification, and is typically performed using prototyping tools. These allow us to ask questions about the specification such as "if I input this value, what will a possible result be?, or, in a Prolog-like fashion, "if I want to obtain this result, what could the inputs be?", also "is the specification consistent?", "can this property be derived from the axioms?", etc. Thus validation

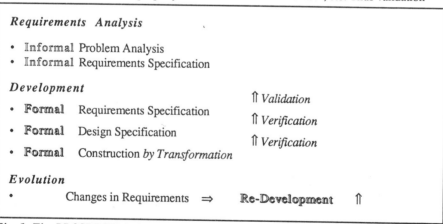

Fig. 1: The PROSPECTRA Development Cycle

subsumes conventional "testing", but at a much higher level of abstraction, in relation to a much more compact description (and less danger of loosing oversight). Moreover, "testing" is done *before* the program is being developed. PROSPECTRA provides support for early prototyping by its verification tools and, in particular, completion, term rewriting and narrowing techniques for conditional equations.

Once the formal requirements specification has been validated, the formal development process starts. First of all, a more constructive specification, called *design specification*, is developed from the requirements specification. Design decisions gradually reduce the set of possible models and make the specification more explicit and operational in terms of an (abstract) implementation; the design specification defines *how* the stated problem is to be solved. The impact of the earliest decisions on efficiency may be of utmost importance, although very little experience is available up to now on this point. The design specification is mainly a set of universally quantified conditional recursive equations, and as such is quite at the same level as a Horn clause logic program with equality.

The design specification can be obtained either by some kind of formal derivation (by a completion procedure, for instance) or informally, in a manual way. In this case, a verification step must be performed to ensure that the design specification is an acceptable model of (i.e., is equivalent to or, most likely, implies) the requirements specification.

Once a satisfactory design specification has been obtained, the transformational development process can start. Each transformation step applies a formally defined, demonstrably correct (i.e., correctness preserving) transformation rule to a previously obtained specification or program, producing a semantically equivalent one or a legal implementation. Applicability conditions for rules are checked during the development process, either automatically or as a proof obligation to be verified interactively, so that rules cannot be applied incorrectly. Transformation rules represent conscious design decisions that improve efficiency of a program or implement abstract data types in terms of more concrete ones. In such a way, a design specification is refined down to the level of a functional or imperative program. Once a level that satisfies the efficiency requirements of the system has been reached, the transformation process stops. The resulting code can be left to a compiler to generate executable machine code.

Because the design specification was either formally derived from the requirements specification or proved to conform to it, and each transformation step preserves the correctness of the previous specification or program, the resulting code is *a priori* correct with respect to the formal requirements specification. No debugging or a posteriori proof (in the traditional sense) is necessary. The whole proof is broken down into a sequence of proof obligations concurrently with the development process.

During the formal development process, each derivation, verification or transformation is recorded. As a result, a development history is obtained that can be used to repeat the development process over a similar specification. In case of a change in the requirements, the development could be replayed (at least partially), taking advantage of the experience of previous developments. This is a basis for knowledge accumulation and reuse, not only at the level of the product, but also at the level of the development process.

An important point is that changes are always made at the level of specifications. If requirements change, the requirements specification is consequently changed and the system re-developed (by replaying the part of the old development that remains applicable). Alternatively, if a design decision turns out to have been bad, it can be tracked back to the point it was made, changed and the development continued from this point. The code is never "patched" to adapt it to new requirements; the specifications are modified and transformed instead.

3.   The Development Language *PAnndA*

PAnndA is derived from Ada [Ada 83] and Anna [Luckham et al. 87], a language for *Ann*otating *A*da programs to support verification. It covers the whole range from loose requirements specifications to applicative or imperative implementations, including constructs for predicative and algebraic specification (conditional (recursive) equations, (algebraically definable) types and subtypes, partial functions, higher order functions, etc) and concurrency (via non-strict functions). Constructs for modularization, reusability, error handling and imperative implementation are those in Ada [Botta et al. 88].

PAnndA-S [Breu et al. 88] is the specification oriented subset of *PAnndA*. It is the only language the developer is allowed to edit directly in the system. All other subsets of *PAnndA* are reached through transformational development. Distinctive features of *PAnndA-S* semantics are partially defined functions, looseness (a specification denotes the set of *all* its models), and higher-order functions.

4.   Requirements Specifications

An informal specification of the GCD of two numbers appears in fig. 2. The formal requirements specification in fig. 3 reads like a simple transliteration into PAnndA-S (or, conversely, fig. 2 as a natural language paraphrasing of fig. 3).

Each specification corresponds to a single package in PAnndA-S. In general, such a specification will include the definition of (private) types and/or functions on these or other visible types. In this case, natural numbers (or integers) are assumed to be already defined (for the specification of Abstract Data Types in PAnndA-S see e. g. [Krieg-Brückner 87a, 88b, 89, Kahrs 86a]). Two functions are specified, one of which (preceded by the symbol - -:) is

---

The *Greatest Common Divisor* of two positive natural numbers X and Y is some natural number N that divides both such that all other positive natural numbers that divide X and Y are smaller.

A positive natural number X *divides* a positive natural number Y if there exists some positive natural number K such that K times X equals Y.

Fig. 2: Informal Requirements Specification of the Greatest Common Divisor

---

```
package GREATEST_COMMON_DIVISOR is
- -: function DIVIDES (X: POSITIVE; Y: POSITIVE) return BOOLEAN;
    function GCD (X: POSITIVE; Y: POSITIVE) return POSITIVE;
axiom for all X: POSITIVE; Y: POSITIVE; N: POSITIVE =>
    DIVIDES (X, Y)  <->  (exist K: POSITIVE => K * X = Y),
    GCD (X, Y) = N  <->   DIVIDES (N, X) ∧ DIVIDES (N, Y) ∧
                      (for all M: POSITIVE =>  DIVIDES (M, X) ∧ DIVIDES (M, Y) → N >= M);
end GREATEST_COMMON_DIVISOR;
```

Fig. 3: Formal Requirements Specification using Predicates

```
package GREATEST_COMMON_DIVISOR is
- -: function DIVIDES (X: POSITIVE; Y: POSITIVE) return BOOLEAN;
    function GCD (X: POSITIVE; Y: POSITIVE) return POSITIVE;
axiom for all X: POSITIVE; Y: POSITIVE; K: POSITIVE; M: POSITIVE =>
    K * X = Y  →  DIVIDES (X, Y) = True,
    DIVIDES (GCD (X, Y), X) = True,     DIVIDES (GCD (X, Y), Y) = True,
    DIVIDES (M, X) = True ∧ DIVIDES (M, Y) = True → GCD (X, Y) >= M;
end GREATEST_COMMON_DIVISOR;
```

Fig. 4: Algebraic Requirements Specification

an auxiliary function; it is only used for specification purposes and need not be implemented by an executable body. Note that the functions are only defined if the arguments are positive natural numbers (that is geater than 0); this is expressed here by the subtype POSITIVE, as usual in Ada.

Fig. 3 specifies GCD using predicates over the arguments in a variant of first order logic for partial functions. Such a predicative style is especially useful for initial requirements specifications for individual functions over an already specified type. In fig. 4, this specification has been transformed to an algebraic style with top-level universal quantification only. In general, transformations at this level would include skolemization, for example.

Loose Specifications

If we omitted the last equation in fig. 4, GCD would be loosely specified; it would correspond to a function returning an arbitrary common divisor, not necessarily the greatest. A specification is said to be *loose* if it allows more than one distinct (non-isomorphic) models. In general, loose requirements specifications are preferable since they avoid overspecification and leave room for further design decisions during the development process while keeping rigour and formality. In the implementation of a loosely specified priority queue, for example, one would be able to choose between a search for the minimal element upon addition to the queue, or removal from it (cf. [Krieg-Brückner 88b]).

Looseness is not the same as non-determinism. A function returning a common divisor will always have the same result for given arguments (the design decision will eventually be to return, for example, the greates, or the smallest, or any other, but a fixed one). A non-deterministic "function" would return an unpredictable result among the legal ones satisfying the specification, even for the same arguments. The concept of non-determinism is not necessary in PROSPECTRA; even for specifying concurrency, looseness (with arbitrary choice among a set of models) is sufficient, cf. [Broy 87, 88].

5.   Design Specifications

The requirements specification of fig. 4 is not constructive; it gives no clue for an algorithmic solution. We may obtain a design specification in several ways (following the approach of algebraic implementation, cf. [Broy et al. 86]):

- by fomally deriving new axioms using, say, a completion process [Ganzinger 87],
- by adding more equations (and, possibly, auxiliary functions) to represent design decisions, thereby restricting the set of possible models, and proving their consistency,
- by (mapping to) another specification and proving that it is a legal implementation (essentially, its axioms must imply those of the given specification).

Here, we could prove the correctness of Euclid's algorithm (fig. 5). Alternatively, we could provide a distinct algorithm as in fig. 6, or derive it formally. Note that we are now embedding the original function into a more defined one (there is no restriction on the parameters to be greater than 0; in fact, Y must become 0 eventually); this is compatible with the usual notion of implementation. Further algebraic simplification by transformation, using equations for natural numbers and **mod**, yields the version of fig. 7 [Bauer & Wössner 82].

Constructive Specifications

The above design specifications are *constructive*, they consist of conditional recursive equations. Constructive design specifications could be implemented by translation to a functional programming language or by some rewriting technique, if they satisfy certain properties, e.g. that the set of equations is complete, and the result is the same on overlapping cases.

Algorithmic Specifications

However, we want to arrive at an executable program in a conventional algorithmic language, for example Ada. Thus we need to transform the equations defining GCD in such a way, that only distinct variables for the arguments of GCD remain on the left hand side of the definitional equations (the constructor 0 or any other functions have to be removed). In general, pattern matching or unification needs to be replaced by explicit case analysis and selection. Constructors or other functions on the left have to be eliminated by selectors or inverse functions on the right and primitive predicates as preconditions, cf. [Kahrs 86b]. Also, the definitonal equality =, used as a meta operation in specifications, must be replaced by an explicit abstract equality operation that is given on the type. In our case, a simple predicate testing for 0, or the relation > 0, will do, see fig. 8.

6.   Applicative and Imperative Programs

We now proceed in the transformation process using the transformation rules in fig. 11 to 13 to arrive at an efficiently executable Ada program (fig. 9, 10). We will give the rules in a semi-formal notation here for illustration; see also chapter 7 below. The rule in fig. 11 illustrates the transition from the specification language PAnndA-S to full PAnndA, that is the generation of Ada bodies.

We could be content with a recursive function in Ada since it is executable, see fig. 9. However, an imperative program using loops might be more suggestive for a conventional programming style, see fig. 10 (an unfold (inline expansion) of GCD2 in GCD has also been made). The rule in fig. 12 transforms a tail-recursive function to a while loop, introducing a local variable. It treats the special case of one parameter; for several parameters, the sequentialisation of the collective assignment to the resp. variables in the loop requires temporary variables unless the expressions are independent (cf. [Krieg-Brückner 88a]).

```
package GREATEST_COMMON_DIVISOR is
    requirements specification as above
private
axiom for all X: POSITIVE; Y: POSITIVE =>
            GCD (X, X) = X,
    X > Y →  GCD (X, Y) = GCD (X–Y, Y),
    Y > X →  GCD (X, Y) = GCD (X, Y–X);
end GREATEST_COMMON_DIVISOR ;
```

Fig. 5: Design Specification

```
private
    function GCD2 (X: NATURAL; Y: NATURAL) return NATURAL;
axiom for all X: POSITIVE; Y: POSITIVE =>
            GCD (X, Y) = GCD2 (X, Y);
axiom for all X: NATURAL; Y: NATURAL =>
            GCD2 (X, 0) = X,
    ¬ (Y = 0) ∧ X < Y →   GCD2 (X, Y) = GCD2 (Y, X),
    ¬ (Y = 0) ∧ X >= Y →  GCD2 (X, Y) = GCD2 (X–Y, Y);
end GREATEST_COMMON_DIVISOR ;
```

Fig. 6: Alternative Design Specification Using Embedding

```
axiom for all X: NATURAL; Y: NATURAL =>
            GCD2 (X, 0) = X,
    ¬ (Y = 0) →  GCD2 (X, Y) = GCD2 (Y, X mod Y);
```

Fig. 7: Design Specification Transformed Using Algebraic Reasoning

```
axiom for all X: NATURAL; Y: NATURAL =>
    not Y > 0  →   GCD2 (X, Y) = X,
        Y > 0  →   GCD2 (X, Y) = GCD2 (Y, X mod Y);
```

Fig. 8: Algorithmic Design Specification

Further transformation to a machine-oriented level with labels and conditional jumps is achieved using the rule in fig. 13; it corresponds to the usual implementation of loops in compilers if no special machine operations are available.

7.   Development of Transformation Rules and Functions

Transformation rules can be seen as equations (relations) in an algebra of programs (see [Krieg-Brückner 88a, 89]). Basic rules must be proved correct against the language semantics. New rules can then be derived from these basic rules by algebraic reasoning (substitution, application of an equation, completion, induction). Thus we can combine the rules in fig. 11 and 12 to a rule from specifications with tail recursion to loop programs, and, combining with rule 13, by a transitive step to goto programs, see fig. 14. Some further rules on conditional statements have been used for the derivation.

The special case of one terminating and one tail-recursive case can be generalized to an arbitrary number (even further to a set of mutually recursive functions); thus it could be applied to fig. 6. Note that this is not possible for loops unless some code is duplicated. We shall show an implementation for this generalized case below.

Programs can be represented as abstract syntax trees; since such trees can be specified as any other abstract data type in PAnndA-S, we can develop transformation programs or "meta programs" in the same way as other programs in PAnndA-S; in fact the whole PROSPECTRA methodology and system carry over (cf. [Krieg-Brückner 88a, 89]).

Meta programs are written in italics here for distinction. Phrases for program fragments in the resp. concrete syntax can be used (using a notation with ⌈...⌋ brackets [De la Cruz 89]); they allow a considerable abbreviation of constructor terms, see fig. 15.

```
package body GREATEST_COMMON_DIVISOR is
  function GCD (X: POSITIVE; Y: POSITIVE) return POSITIVE is
  begin
    return GCD2 (X, Y);
  end GCD;
  function GCD2 (X: NATURAL; Y: NATURAL) return NATURAL is
  begin
    if not (Y > 0) then
      return X;
    else
      return GCD2 (Y, X mod Y);
    end if;
  end GCD2;
end GREATEST_COMMON_DIVISOR ;
```

Fig. 9: Applicative Body

```
package body GREATEST_COMMON_DIVISOR is
  function GCD (X: POSITIVE; Y: POSITIVE) return POSITIVE is
    VX: NATURAL; VY: NATURAL; VT: NATURAL;
  begin
    VX := X; VY := Y;
    while VY > 0 loop
      VT := VY; VY := VX mod VY; VX := VT;
    end loop;
    return VX;
  end GCD ;
end GREATEST_COMMON_DIVISOR ;
```

Fig. 10: Imperative Body

```
package p is
  decls1
  function f (x: S) return R;
  axiom for all x: S =>
        B1 (x) = True →   f (x) = K1 (x),
  {     Bi (x)  = True →   f (x) = Ki (x),      }
        Bn (x) = True →   f (x) = Kn (x);
  end p;
  package body p is
    decls2
  end p;
```

```
same package specification as on left side
package body p is
  decls2
  function f (x: S) return R is
  begin
      if B1 (x) then
          return K1 (x);
      else
  {         if Bi (x) then
                return Ki (x);
            else                         }
                return Kn (x);
  {         end if;                      }
      end if;
  end f;
end p;
```

Fig. 11: Transformation Rule from Algorithmic Specification to Applicative Program

```
function f (x: S) return R is
begin
    if B (x) then
        return T (x);
    else
        return f (H (x));
    end if;
end f ;
```

```
function f (x: S) return R is
  vx: S;
begin
    vx := x;
    while not B (vx) loop
        vx := H (vx);
    end loop;
    return T (vx);
end f ;
```

Fig. 12: Transformation Rule from Tail-Recursive Applicative Program to Loop Program

```
while B loop
    S
end loop;
```

```
«l»if B then
        S goto l;
    end if;
```

Fig. 13: Transformation Rule from Loop to Goto Program

```
package p is
  decls1
  function f(x: S) return R;
  axiom for all x: S =>
      B(x)=True → f(x)=T(x),
  notB(x)=True → f(x)=f(H(x));
  end p;
  package body p is
    decls2
  end p;
```

```
same specification as left
package body p is
  decls2
  function f(x: S) return R
  is
    vx: S;
  begin
    vx := x;
    while not B (vx) loop
        vx := H (vx);
    end loop;
    return T (vx);
  end f ;
end p;
```

```
same specification as left
package body p is
  decls2
  function f (x: S) return R
  is
    vx: S;
  begin
    vx := x;
    «l»if B (vx) then
        return T (vx);
    end if;
    vx := H (vx); goto l;
  end f ;
end p;
```

Fig. 14: Transformation Rule from Tail Recursion to Goto Program

⌈ f (x) = f (hx) ⌋

mkCall (mkName (logicalEq),
    cons (mkCall (mkName (f), cons (mkName (x), empty)), cons (mkCall (mkName (f), hx)

Fig. 15: Fragment in Phrase Notation and as Constructor Term over the Abstract Syntax

function Map (f: EXP **return** STMT) **return** (el: EXP_LIST) **return** STMT_LIST;
axiom for all   f: EXP **return** STMT;   e: EXP; el: EXP_LIST =>
    Map (f) (empty) = empty,   Map (f) (cons (e, el)) = cons (f(e), Map (f) (el));

Fig. 16: Homomorphic Extension Functional

with ABSTRACT_SYNTAX; **use** ABSTRACT_SYNTAX;
package SPEC_TO_IMPERATIVE_TRAFOS **is**
    function eqnToIf(f: NAME; x: NAME; vx: NAME; l: NAME) **return** (eqn: EXP) **return** STMT;
axiom for all f: NAME; x: NAME; vx: NAME;   l: NAME;
         bx: EXP; tx: EXP; hx: EXP; bvx: EXP; tvx: EXP; hvx: EXP =>
bvx = substByIn (x, vx, b) ∧ tvx = substByIn (x, vx, tx) →
   eqnToIf (f, x, vx, l) (⌈ bx = True → f (x) = tx ⌋) =
            ⌈ **If** bvx **then return** tvx ; **end If;** ⌋ ,
bvx = substByIn (x, vx, b) ∧ hvx = substByIn (x, vx, hx) →
   eqnToIf (f, x, vx, l) (⌈ bx = True → f (x) = f (hx) ⌋) =
            ⌈ **If** bvx **then** vx := hvx; **goto** l ; **end If;** ⌋ ;
end SPEC_TO_IMPERATIVE_TRAFOS;

Fig. 17: Primitive Transformation Function (without Higher Order Matching)

with ABSTRACT_SYNTAX; **use** ABSTRACT_SYNTAX;
package SPEC_TO_IMPERATIVE_TRAFOS **is**
    function tailRecToGoto (p: PROGRAM) **return** PROGRAM;
axiom for all f: NAME; x: NAME; vx: NAME; l: NAME; s: NAME; r: NAME; p: NAME;
         decls1: DECL_LIST; decls2: DECL_LIST; eqns: EXP_LIST =>
vx = SimilarName (x) ∧ l = NewName ∧ isExhaustiveDef (f, x, eqns) →
tailRecToGoto (

⌈**package** p **is**	⌈**package** p **is**
decls1	decls1
function f (x: s) **return** r;	**function** f (x: s) **return** r;
axiom for all x: s =>	**axiom for all** x: s =>
eqns	eqns
end p;	**end** p;
package body p **is**	**package body** p **is**
decls2	decls2
end p; ⌋) =	**function** f (x: s) **return** r **is**
	vx: s;
	begin
	vx := x;
	«l» Map (eqnToIf (f, x, vx, l)) (eqns)
	end f;
	end p; ⌋

end SPEC_TO_IMPERATIVE_TRAFOS;

Fig. 18: Composite Transformation Function

Higher Order Functions

PA^nndA-S also includes higher order functions, that is functions with functions as parameters or results. These allow for a considerable increase in abstraction and consequently compactness of programming, reuse etc., in analogy to generics. The paradigm of functional programming can thus be used in PROSPECTRA together with the combined advantages of algebraic specification. This aspect is described in more detail in [Krieg-Brückner 89, Möller 87, Karlsen et al. 88, Nickl et al. 88]. Here, we give an example of a well known functional on lists, instantiated for the special case of mapping from a list of expressions to a list of statements, by homomorphic extension [von Henke 76] of a primitive function from expressions to statements, see fig. 16. It allows us to concentrate on this primitive function; the effect on the lists is automatic.

We can use this functional to implement the curly brackets denoting iteration in the semi-formal notation of the transformation rules. The primitive function eqnTolf treats the generalized cases of termination and tail-recursion, resp. The notation for higher-order matching, e.g. *B (x)* to denote an expression containing an arbitrary number of occurrences of *x*, is then transformed into an expression *bx* in fig. 17. Finally, it is used in fig. 18 for a composite transformation function implementing the rule generalized from fig. 14.

8.   The Replay of Developments

During the transformational development, every operation is automatically recorded by the system. So, at the end of the development process, not only an executable program is obtained, but also a development history of such a program.

Moreover, a development history can be seen as a kind of meta-program, made of individual transformations, over the data type of specifications and programs.

Taking this point of view, a development (history) can be applied to a similar specification, as long as the individual steps of the development are applicable. This provides a basis for replay and reuse of developments, upon change of specifications or when the initial specification exhibits similar properties.

Also, developments can be composed to produce more complex ones. This leads to an algebra of developments (or development scripts), in much respects similar to those of data or programs [Krieg-Brückner 88a]. It is possible to specify development goals, implement them by using available transformations, simplify development terms, and abstract from developments to development methods incorporating development strategies. This may provide a basis for a knowlege base about program development, development strategies, etc.

9.   The PROSPECTRA System

By taking the approach described above, every operation in the system can be seen as a transformation of some kind of "program" (represented as an attributed abstract syntax tree). This leads to a uniform treatment of programming language, transformation language and command language. Components of the system may be classified according to the kind of activity they are mainly devoted to:

System Generation components: the Editor Generator and the Transformer Generator. For the moment, the two roles are played by the Cornell Synthesizer Generator (CSG) [Reps & Teitelbaum 87]. All other components of the system are either generated by CSG or developed using other techniques but driven from a CSG generated interface.

Program Development components: the *PAnndA-S* Editor [Bendix et al. 87], the *PAnndA* Transformer(s), and the *TrafoLa-H* interpreter [Heckmann 87]. Both the *PAnndA-S* Editor and *PAnndA* Transformers are generated by CSG.

Transformation Development components: the *TrafoLa-S* editor [De la Cruz 89], the *TrafoLa-S* Transformer(s) and the *TrafoLa-S* to SSL and *TrafoLa-H* translators [Gersdorf 89]. All are generated by CSG.

Verification components: the Verifier [Traynor 88] and the Conditional Equational Completion (CEC) system [Bertling et al. 88]. They support both the transformation development and the program development processes. The CEC system provides conditional rewriting and therefore can also be used for prototyping purposes. The Verifier is generated by CSG.

Control and Support components: the Log and Replay Controller, the *ControLa* to *TrafoLa* Translator, the Library Manager [Mathae 87] and the Method Bank [Fermaut & Boulle 89]. The Library Manager, implemented using the European standard Portable Common Tool Environment, is in charge of storage and retrieval of all objects managed in the system. The Method Bank provides for intelligent search in the Library. The *ControLa* Editor and the Library Manager interface are generated by CSG.

10.   Reuse in PROSPECTRA

The PROSPECTRA System Library is a central repository where every object produced during the program development process is stored. This includes specifications / programs and transformations / developments. The availability of such objects, together with the common compositional mechanisms available in *PAnndA* and *TrafoLa*, provide good opportunities for several dimensions of reuse.

At the program component level: Specifications and programs may be reused as pieces for constructing (specifying or implementing) more complex specifications or programs. Generic specifications and programs can be instantiated and thus reused for different applications.

At the program development level: Transformations and developments may be reused as components for specifying or implementing more complex transformations or developments.Transformations and developments may be applied to different input specifications or programs. Moreover, many transformations or developments may be used both in developing programs and transformations.

References

Bauer, F.L., Berghammer, R., Broy, M., Dosch, W., Gnatz, R., Geiselbrechtinger, F., Hangel, E., Hesse, W., Krieg.-Brückner, B., Laut, A., Matzner, T.A., Möller, B., Nickl, F., Partsch, H., Pepper, P., Samelson, K., Wirsing, M., Wössner, H.: *The Munich Project CIP, Vol. 1: The Wide Spectrum Language CIP-L. LNCS 183,* Springer 1985.

Bauer, F.L., Ehler, H., Horsch, B., Möller, B., Partsch, H., Paukner, O., Pepper, P.,: *The Munich Project CIP, Vol. 2: The Transformation System CIP-S. LNCS 292,* Springer 1987.

Bauer, F.L., Wössner, H.: *Algorithmic Language and Program Development.* Springer 1982.

Bauer, F.L.: Program Development by Stepwise Transformations - The Project CIP. in: Bauer, F. L., Broy, M. (eds.): Program Construction. *LNCS 69,* Springer 1979.

Bendix Nielsen, C., Botta, N., Karlsen, E.: The PA^{nn}dA-S Editor and Front End: Rationale; Specification. PROSPECTRA Study Notes S.3.1.C1-SN-5.0, 6.0, Dansk Datamatic Center, 1987.

Bertling, H., Ganzinger, H., Schäfers, R.: CEC, A System for Conditional Equational Completion - User Manual (version 1.0). PROSPECTRA Report M.1.3-R-7.0, Universität Dortmund, 1988.

Botta, N., Karlsen, E., Joergensen, J.: Abstract Syntax of PA^{nn}dA. PROSPECTRA Study Note S.3.2.S2-SN-1.2, Dansk Datamatic Center, 1988.

Breu, M., Broy, M., Grünler, Th., Nickl, F.: PA^{nn}dA-S Semantics. PROSPECTRA Study Note M.2.1.S1-SN-1.3, Universität Passau, 1988.

Broy, M., Möller, B., Pepper, P., Wirsing, M.: Algebraic Implementations Preserve Program Correctness. *Science of Computer Programming 7* (1986) 35-53.

Broy, M.: Predicative Specification for Functional Programs Describing Communicating Networks. *Information Processing Letters 25:2* (1987) 93-101.

De la Cruz, P.: The TrafoLa-S Editor (Version 5.2). PROSPECTRA Report S.2.1.I2-R-2.2, ALCATEL-Standard Electrica S.A., February 1989.

Fermaut, E., Boulle, P.: The PROSPECTRA Method Bank User Guide. PROSPECTRA Report S.2.2-UG-1.0, SYSECA Logiciel, February 1989.

Ganzinger, H.: Ground Term Confluence in Parametric Conditional Equational Specifications. in: Brandenburg, F.J., Vidal-Naquet, G., Wirsing, M.(eds.): Proc. 4th Annual Symp. on Theoretical Aspects of Comp. Sci., Passau '87. LNCS 247 (1987) 286-298.

Gersdorf, B. Translating TrafoLa-S to SSL and TrafoLa-H. PROSPECTRA Report M.1.1.S3-R-49.0, University of Bremen, February 1989.

Heckmann, R.: Language Reference Manual for TrafoLa-H. PROSPECTRA Report S.1.6-R-14.0, Universität des Saarlandes, 1988.

Kahrs, S.: From Constructive Specifications to Algorithmic Specifications. PROSPECTRA Study Note M.3.1.S1-SN-1.2, Universität Bremen, 1986.

Kahrs, S.: PA^{nn}dA-S Standard Types. PROSPECTRA Study Note M.1.1.S1-SN-11.2, Universität Bremen, 1986.

Karlsen, E., Joergensen, J., Krieg-Brückner, B.: Functionals in PA^{nn}dA-S. PROSPECTRA Study Note S.3.1.C1-SN-10.0, Dansk Datamatic Center, 1988.

Krieg-Brückner, B., Hoffmann, B., Ganzinger, H., Broy, M., Wilhelm, R., Möncke, U., Weisgerber, B., McGettrick, A.D., Campbell, I.G., Winterstein, G.: PROgram Development by SPECification and TRAnsformation. in: Rogers, M. W. (ed.): Results and Achievements, Proc. ESPRIT Conf. '86 . North Holland (1987) 301-312.

Krieg-Brückner, B.: Algebraic Formalisation of Program Development by Transformation. in: Proc. European Symposium On Programming '88, LNCS 300 (1988) 34-48.

Krieg-Brückner, B.: Algebraic Specification and Functionals for Transformational Program and Meta-Program Development. Proc. TAPSOFT'89 (Barcelona), LNCS (to appear).

Krieg-Brückner, B.: Integration of Program Construction and Verification: the PROSPECTRA Project. in: Habermann, N., Montanari, U. (eds.): Innovative Software Factories and Ada. Proc. CRAI Int'l Spring Conf. '86. LNCS 275 (1987) 173-194.

Krieg-Brückner, B.: The PROSPECTRA Methodology of Program Development. in: Zalewski (ed.): Proc. IFIP/IFAC Working Conf. on HW and SW for Real Time Process Control (Warsaw). North Holland (1988) 257-271.

Luckham, D.C., von Henke, F.W., Krieg-Brückner, B., Owe, O.: Anna, a Language for Annotating Ada Programs, Reference Manual. LNCS 260, Springer (1987).

Mathae, B.: Library Manager User Guide. PROSPECTRA Report S.4.4-UG-2.0, SYSECA Logiciel, 1987.

Möller, B.: Algebraic Specification with Higher Order Operators. in: Meertens, L.G.T.L. (ed.): Program Specification and Transformation, Proc. IFIP TC2 Working Conf. (Tölz '86). North Holland (1987) 367-398.

Nickl, F., Broy, M., Breu, M., Dederichs, F., Grünler, Th.: Towards a Semantics of Higher Order Specifications in PA^{nn}dA-S. PROSPECTRA Study Note M.2.1.S1-SN-2.0, Universität Passau, 1988.

Reps, T.W., Teitelbaum, T.: The Synthesizer Generator, A System for Constructing Language-Based Editors. Springer, 1988.

Reference Manual for the Ada Programming Language. ANSI/MIL.STD 1815A. US Government Printing Office, 1983. Also in: Rogers, M. W. (ed.): Ada: Language, Compilers and Bibliography. Ada Companion Series, Cambridge University Press, 1984.

Traynor, 0.: A specification for a Cornell based proof editor for PROSPECTRA. PROSPECTRA Study Note S.3.4-SN-10.0, University of Strathclyde, September 1988.

von Henke, F.W.: An Algebraic Approach to Data Types, Program Verification and Program Synthesis. in: Mazurkiewicz, A. (ed.): Mathematical Foundations of Computer Science 1976. LNCS 45 (1976) 330-336.

Part 5 Implementation Issues

Design for High Performance

Sabina H. Saib and Richard J. Gilinsky

with PSS, 429 Santa Monica Boulevard 430, Santa Monica, California 90401, USA. Tel.: 01 213 394 5233

Abstract.
The primary application area for Ada is real-time, embedded systems. For this area there is a great need for high performance in the generated code. In fact, a primary concern of system developers is the expected performance of Ada applications. This concern has slowed the acceptance of Ada in real-time systems. There are at least four ways of achieving high performance with Ada applications. The first is to have a computer architecture that directly supports Ada features. This paper covers three other methods of achieving high performance: compiler technology, support tool technology, and the careful use of Ada features.

Compiler Technology.

Given a target machine, an Ada user today often has a choice of several Ada compilers. By performing a few well chosen tests and by examining the documentation that is available with each Ada compiler, an Ada user can evaluate these compilers to determine how well they will perform in an application. Some of the compiler aspects fall under the area of compiler optimization [1] and some fall under the area of optional features available to the user. Table I lists standard known optimization features that could be tested in an Ada compiler. Several of these features are discussed in the body of this paper along with suggestions for simple tests that can be used to demonstrate the existence of the optimization technique. A compiler can be evaluated by how well it supports each feature. Other aspects of compiler technology that may be evaluated are listed in Table II.

Almost every real-time program has parts that are very time critical. For these parts of the program, the user may feel the need to make use of previously prepared programs. These may take the form of calls to underlying system functions that are not part of the standard run-time, to previously prepared libraries for the target machine, or for individual procedures that are written in assembly code. In addition, some target machines may have specified instructions to speed up time-critical functions such as the trigonometric functions. There is a provision in the Ada language to support with in-line code with the package Machine_Code if the vendor has supplied it. The size of executable programs and of the Ada run-time can be important in embedded applications where memory often is limited. Most Ada binders are able to select the portions of the Ada library that are needed for a particular application.

Table I Ada Optimization Features

In-line Subroutine Calls	Library Optimization
Register Utilization	Dead Variable Elimination
Stack Allocation	Inter-unit Optimization
Constraint Elimination	Generic Sharing
Constant Evaluation	Constant Propagation
Loop Optimization	Literal Pooling
Loop Invariants	Strength Reduction
Loop Interchange	Common Subexpression
Loop Fusion	Elimination
Loop Expansion	Test Merging
Compile Time Evaluation	Boolean Expression
of Constants	Optimization
Algebraic Simplification	De Morgans
Expression Order	Packing
Branch Elimination	Static Elaboration
Dead Code Elimination	

Table II Ada Performance Characteristics

Size of Objects	Ability to Access System Functions
Size of Executable	Ability to Access System Libraries
Size of Run-Time	Ability to Access Machine Code
Ability to Access Assembly Language	
Alternative Tasking Implementations	

Support Tool Technology.

Support tool technology can advance the cause of program measurement and analysis. Tools can be applied at certain strategic points in the design process to provide system architects with objective data to improve the selection of approaches and alternatives. For example, a system upgrade may be developed using a navigation package from a previous system, and measurements applied may be used as benchmarks for the Ada implementation. Measurement tools may also analyze various Ada compilers to obtain performance data on critical items such as rendezvous timing and context switches.

In-line Subroutine Calls.

In-line subroutine calls can save both space and time. An optimizing compiler can provide automatic in-lining. Many Ada compilers also provide user control for in-lining through pragma inline. In cases where a subroutine with no parameters is called only once, the instructions for the subroutine call, the saving of the return address, and the return jump are all eliminated from the code when a subroutine is in-lined. In cases where a subroutine is called from several places, the savings in time must outweigh the cost in space for in-lining to be worthwhile. Time critical programs should consider this savings. Tests for in-line subroutine calls are provided in the PIWG [2] and ACEC [3] test suites. If automatic inlining is done, the PIWG test, P000001, that tests the time for execution for a procedure call and return will report a time of 0.0 microseconds. In the PIWG test, the procedure contains the following statements:

```
procedure PROC_0 is
begin
   GLOBAL := GLOBAL + A_ONE;
   REMOTE;
end;
```

The time it takes to execute the two statements in the procedure inside a loop (~1000 times on a VAX780 to obtain a measurable amount of time) is subtracted from the time it takes to execute the procedure in the same type of loop. In the PIWG tests, most tests put the timing tests in two loops. The first is a control loop and the second is a test loop:

```
for j in 1..ITERATION_COUNT loop        for j in 1..ITERATION_COUNT loop
   GLOBAL := 0;  -- initialization          GLOBAL := 0;  -- initialization
   for   INSIDE_LOOP                        for  INSIDE_LOOP
      in 1..CHECK_TIMES loop                   in 1..CHECK_TIMES loop
      -- statements for which time            -- statements to be timed
      -- is not of interest                   PROC_0;
      GLOBAL := GLOBAL + A_ONE;
      REMOTE;
   end loop;                                end loop;
end loop;                                 end loop;
```

The time for a feature is thus the difference in time between the execution of the two loops. In the ACEC tests, the difference in times between the tests named loop4b and loop4c will be zero if either automatic in-lining is used or the compiler supports pragma inline. The ACEC tests provide a random number generator as documented by Knuth [4]. In the loop4c version of the test, the code for the procedure in loop4b is expanded.

It is often necessary to look at an assembly language listing of the generated code that calls a single procedure to determine whether of not automatic in-lining is used. As in all tests for optimization, some care must be used that the procedure itself is not eliminated because of other possible optimizations.

Register Utilization.

In-line subroutines that can use registers for parameters can gain further savings because additional space need not be allocated for the parameters. Since operations on registers generally execute faster than operations on memory; and since register instructions are generally shorter than instructions that use memory, good register utilization results in savings both in time and space. Register use for temporary variables rather than allocation of space from a stack is normally faster during the allocation process and results in faster operations on temporary variables.

If the computer has instructions that directly operate on memory, it may be even more efficient to directly operate on the data item itself. For example, the PIWG test P000005 has a single in parameter that is added to a global variable. This may be compiled into one VAX instruction that references the global variable and the parameter. The ACEC tests SS442 and SS443 were designed to demonstrate register utilization by comparing the time between statements that could use registers and those that could not.

Constraint Elimination.

Ada has powerful, but possibly redundant constraint checks. A good optimization technique that is found in mature Ada compilers is the elimination of such checks. An excellent Ada compiler will not only eliminate constraint checks but detect constraint violations where they occur and warn the user at compile time.

In the text of a program that has

```
x : integer range 1..3;
y : constant := 4;
         .
         .
x := y;
```

the user should be warned that a constraint error will be raised during execution. A compiler will in fact substitute the assignment with a raise exception if it is able to eliminate constraint checks. The PIWG tests B000001 to B000004 show the differences between executing with and without constraint checks for a computational application.

Constant Evaluation.

Constant evaluation should be done at compilation time. Expressions that involve compile time constants and operations on these constants should be computed at compile time. Some compilers are able to evaluate constant expressions at compile time within a compilation unit. Other compilers are able to perform this evaluation across compilation units thus providing additional savings in execution time. The same is true for the pooling of literals. Literals that are the same in one compilation unit should occupy the same space. A more sophisticated compiler will be able to provide the same space for literals that appear in more than one compilation unit. A test for this optimization would measure the object space of two units that in one version have different constants that can be shared and the other version will have the same constants that cannot be shared. To test constant evaluation, a program that assigns a value to a constant with an expression such as

> x : **constant** := 2 * 3;
> y : integer **range** 5..10;
>
> .
>
> .
>
> y := x;

should translate into an instruction that performs an immediate move of the literal 6 into the variable y or the register assigned to y. The ACEC tests SS8, SS41, SS42, SS55, and SS60 check for constant evaluation under several conditions.

Loop Optimization.

Loop optimization techniques that move statements outside of a loop can result in significant time savings. Such techniques can be done manually or by a compiler. When loops operate on multi-dimensional arrays, the order of the indices should match the order of the loop increments so that multiplications can be avoided in computing the address of the array element. Normally this is done manually during program design, but a compiler can also give guidance to a user for such an optimization through adequate documentation and/or warning messages. Loop expansion of short loops trades off space versus time and might be selected as a result of the optimize (space) pragma. The PIWG tests L000001 to L000005 measure loop times. The ACEC tests contain numerous tests with loops. The ACEC test SS180 can be used to check for merging loops. Such optimizations can be detected by comparing loops where:

a.   Expressions that do not depend on the loop parameter are inside and
      outside the loop:

```
for i in 1..100 loop            x := y * z;
  x := y * z;                   for i in 1..100 loop
  m := m + i;                     m := m + i;
end loop;                       end loop;
```

b.   The array element order is reversed:

```
for i in 1..100 loop            for j in 1..100 loop
  for j in 1..100 loop            for i in 1..100 loop
    c(i,j) := a(i,j) + b(i,j);     c(i,j) := a(i,j) + b(i,j);
  end loop;                      end loop;
end loop;                       end loop;
```

c.   A short loop can be expanded:

```
for i in 1..3 loop              x := x + y;
  x := x + y;                   x := x + y;
end loop;                       x := x + y;
```

d.   Independent loops can be merged:

```
for i in 1..100 loop            for i in 1..100 loop
  x(i) := 0.0;                    x (i) := 0.0;
end loop;                         y (i) := 1;0
for j in 1..100 loop            end loop;
  y(j) := 1.0;
end loop;
```

e.   Nested loops can be fused:

```
for i in 1..100 loop            for i in 1..10000 loop
  for j in 1..100 loop            d(i) := 0.0;
    c(i,j) := 0.0;              end loop;
  end loop;
end loop;
```

The most difficult optimizations, but the most powerful optimizations are those that go across multiple compilation units. When multiple units can be analyzed to determine the variables that are most frequently used, these variables can be assigned to registers.

Generic Sharing.

Some compilers provide the ability to share the code that is generated for a generic body. This saves space if the generic is used for many different types and in many places. Other compilers generate code for each instantiation. When code is generated for each instantiation, this code should be in-lined. When the code is shared, it means that it is not in-lined. The use of a pragma that designates that the code is shared or not allows the user to make this time/space trade-off. For example, when a generic is very short, it is best if the code is not shared, but in-lined to remove the overhead of subroutine calls.

Strength Reduction.

Major savings can be achieved by reduction in the strength of operations via algebraic simplification or via DeMorgan's law. For example, most optimizing compilers will replace $x**2$ with $x*x$ or $x*2$ with $x+x$. In an extreme but very useful case, Boolean arrays may be mapped to adjacent bits in a byte or word so that operations on them may use a single instruction rather than a loop during evaluation. Such efficiencies may or not be subverted when representation clauses are used instead of the pack pragmas. The ACEC test suite has several algebraic simplification tests in the series ss47..ss51; ss61..ss67; and ss71..ss74. The two PIWG tests H000003 and H000004 show the difference between using the pack pragma and representation clauses.

Dead-Variable Elimination.

Savings in time and space are also possible with dead-variable elimination -- i.e., detecting and eliminating variables for which no subsequent use is found. Such eliminations are possible on a local and or global basis with the latter being more difficult to achieve. Even in a single unit, data flow analysis to detect and eliminate variables that are set and never used is a powerful optimization technique. This feature can be tested by examination of the code that only sets a variable. If this feature is not available in a compiler, support tools that perform data-flow analysis may determine the location of dead variables that can then be eliminated manually. If dead-variable elimination is present, the ACEC test ss68 will show it.

Common Subexpression Elimination.

The elimination of redundant occurances of subexpressions in a compilation unit also allows significant savings not only in time but in the space required for the unit. A powerful optimizing compiler can detect such expressions even when embedded in another expression or when the expression has a different order of operands. When common subexpression elimination is combined with algebraic simplification and constant folding, an Ada compiler will be able to recognize that the second assignment statement in:

    a := 1.0/ 2.0*pi;
    b := 2.0*pi*a;

is the same as

    b := 1.0;

The ACEC tests ss75, ss76, ss172, ss174 check for common subscript expressions.

Use of Ada Features.

The user also has some control in program design to achieve high performance no matter what compiler has been chosen. The list of guidelines to the use of Ada features appears in Table III.

Table III Ada Feature Use

Instantiation	Numerics
Allocation	Tasking
Arrays	Loops
Procedure vs Function	
Separate vs In-line	Short-Circuit Evaluation
Operations	Case versus If
Logical	True versus False If
Numeric	Exceptions

While some use of Ada features will depend on a particular compiler such as the order of evaluation in expressions, the method of code generation for control statements and the method for handling exceptions, there are some characteristics that will apply to all programs written in Ada.

Some Ada features are also important for compilation speed. For example, instantiation outside a main program versus instantiation in a main program can cause a factor of two in compilation time. This is a function of the librarian.

Dynamic allocation is inherent to Ada. A real-time program should avoid dynamic allocation. If necessary, a real-time program should make the memory global and manage it separate from the Ada run-time. For example, allocation of a block of 1000 elements versus allocation of 1 element at a time in a loop can require a factor of 3 less in execution time.

The order of subscripts in arrays has always been of importance in programming languages. The time to access array elements in a loop can be an order of magnitude different if the array is accessed with an expression of a(j,i) versus a(i,j) depending on whether the array is stored in row order or column order.

Most compilers should not generate different code between the use of CASE statements or IF statements if the number of possible cases is small, but the only way to be sure is to test your compiler. The code on the left should execute the same as the code on the right if the variable v can take on the values of a,b, and c.

```
case v is                    if v = a then p1;
when a => p1;                elsif v = b then p2;
when b => p2;                elsif v = c then p3;
when c => p3;                end if;
end case;
```

When the number of possible cases is large, it is then better if the compiler makes use of an indexed address or a jump vector to implement the case statement.

In trying to squeeze every last microsecond out of an application, it is important to realize that knowing the number of times that an application will access the false side of a test versus the amount of times that an application will access the true side of a test can make a difference. For the following code segment:

```
if a then                    -- compute a
    p1;                      -- branch if false
else                         -- do true side
    p2;                      -- branch around false side
end if;                      -- do false side then join together
```

The common method of translation is shown on the right. Note that if the expression a is true, an extra branch instruction is necessary. Hence, if time is really tight, one should try to make the test so that the % of time that the test is true is less than the time that the test is false. Support tools that provide results on branch executions can be used to provide this data. The same is true for the use of short circuit tests. In statements such as

if a and then b then

and a and b are of equal computational complexity, try to make the percentage of time that a is true less than the percentage of time that b is true.

On most computers, it can be expected that the compiler will make use of the computers built-in numerics for floating point. However, some care is still necessary. In fact on many microprogrammed computers, such as the VAX, microprogrammed instructions that are expensive computationally might be used by a compiler. For example, the VAX has D,F,G and H floating point formats. The G and H floating point formats are examples of expensive formats on the VAX 780.

A compiler may generate different code for procedures versus functions. For example the code to generate a procedure with two parameters, one an input and one an output parameter, might be more efficient than code that uses a function where i is an input and o is an output:

p(i,o);   o := f(i);

The only way to determine this is with a user defined test.

In most cases, real-time programs will want to use global data areas with assigned locations via representation clauses or via special loaders. However in some cases, the user may find that it is faster to use parameters rather than global data. The reason is that global data can not be addressed locally with short instructions and handled as well in registers.

A real-time program will want to avoid causing tasks to be initiated and terminated in a dynamic manner. If a decision is made to use Ada tasking, the program will probably initiate all tasks at the level of the main program. Wherever possible, the programmer will try to make use of short-circuit evaluation causing the most common predicate to make the decision as the first predicate in the test. One can use Ada in an application and reuse executives that have proved efficient in the past. This can be done if the compiler supports pragma interface.

Exceptions cause little or no time when there are no errors. What takes time are the tests to raise an exception. Although the checks that Ada provides are extremely valuable in ensuring the correct operation of a program, it may be necessary to eliminate the checks during the portions of a program that are time critical. Depending of the compiler, from 10 to 30% of the execution time can be saved by suppressing such checks.

Summary.

In summary, examination of the Ada compiler optimization features will aid in compiler selection. In addition the careful choice of Ada features and application architecture is important for applications where high performance is required.

References.

1. A. Aho, R. Sethi, and J. Ullman, *Compilers: Principles, Techniques, and Tools*, Addison-Wesley, 1986.
2. Performance Issues Working Group (PIWG), *PIWG Test Suite*, SigAda, 1987.
3. T. Leavitt and K. Terrell, *Ada Compiler Evaluation Capability (ACEC) Reader's Guide*, Boeing Military Airplane, Wichita, Kansas, 1988.
4. D. Knuth, "An Empirical Study of FORTRAN Programs," *Software: Practice and Experience*, Volume 1, Number 2, 1971.

ELABORATION AND TERMINATION OF DISTRIBUTED ADA PROGRAMS

A.D. Hutcheon
A.J. Wellings
Department of Computer Science, University of York, Heslington, York, Y01 5DD, UK

Abstract

The virtual node approach has been proposed as an effective means to program loosely coupled distributed systems in Ada. This paper discusses the implementation of Ada elaboration and termination requirements with respect to the virtual node distribution approach. Parallel elaboration of distributed programs is shown to raise complex issues, while the virtual node approach to distribution allows the use of simple termination algorithms.

INTRODUCTION

There are many different ways in which a single Ada program can be partitioned for execution on a loosely coupled distributed system. Very few of these partitionings can be achieved without compiler support; consequently there is a lack of any real implementation experience. An exception to this is the *virtual node* approach which has been proposed by a variety of groups. The characteristics of virtual nodes are as follows:[Hutcheon1988a]

- They are the units of modularity in a distributed system.
- They are also the units of configuration and reconfiguration.
- They provide well defined interfaces to other virtual nodes in the system.
- They encapsulate local resources. All access to these resources from remote virtual nodes is via the virtual node interface.
- Each can consist of one or more processes. These processes may communicate with each other using shared memory. They can also communicate with processes in other virtual nodes via the interfaces provided. This communication is normally via some form of message passing protocol.
- More than one virtual node can be mapped onto a single physical node. However, it is worth emphasising that a virtual node can not be distributed between machines. Decomposing programs into virtual nodes therefore defines the granularity of potential distribution of the application.
- They are the units of reuse — wherever possible programs should be composed of off-the-shelf virtual nodes.

In applying the virtual node idea to Ada, it is necessary to associate some language construct(s) with a virtual node. The most obvious candidates are the task, the package, the procedure or a collection of library units. It is the last that appears to offer the most potential (a task cannot be compiled separately as a library unit, a package is static and a procedure does not providing adequate encapsulation facilities). Furthermore it can be supported easily by tools in the project support environment *without* modification to the compiler.[Atkinson1988, Hutcheon1987, Hutcheon1988b, Hutcheon1989a]

The two main proponents of the virtual node approach are the DIADEM[Atkinson1988] project and the York Distributed Ada project. (The YDA project was originally funded through the UK's Alvey Software Engineering Directorate as part of the ASPECT [Hutcheon1989b] project. It is currently funded by the Admiralty Research Establishment.) Although they are similar in many ways, they do differ in their detailed approach.[Hutcheon1988a] Although much has been written about distributed Ada in general and virtual nodes in particular, most papers concentrate either on the implementation and semantics of remote selective rendezvous, or on the tools necessary to enforce a restricted use of Ada. There has been little analysis of the algorithms necessary to support elaboration and termination of distributed Ada programs. In this paper we first describe briefly the YDA approach to distribution and then concentrate on the possible options in the design and implementation of these algorithms.

VIRTUAL NODES IN YDA

We have suggested that virtual nodes are an appropriate abstraction for programming distributed systems and that a virtual node in Ada can be represented by a collection of Ada library units. In general in order to identify which library units are associated with which virtual nodes, a *root* library unit is specified. The **WITH** clauses of the root specify all the library units which are components of the virtual note. Note that this includes all the library units which are **WITH**ed by the library units which are **WITH**ed by the root library unit, and so on. One of these library units provides an interface to the virtual node, with all communication between virtual nodes taking place by remote procedure call (RPC).

In the YDA project, the root of and the interface to a virtual node is the same library unit. This is a package which contains procedures and their associated type declarations, constants whose values can be fixed when the package is compiled, and any embedded packages. The thread of control of the virtual node is the elaboration of the interface package. It is expected that the main processing of the virtual node will be performed by tasks declared local to it. Communication between virtual nodes is by remote procedure call.

It is possible that two virtual node roots have **WITH**ed the same library unit; that is the virtual nodes share a library unit. In these cases, in order that the configuration can be allocated to physical nodes, the library units must either be the interfaces to other Virtual Nodes or must be templates, in which case they can be replicated on each Virtual Node without violating their semantics. Template library units are defined to be without any global state. This means that they are either generics; or packages with only type declarations (including task types) and subprogram which do not access any global memory; or subprograms by themselves.

Once a group of library units have been written and grouped together as virtual nodes, it must be possible to configure them into virtual nodes for execution on the available processors. Consider a system of three virtual nodes: V1, V2, V3. An YDA program takes the form shown in Example 1 (V1_INTERFACE is the root and interface package for V1 etc.).

```
with V1_INTERFACE, V2_INTERFACE, V3_INTERFACE;
procedure MAIN is
begin
     null;
end;
```
Example 1: Main Program for Three Virtual Node System

The program will not terminate until all tasks in the called library unit terminate (see later section on Program Termination). Tools are used to transform the program (transparently to the programmer) into the required number of different load modules; however, it should be stressed that YDA still views the program as a *single* Ada program although from the viewpoint of the host development tools (compiler, linkers etc) it is three Ada programs. For full details of this transformation see Hutcheon and Wellings.[Hutcheon1989a]

ELABORATION OF VIRTUAL NODES

As was stated in the introduction one of the problems of executing Ada in a distributed environment is that of the program's elaboration. The ALRM states in section 10.5 that elaboration of a program must conform to a partial ordering in which no unit is elaborated until all units which it names in **WITH** clauses have been elaborated (note that if both a specification and body exist then only the specification is actually referred to by a **WITH** clause). This ordering ensures that no specification is used before it has been elaborated, while "**pragma ELABORATE**" can be used to force prior elaboration of the bodies of units named in **WITH** clauses if this is also required. For example if the "**pragma ELABORATE(B);**" line was removed from Example 2 then the Ada system could choose to elaborate package body A before package body B, so causing the exception "PROGRAM_ERROR" to be raised by the call of B.IN_B as the procedure body was not elaborated when it was used. If the dependencies introduced by **WITH** clauses and "**pragma ELABORATE**"s produce cycles in the required elaboration order then the program is erroneous. This situation, which can be detected by the compiler, is illustrated by Example 3.

On a single processor a common approach to elaboration is to determine a fixed elaboration order which conforms to the partial ordering explained above, then to elaborate the units of a program in this order and raise "PROGRAM_ERROR" if anything is used before it has elaborated. It would be possible to produce similar behaviour in a distributed Ada program by passing messages between processors to indicate that particular units had elaborated and using these to drive elaboration in the same order as on a single processor and with only one processor active at any time.

```
package A is                      package B is
   A_NUM : INTEGER := 1;             procedure IN_B;
end A;                            end B;

with B;
pragma ELABORATE(B);              with A;
package body A is                 package body B is

begin                                B_NUM : INTEGER;
   B.IN_B;
end A;                               procedure IN_B is
                                        begin
                                           B_NUM := B_NUM + 1;
                                        end IN_B;

                                     begin
                                        B_NUM := A.A_NUM + 3;
                                     end B;
```

Example 2: Use of pragma ELABORATE

However such an approach involves a complex mechanism and run-time overhead, and much better use can be made of the available processing power if elaboration is performed in parallel. This leads us to consider mechanisms which seem more suitable for distributed systems.

```
package C is                      package D is
   procedure IN_C;                   procedure IN_D;
end C;                            end D;

with D;                           with C;
pragma ELABORATE(D);              pragma ELABORATE(C);
package body C is                 package body D is

   procedure IN_C is                 procedure IN_D is
      begin                             begin
         null;                             null;
      end IN_C;                         end IN_D;

begin                             begin
   D.IN_D;                           C.IN_C;
end C;                            end D;
```

Example 3: Cycle in elaboration

Simple Parallel Algorithms

The two mechanisms described here have been implemented in experimental virtual node distribution approaches. The program transformations to enable distributed execution of virtual nodes produce a program for each processor in the system. These programs include the virtual nodes placed on that processor, plus a copy of each remote server interface specification named in **WITH** clauses by those virtual nodes. This allows remote procedure calls to be carried out as shown in Figure 1 below:

Figure 1: Server Specification Used as Interface to RPC Mechanism

As remote server specifications are included in the same program as each of their clients, the elaboration mechanisms are concerned only that remote server bodies may not have elaborated when they are called. However, the transformation into multiple programs effectively removes any "pragma ELABORATE" directives which cross processor boundaries. Neither elaboration mechanism described here requires actual compiler support, but neither conform exactly to the elaboration requirements described above.

Elaboration without Synchronisation.

If remote calls arrive at a server before the server has been elaborated then an exception is returned to the client. The client must therefore be aware that if it tries again later the call may succeed. If the client after several calls still receives an exception then it may assume that there is no elaboration order for the distributed programs and it can initiate some recovery action. The drawbacks of this approach are that the application programmer is required to decide on an elaboration retry strategy and program it for each remote call which may fail during elaboration, and that the startup order of the processors may cause elaboration problems which would not occur in a single processor system, for example if a client is started before a server which it calls. This is the approach adopted by the DIADEM project.[Atkinson1988]

Lazy Synchronisation.

In this approach, adopted as an interim measure by the YDA project, if a processor receives an RPC request for a server which has not yet been elaborated then the call is blocked until the server has finished its elaboration. When the server completes elaboration the blocked call is carried out. If we consider Example 2 above and assume that packages A and B are virtual nodes residing on different processors then the approach can be illustrated. Presuming that package A elaborates first and makes the call B.IN_B before package B has elaborated then the arriving RPC request is deferred until package B has elaborated. After this has occurred the requested procedure call is carried out and returns, allowing the elaboration of package A to continue. If a distributed program does have a valid elaboration order then the program will elaborate without the application software's help. Unfortunately, if the program does not have an elaboration order due to circular dependencies in subprogram calls during elaboration then remote calls will be stalled permanently, whereas "PROGRAM_ERROR" should be raised according to the ALRM. This may lead to deadlock of the entire program, as would be the case if packages C and D of Example 3 above were the only two virtual nodes of a distributed program and were placed on different processors. The result would be that the calls during the elaboration of each package would be stalled awaiting the completed elaboration of the other package, this in turn being prevented by its own stalled call. In this special case of complete deadlock with RPC requests stalled awaiting elaboration "PROGRAM_ERROR" could be returned as the result of the blocked calls. However, this would be of limited usefulness as complete deadlock may never occur despite the presence of permanently blocked calls, or may develop long after the initial elaboration failure when the program may no longer be in a suitable state to recover from the exception.

Parallel Algorithms with Full Synchronisation

In order to meet the full Ada semantics for elaboration in a distributed system, including honouring "pragma ELABORATE" directives which cross processor boundaries, messages must be passed between processors so that the elaboration of units on different processors can be synchronised to conform to the required partial ordering. This introduces complexity in the message passing protocol and in the mechanism which performs elaboration, but is necessary in order to raise PROGRAM_ERROR if anything is used before it has elaborated.

A static analysis of the program determines the required elaboration partial ordering and signals an error if this contains any circular dependencies — if no cycles are detected then no permanent waits for elaboration messages can occur. Although this analysis could be performed in the two approaches described above it fails to detect those programs which must fail to elaborated, despite there being a valid elaboration order, due to cycles in calls made during elaboration. Such a program would be produced if the "pragma ELABORATE" lines were removed from Example 3 above. In parallel algorithms with full synchronisation, messages are passed during elaboration to ensure that no unit is elaborated until all units on remote processors, which appear before it in the partial ordering, have elaborated. The exception "PROGRAM_ERROR" is raised if any use before elaboration occurs despite this. Two basic approaches to synchronised parallel elaboration can be identified:

Fixed Elaboration Order with Synchronisation

In this approach an elaboration order is worked out for each processor, and synchronisation messages are used to suspend the elaboration on each processor until messages have been received to indicate that required remote units have elaborated. To illustrate this, consider the packages allocated to three processors in Example 4. The elaboration mechanism might decide that, on processor 1, package A_1 will be elaborated before package B_1. At runtime the elaboration on processor 1 will await the arrival of a message from processor 2 indicating that package C_2 has elaborated before elaborating package A_1. Once this has completed the elaboration thread will, if the message has not already arrived, await a message from processor 3 indicating that package D_3 has elaborated before continuing to elaborate B_1.

Processor 1

```
with C_2;                          with D_3;
package A_1 is                     package B_1 is
    ...                                ...
end A_1;                           end B_1;
```

Processor 2   Processor 3

```
package C_2 is                     package D_3 is
    ...                                ...
end C_2;                           end D_3;
```

Example 4: Elaboration on multiple processors

Runtime Determination of Elaboration Order

The algorithm above uses the precondition that a unit cannot be elaborated until all those which it names in **WITH** clauses have elaborated to determine a fixed elaboration order in advance. In contrast runtime determination of elaboration order uses the preconditions themselves to determine elaboration order at runtime. An elaboration scheduler on each processor selects for elaboration any unit whose elaboration precondition is met, with synchronisation messages being passed to complete preconditions involving remote units. Considering Example 4 again, the runtime elaboration mechanism on processor 1 will await messages from both processor 2 and processor 3, indicating that package C_2 and package D_3 have elaborated. Dependent upon which message arrives first either package A_1 or package B_1 will be elaborated first, rather than possibly having to idle awaiting the message corresponding to C_2 despite the fact that the message indicating D_3's elaboration has arrived and so B_1 could be elaborated. Although complex, this mechanism does allow as much parallel elaboration as possible to take place while some units are blocked awaiting synchronisation messages.

When elaboration is carried out in parallel there is much more opportunity for unit bodies to be called before they have elaborated, so requiring more use of "pragma ELABORATE" and explicit initialisation synchronisation of tasks than would be required under sequential elaboration. This does not indicate a problem with parallel elaboration — any program whose correct operation relies on assumptions about elaboration order beyond those given in the ALRM is erroneous.

PROGRAM TERMINATION

The ALRM does not define currently the relationship between the termination of the main program and the termination of library units. However, we understand Ada 9x will require termination of the main program only when all library tasks can terminate. The YDA approach enforces that the main program will not terminate until *all* the library tasks can terminate.

Task termination in Ada can be considered in two parts: one is that a task in general cannot terminate until all of its children are willing to do so; the other that a task suspended on a select statement with a terminate alternative cannot terminate while its entries can still be called by any other task. As the unit of distribution is based on library packages the first task termination mechanism is local to each processor — no exchange of messages through a distributed task hierarchy is required. As mentioned above, a distributed YDA program terminates when all library tasks have terminated. This is based on an implementation of the second task termination mechanism whereby any task which wishes to terminate "pretends" to do so and and becomes inactive, reactivating if it is called at a later time. Distributed termination then requires an algorithm which can detect that all tasks on all processors have become inactive.

YDA has experimentally implemented two distributed termination algorithms, one simple and the other both more complex and more general. Before these are described it is necessary to note some points relevant to distributed termination:

- A processor is considered to be passive if it holds no executable tasks, or tasks awaiting the expiry of delays. In this state it can never again have an executable task without the prior arrival of a message from another processor resulting in the unblocking or creation of a local task. (The implications of interrupt entries are considered later.)

- The algorithms considered here do not directly detect termination. Instead they detect that a distributed system has become stable — that no further change in its state will take place. One such condition is termination of the program, the other is that deadlock has occurred. These can be differentiated once stability has been detected as in the case of deadlock some tasks will be suspended awaiting events which will never occur.

The simple algorithm is described first: Each processor in the distributed system maintains a count of the number of currently active processors in the system, initially set to be the number of processors in the system. When a processor becomes passive it sends a message to all other processors to indicate this, and each decrements its active processor count. When all processors have no active tasks the count reaches zero and all processors recognise stability, check for termination or deadlock, then take appropriate action. If a passive processor receives an RPC request then any required tasks are reactivated, returning the processor to active status, and a message is sent to the other processors instructing them to increment their counts of active processors. This algorithm relies on messages being delivered in the order in which they are sent, as out of order delivery of passive and active messages would result in inconsistent active processor counts and possible premature termination of some processors. It also fails to detect deadlock which occurs while RPCs are in progress as it assumes that a task suspended while an RPC takes place will always be restarted. This is necessary to avoid a system, which contains no other activity, erroneously terminating while an RPC call or reply message is in transit, although the message will cause the receiving processor to become active. Thus in this algorithm a processor which has tasks suspended awaiting the return of RPC results is not considered passive.

A slightly more complex algorithm is based on the algorithm proposed by Helary, Jard, Plouzeau and Raynal.[Helary1987] Each processor maintains its local view of the message state in the system, in the form of a count of the number of messages that it has sent to and received from every other processor. When a processor becomes passive it broadcasts a "passive" message containing its local message state view to all processors. The processor then checks its local sent and received message counts, and those broadcast by other processors in "passive" messages, against each other. If all corresponding "sent to" and "received from" counts for pairs of processors match then the processor making the check recognises that the system has become stable. Otherwise it remains idle, repeating the stability check each time a "passive" message arrives until it either discovers stability or a message arrives and causes it to become active by either requesting an RPC execution or returning a result and unblocking the waiting task. After reactivating it may again become passive and broadcast its message view. The explanation of the correctness of the stability condition is as follows:

- In order for the local and broadcast message states to match each processor must have become passive at least once.

- If the local and broadcast states match then there are no outstanding messages in transit so no currently passive processor can become active.

- All processors must currently be passive otherwise there would be a disagreement between one or more "sent to" counts from passive processors to the currently active processor and the last "passive" message which it broadcast before reactivating, as the last passive message view would not include the message which reactivated the processor.

All processors will recognise stability together when the appropriate conditions arise as they perform the stability test when either they become passive or are passive and receive a passive message state broadcast. Once stability has been detected then termination and deadlock can be distinguished because in the latter case at least one task will be awaiting an expected event, e.g. the return of a remote procedure call. Although the message size and processing cost is slightly higher than in the simple approach described above, this algorithm does not rely on ordered message delivery and can detect deadlock which occurs while an RPC is in progress. Although deadlock detection is not required by Ada, it is a condition which it is useful to detect and report.

An issue which is likely to arise in embedded systems is that of termination in the presence of interrupt-handling tasks. These can be regarded either as services which disappear when the rest of the program terminates or as persistent tasks which may prevent program termination, and treated appropriately by the runtime system on each processor in a distributed system. In either case they are easily handled as required by the above mechanisms.

CONCLUSIONS

The Ada elaboration mechanism is complex, and indeed presents perhaps the greatest problems in our implementation of distributed Ada. Parallel elaboration, although allowed by the ALRM, would appear to make it much more likely for "PROGRAM_ERROR" to arise during elaboration.

In comparison our choice of distribution approach localises the complex part of Ada termination to lie within single processors, so allowing distributed termination (and deadlock) detection to be carried by comparatively simple and well understood algorithms.

ACKNOWLEDGEMENT

We would like to acknowledge the Alvey Directorate and the Admiralty Research Establishment, who have partially funded this work, and Yvon Kermarvec, for his helpful discussions of distributed termination algorithms.

REFERENCES

Atkinson1988.   Atkinson, C., Moreton, T. and Natali, A., *Ada for Distributed Systems*, Ada Companion Series, Cambridge University Press (1988).

Helary1987.   Helary, J.-M., Jard, C., Plouzeau, N. and Reynal, M., "Detection of Stable Properties in Distributed Applications", *Proceedings of the Sixth ACM Symposium on Principles of Distributed Computing*, Vancouver, pp. 125-136 (August 1987).

Hutcheon1987.   Hutcheon, A.D. and Wellings, A.J., "Ada for Distributed Systems", *Computer Standards and Interfaces* **6**(1), pp. 71-82 (1987).

Hutcheon1988a.   Hutcheon, A.D. and Wellings, A.J., "The Virtual Node Approach to Designing Distributed Ada Programs", *Ada User* **9**(Supplementary) (December 1988).

Hutcheon1988b.   Hutcheon, A.D. and Wellings, A.J., "Supporting Ada in a Distributed Environment", *Proceedings of the 2nd International Workshop on Real Time Ada Issues, Ada Letters*, Devon **8**(7), pp. 113-117 (1988).

Hutcheon1989a.   Hutcheon, A.D. and Wellings, A.J., "Distributed Embedded Computer Systems in Ada - An Approach and Experience", pp. 55-64 in *Hardware and Software for Real Time Process Control, Proceedings of the IFIP WG 5.4/IFAC/EWICS Working Conference*, ed. Ehrenberger, J. Zalewski and W., North-Holland (1989).

Hutcheon1989b.   Hutcheon, A.D., Snowden, D.S. and Wellings, A.J., "Programming and Debugging Distributed Target Systems", in *ASPECT: An Integrated Project Support Environment*, ed. Hitchcock, P., MIT Press (1989).

A Storage Model for Ada on Hierarchical-Memory Multiprocessors

Susan Flynn Hummel
Vrije Universiteit
Faculteit Wiskunde en Informatica
De Boelelaan 1081
1081 HV Amsterdam, The Netherlands

Robert B. K. Dewar
Edmond Schonberg
New York University
Courant Institute of Mathematical Sciences
251 Mercer Street
New York, NY 11012

Abstract

The management of storage for parallel block-structured languages such as Ada in a multiprocessor environment is complicated by the presence of several active tasks and possibly more than one memory (i.e., local memories and a global memory). Common storage management schemes (e.g., activation stacks with displays) assume a linear address space and therefore do not provide an obvious mapping of languages that allow tasks to share variables onto machines with a hierarchical memory. In this paper, we describe an alternative storage management model based on *relay sets* that extends quite naturally to parallel languages implemented on multiprocessors. Our *modified relay sets* provide a means not only for efficiently managing the variables of parallel block-structured languages in a hierarchy of memories, but also for identifying shared variables.

1. Introduction

In order to reduce memory access times, uniprocessors often use a hierarchy of memories — expensive, fast, small memories reside closest to the processor, while cheap, slow, large memories reside further away. Each level of memory functions as a cache for the next higher level. Since data references exhibit a high degree of spacial and temporal locality, by the judicious caching of data, the average data access time can approach that of the fastest memory. On multiprocessors, a hierarchical memory is motivated by data sharing between concurrently executing tasks: a consistent view of shared data can be ensured by storing the data in a memory that is common to the processors that execute the tasks. While it is desirable to (temporarily) cache shared data in lower levels of the hierarchy to reduce access times, shared data must be cached cautiously lest processors touch stale (inconsistent) copies. For example, if a processor updates a cached shared datum, then this change may not be reflected in other caches.

The efficient resolution of non-local references to shared data in tasks running on multiprocessors is more problematic than resolving non-local references of subprograms on uniprocessors. Conventional stack management schemes that use activation stacks and rely on displays to resolve references to non-local data assume a linear address space, and do not differentiate between shared and non-shared (private) data allocated within an activation record.

Another method for resolving the non-local references of block structured languages which can be extended to parallel languages and multiprocessors quite naturally is the so called *relay set*[Buroff 1977]. Buroff used relay sets (RSs), or *global displays* as he called them, in an implementation of Algol 68 to eliminate scope and name restrictions. More recently, RSs have been used by Kruchten to resolve the non-local references of subprograms and tasks for a uniprocessor implementation of Ada, namely the NYU Ada/Ed compiler [Kruchten 1985]. The RS of a program unit (subprogram or task) contains all of the non-local variables referenced within the unit. These variables are passed to the unit as if they were parameters passed by reference.

In this paper, we show how to modify RSs to efficiently manage Ada variables in a multiprocessing environment with a hierarchy of memories. The storage management scheme we present is being considered as part of an implementation of the Ada/Ed compiler on two highly parallel machines, the NYU Ultracomputer [Gottlieb 1987] and the IBM RP3 [Pfister *et al.* 1987].

Our modified relay sets (MRSs) also provide a means for calculating *shared sets*. The shared set (SS) of a program unit is the set of variables declared by the program unit that are referenced non-locally by inner tasks. (Not all Ada shared variables must be explicitly declared as shared.) It is imperative that these variables be identified, so that they can be allocated in the proper memory (e.g., global as opposed to local) and cached safely.

In the rest of this paper, we show that once SSs have been indentified, Ada variables can be mapped quite naturally onto a multiprocessor with a three tier memory hierarchy (caches, local memories and a global memory), and moreover, that MRSs provide an efficient mechanism for resolving non-local references in this environment. We begin by giving a brief history of the Ada/Ed project, after which we review the Ada rules for shared variables. Next, we describe our target machine model in more detail, and consider the appropriate mapping of Ada variables onto the memory hierarchy of this machine model. Some of the problems with traditional stack management techniques are then identified. After defining MRSs more precisely, we explain how they can be used to efficiently resolve non-local references appearing in tasks. In §7, we show how to calculate SSs from MRSs, and how SSs can themselves be used to resolve the non-local references of tasks. Finally, we assess the cost of using MRSs and SSs versus conventional displays. An example of the calculation MRSs and SSs is given in the appendix.

1.1. Background — Towards a Highly Parallel Ada

The NYU Ada project began as a large-scale prototyping experiment using the SETL programming language [Schwartz *et al.* 1986]. A prototype Ada compiler, Ada/Ed, was rapidly produced using the high-level features of SETL [Dewar *et al.* 1980]. The next phase of the experiment was to improve the performance of Ada/Ed and bring it closer to an implementation in a more traditional language [Kruchten and Schonberg 1984]. This involved rewriting the compiler using lower level SETL constructs. The memory management scheme for this low-level version was based on RSs (see [Kruchten 1985, Rosen 1985]). Once Ada/Ed was written in low-level SETL it was straightforward to translate it into C. The result of this translation, called Ada/Ed-C, is currently being retargeted to two highly parallel shared memory machines, the NYU Ultracomputer and the IBM RP3.

The tasking idiom favored for this class of machines describes a large number of nearly identical short-lived tasks (e.g., declared with an array in Ada) operating on a shared data structure (such as a matrix). The feasibility of efficiently supporting this paradigm in Ada has been investigated in [Schonberg and Schonberg 1985, Flynn *et al.* 1987, Hummel 1988]. Although the restrictions that Ada places on how shared composite object are accessed (see §2.1 and [Shulman 1987]) seemingly outlaws this style of programming, the storage model we present enables Ada programs to coordinate large numbers of tasks using shared variables without sacrificing efficiency.

2. Data Model

Ada allows tasks to reference variables declared in an enclosing unit in accord with the usual visibility rules for block structured languages. Such variables are said to be *shared*. Variables referenced only by the task that declares them are called *private*.

Task share data either to communicate information or to synchronize. The manner in which tasks access shared data to accomplish these two goals leads to the following classification of shared data: *synchronous* and *asynchronous*. Synchronous shared data is accessed in a disciplined manner between points where tasks synchronize, for instance, either by concurrent readers or by an exclusive writer (CREW). In contrast, asynchronous data is accessed indiscriminately by tasks (i.e., with no discernible coordination). Typically, tasks use synchronous shared variables to communicate information, while asynchronous shared variables are themselves used to implement synchronization mechanisms (e.g., locks). Synchronous data can temporarily reside in fast levels of the hierarchy (e.g., while they are being read) as long as they are flushed to slower levels of memory when tasks synchronize. To ensure that all tasks have a consistent view of asynchronous data, it must always reside at slower levels of the memory hierarchy. As described below, Ada supports both synchronous and asynchronous shared variables.

2.1. Ada Variables

The Ada reference manual (ARM) [DoD 1983] 9.11 (7-8) states that an implementation is allowed to maintain local copies of shared variables, and only need update the variables at points where tasks synchronize. A program is erroneous if keeping local copies of a shared variable produces different results than not keeping local copies, i.e., it is up to the programmer to guarantee that the local copies are consistent between synchronization points.

The relevant synchronization points are defined in the ARM 9.11 (2) to be "*Two tasks are synchronized at the start and end of their rendezvous. At the start and end of its activation, a task is synchronized with the task that causes this activation. A task that has completed its execution is synchronized with any other task.*"

For variables named in a pragma SHARED, every read or write is a synchronization point for that variable. According to our previous definition, shared variables that are not named in a pragma SHARED are synchronous variables while variables that are named in a pragma SHARED are asynchronous variables.

The pragma SHARED can only be applied to variables of scalar or access type. It cannot be applied to composite objects. To allow tasks to access the (scalar or access type) components of composite shared objects asynchronously, i.e., to access them as if they were declared in a pragma SHARED, an implementation must provide a pragma whose meaning is that every read or write of the scalar or access type components of the composite object is a synchronization point for that component (see §4).

Although in direct violation of Steelman (the design requirements document of Ada [DoD 1979]), Ada does not require that a task explicitly declare synchronous variables. Synchronous variables become shared implicitly by virtue of being accessed by a task other than the task that declares the variables.

This has some severe repercussions. In the presence of separately compiled units, a compiler cannot be sure what variables are shared until bind time (since variables declared in one compilation unit could be referenced by tasks declared in a subunit). Either code generation must delayed until bind time, or pessimistic assumptions must be made, e.g., all the variables that appear before the declaration of a stub must be regarded as shared.

3. Memory Model

To keep our storage management scheme as general as possible, we consider a rather generic hierarchical-memory large-scale multiprocessor (of which both the Ultracomputer and RP3 are representative). We assume that each processor of our target machine is paired with a memory module (its local memory), and can access all of the other memory modules (the global memory) via some kind of (unspecified) interconnection network. In addition, each processor has a local cache. The latency of a memory request to the global memory is assumed to be significantly greater than a request to its local cache or memory.

Our target machine can be viewed as having a three tier memory consisting of a global memory, local memories and caches. Data that is shared by tasks that are executed on distinct processors can be stored in the global memory. If tasks are not migratory, that is, a task only executes on a single processor throughout its lifetime, then the private variables of the task can be stored in the local memory of the processor that executes the task. Private variables can always be cached, while some shared data (e.g., synchronous variables) may be cached temporarily. (Note that when a write-through caching policy is used, synchronous shared variables will not have to be evicted from the cache at points where tasks synchronize, only invalidated.)

The cache coherence of a modest number of processors can be maintained in hardware, e.g., with snoopy caches. However, it is predicted that all (currently known) hardware cache coherence solutions will not scale up [Gottlieb 1987]. Thus, it has been suggested that ensuring the cache coherence of large-scale multiprocessors should be the responsibility of software [McAuliffe 1986]. That is, the software should be able to specify where a datum resides in the memory hierarchy.

Accordingly, we assume that data can be labeled as global or local, and as cacheable, temporarily cacheable or non-cacheable by software. We will use *global, local, cacheable, marked* and *noncacheable* to denote these data attributes (respectively). We also permit software to selectively flush a particular class of data from a cache (say, *global marked* at synchronization points). Both the Ultracomputer and RP3 have instructions for specifying these data attributes and for selectively flushing data from caches.

There are thus six combinations of data attributes corresponding to the cross product: {*local, global*} × {*cacheable, marked, noncacheable*}. (Note that a datum may be further classified by how it is accessed, read/write or read-only, resulting in twelve combinations.) The tuple <*location, cacheability*> is called the *storage mode* of a datum [Edler *et al.* 1987]. The virtual address space of our target machine is composed of segments that have storage modes corresponding to these data storage modes. The memory mapping unit maps each virtual segment to the appropriate physical segment.

4. Storage Modes of Ada Variables

Of the six possible storage modes, only the following are of interest for Ada:
a)   Asynchronous Variables are <*global, noncacheable*>;
b)   Synchronous Variables are <*global, marked*>;
c)   Private Variables are either:
    i)   <*local, cacheable*> if tasks can migrate,

ii)   <*global, cacheable*> if tasks are non-migratory.

The advantage of labeling synchronous shared variables with the attribute *marked* is that we can selectively flush these variables from the cache at synchronization points. If tasks are migratory, then their private variables must be flushed from the cache at scheduling points, i.e., at points where the tasks relinquish their processors. Hence, there are at least three different types of virtual address segments that must be managed by an Ada compiler for our target machine. (Later, we see that the cost of stack management schemes is proportional to the number of storage modes supported.)

It is conceivable that an optimizing Ada compiler might support other storage modes. For instance, if a task references enough synchronous shared variables to fill an entire cache, then the compiler might decide to label the private variables of the task as <*local, noncacheable*>, since caching private data might evict shared data from the cache. (The cache is a scarce resource.) Moreover, to allow users to experiment with various storage strategies, Ada/Ed will provide a pragma for each storage mode, e.g., a pragma GLOBAL_MARKED. (Note that a pragma GLOBAL_NONCACHEABLE has the same affect as the pragma SHARED; however, the former can be applied to composite objects.) In addition, Ada/Ed will provide the pragma SHARED_VARIABLES_MARKED, to assert that all shared variables have been otherwise declared, so that subunits can be compiled separately without incurring a performance penalty.

The storage management schemes based on MRSs and SSs that we describe in §6 and §7 assume that either the pragma SHARED_VARIABLES_MARKED is in effect or all separately-compiled subunits of a unit being processed have been compiled. If such is not the case, then the actual calculation of the MRS of the unit must be delayed until bind time; however, code for the unit can still be generated at compile time (at the price of some contortions: see [Kruchten 1985]). Unfortunately, to be able to generate code at compile time for a unit whose subunits have not been compiled, we must be overly pessimistic about the contents of its SS.

5. Storage Modes and Stacks: The Data Placement Problem

In this section, we consider some of the difficulties of managing variables with different storage modes. Block structured languages that support recursive subprograms are usually implemented with an activation stack. Non-local references are resolved using a display. For languages with parallel constructs, such as Ada, the activation stack of a program becomes a cactus stack. The branches of the cactus stack are the activation stacks of individual tasks. A snapshot of the activation stack that could result from the execution of the program given in the appendix appears in the diagram below.

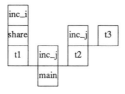

Figure 1. Displays: A Cactus Stack

Maintaining a display for a cactus stack is problematic as there may be more than one display pointer per nesting level (one for each active task at the same level). Thus, a single global display (which is the typical implementation of displays for languages without parallel constructs) cannot be used for languages with parallel constructs. Instead, each task must keep a local copy of its display which is more expensive in terms of both time and storage than keeping a global display.

A more serious problem with cactus stacks (as they have traditionally been implemented) is that there is no clear demarcation between data with different storage modes within an activation record. Consecutive stack locations may contain data with different storage modes. But, data of different storage modes must be allocated in different segments. Furthermore, as a stack grows and shrinks, the same stack location may refer to data of different storage modes at different times. We will call this the data placement problem.

One possible solution to the data placement problem is to maintain a separate cactus stack, and hence display, for each storage mode. Assuming we support m storage modes, this would mean keeping m local displays and stack pointers per task, which is quite expensive in terms of storage and registers. In the following two sections, we present two schemes for solving the data placement problem that do not consume large amounts of storage (at the cost of an extra level of indirection to access the non-local references of tasks).

6. Modified Relay Sets

An alternative to displays for resolving the non-local references of block structured languages are the aforementioned RSs. The RS of a subprogram identifies the non-local variables referenced within the subprogram. These variables are passed to the subprogram during its elaboration as if they were reference parameters. Using RSs for block structured languages leads to a rake of scopes in which the stacks of the subprograms are the prongs. Each subprogram maintains a relay table (RT) where the addresses of its RS are stored. When RSs are applied to a parallel block structured language, the prongs become the stacks of subprograms and tasks.

RTs and displays are for the most part orthogonal, in that RTs can be used for tasks while displays are used for other program units. However, RTs and displays are not completely separable, as tasks can call subprograms that are local to enclosing tasks: the non-local variables referenced by a shared subprogram will not necessarily be in the RS of (or local to) a calling task. To resolve the non-local references of shared subprograms the RS of a shared subprogram must be added to the RS of any task that calls the subprogram. (Adding the RSs of shared subprograms to the RSs of any task which calls the subprogram also simplifies the calculation of SSs.)

To reflect this change, we formally define the modified relay set MRS_t of a task t as

$$MRS_t = \left[\bigcup_{p \in L_t} MRS_p \right] \cup R_t - L_t - G \cup \left[\bigcup_{s \in CS_t} MRS_s \right],$$

where p is a program unit, L_t is the set of entities local only to t, R_t is the set of entities referenced by t, G is the set of global entities, s is a subprogram, and CS_t is the set of non-local subprograms called by t. (The MRSs of program units that are not tasks are defined analogously.)

An algorithm can be derived from the above definition to calculate MRSs in a single pass (see [Hummel 1988]). When the compiler processes the body of a task type tt, its MRS is calculated. When tt is elaborated, a task template is created containing a RT where the actual addresses of the MRS are stored. All of the task objects created from this template will share the RT. More specifically, when a task of type tt is activated its RT pointer (RTP) is set to the RT. (Although it is possible to store the RT in the first activation record of a task [Kruchten 1985] thereby saving a register, this would prohibit tasks from sharing a RT.)

As shown in the next section, the variables in the SS of a program unit are readily identifiable from the MRSs of its inner tasks; hence, these variables can be allocated in the heap of the appropriate mode. Pointers to the variables are kept in the unit's activation record. Thus, MRSs and SSs elegantly solve the data placement problem. Hereafter this approach will be called the *RT scheme*. A snapshot of the rake of stacks that could result from the execution of the program given in the appendix using RTs appears in figure 2.

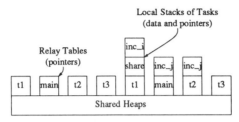

Figure 2. Relay Tables for Tasks

Note that two levels of indirection are required to access a non-local shared variable (one via the RTP and another via the RT entry), whereas only one level of indirection is needed for multiple cactus stacks. However, as the addresses of the shared variables are read-only (after being written by the unit that declares them), local copies of the addresses can be cached or kept in registers. Hence, the penalty of the extra level of indirection need only be paid the first time a shared variable is referenced (at the cost of extra storage).

7. Shared Sets

The SS of a task is the set of variables local to the task that are referenced by inner tasks. That is, the set of variables local to the task that are included in the MRSs of its inner tasks. A slight complication is that it is difficult to determine when the designated object of a access object is shared. For instance, during an entry call, the called task can assign an access object parameter to a local variable. After the call, the called task can access the designated object through this variable. Thus, we (pessimistically) add to the SS of a program unit the entire collection of objects designated by access objects that are either entry call parameters or shared.

Formally the shared set SS_t of a task t is defined as

$$SS_t = \left[\bigcup_{tt\, \in\, DT_t} MRS_{tt} \cap L_t \right] \cup \left[\bigcup_{ao\, \in\, PSS_t} type\,(o,\, t) \right],$$

where tt is a task type, DT_t is the set of task types defined within t (but not within an inner task), MRS_{tt} is the MRS of tt, L_t is the set of entities declared immediately in t, PSS_t (the potentially SS) is $SS_t \cup MRS_t$ augmented with the access objects of t that are actual or formal parameters of entry calls, ao is an access object, and $type(o,\, t)$ is the set of objects declared in t that are designated by access objects of the same type as ao. (The SSs of program units that are not tasks are defined in a similar manner.) Like MRSs, SSs can be calculated in a single pass.

SSs can be used in conjunction with displays to solve the data placement problem for cactus stacks: Each task maintains two stacks, one for private data and the other for shared data. The shared stack is a cactus stack that consists of shared tables (STs). The ST of a program unit contains an entry for each element of its SS. Rather than allocating the elements of its SS in an activation record, a program unit allocates these elements in a heap of the appropriate storage mode, and stores pointers to these heap objects in its ST.

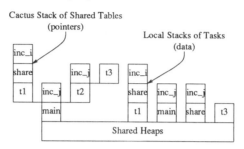

Figure 3. Shared Tables: Cactus Stack and Rake of Stacks

If tasks are migratory, then the private and shared stacks can be coalesced, since they both will be allocated in the global memory. In this case, the STs would be stored in activation records. As with RTs, two levels of indirection are required to access a non-local shared variable. The relative costs of using multiple stacks, RTs and STs are examined in more detail below.

8. Cost Comparisons

Table 1 summarizes the costs of using multiple cactus stacks, STs and RTs to resolve the non-local references of tasks. (For a comparison of the subprogram case see [Hummel 1988].)

	Display	Shared Table	Relay Table
Number of Heaps	0	$SM-1$	$SM-1$
Number of Stacks per Task	SM	2	1
Elaboration Storage Overhead	0	0	SVR
Execution Storage Overhead	$SM*LNL + (SM-1)*GNL$	$2*LNL + GNL$	$LNL + 1$
Registers for Local Data	$SM*LNL$	$2*LNL$	LNL
Registers for Non-local Data	$(SM-1)*GNL$	GNL	1
Non-local Data Indirection	1	2	2

SM is the number of storage modes.
GNL is the number of statically nested enclosing scopes.
LNL is the number of static nesting levels within a task.
SVR is the number of shared variables referenced within a task.

Table 1. Comparison of Stack Management Schemes for Tasks

(It is assumed that pointers to activation records and tables are held in registers whenever possible.)

As can be seen from the table, there is a clear space/time tradeoff between displays and RTs (with STs falling somewhere in between): RTs tie up at most two registers to access both local and non-local variables; displays incur only a single level of indirection when accessing non-local variables. However, by using additional registers to hold the addresses of non-local variables, the level of indirection to access non-local variables can be reduced to one for RTs and STs. (These addresses can also be cached as they are read-only.)

While the (minimal) register consumption of RTs is small, their overall storage costs will depend of the number of non-local variables referenced within a task. Although more experience with actual parallel programs is necessary, studies of the reference patterns of programs written in sequential languages suggest that the number of non-local references made by tasks could be small (see for example, [Magnusson 1982]).

A clear benefit of using RTs is that optimizations wherein accept statements are executed by the calling task are facilitated: the environment of an accept statement can be captured simply by adding the MRS of the accept statement to the MRS of a calling task. While a display can also be used to capture the environment of an accept statement, the display of the accept statement may include scopes that are not in the local display of the calling task. Thus, when the entry is called the local display of the calling task would have to be swapped with the display of the accept statement.

In general, however, RTs are not very amenable to compiler detected optimizations, since every variable in the RT is used (when it is passed to an inner task if nowhere else). Whereas, an argument in favor of using displays is that we tap into a large body of results on their efficient implementation.

As none of the schemes is categorically better than the others for resolving the non-local references of tasks, the appropriate scheme for a given environment will depend upon what programming paradigms are preferred by its programmers. For the favored tasking idiom of highly parallel machines, an array of tasks operating on a shared matrix, RTs seem particularly apt: All of the tasks share a RT in which the matrix will occupy a single entry. Moreover, this overhead is independent of the (local) nesting level of the array of tasks and of the matrix. Furthermore, as MRSs are needed to calculate SSs, which in turn are integral to an efficient mapping of Ada variables onto the hierarchy of memories typical of this class of machines, there is no extra compile-time penalty for using RTs. Thus, we are optimistic that the storage management scheme we have presented, taken together with the pragmas that will be supported by our implementation of Ada/Ed on the Ultracomputer and RP3, constitute a step toward enabling Ada programs to effectively harness the power of these highly parallel machines.

References

Buroff 1977. S. J. Buroff, "Algol 68 implementation techniques," Ph.D. Thesis, Illinois Institute of Technology (1977).

DoD 1979. United States Department of Defense, "Preliminary Ada Reference Manual," *SIGPLAN Notices* **16** (June, 1979).

DoD 1983. United States Department of Defense, *Reference Manual for the Ada programming Language, ANSI/MIL-STD-1915*, United States Government (January, 1983).

Dewar *et al.* 1980. R. B. K. Dewar, G. A. Fisher Jr., E. Schonberg, R. Froehlich, S. Bryant, C. F. Goss, and M. G. Burke, "The NYU Ada translator and interpretter," *The Proceedings of the Compsac'80 conference, IEEE* (October, 1980).

Edler *et al.* 1987. J. Edler, J. Lipkis, and E. Schonberg, "Issues in the parallel runtime environment," *Private Communication* (December 15, 1987).

Flynn *et al.* 1987. S. Flynn, E. Schonberg, and E. Schonberg, "The efficient termination of Ada tasks in a multiprocessor environment," *Ada LETTERS* **VII**, pp. 55-76 (November, December 1987).

Gottlieb 1987. A. Gottlieb, "An overview of the NYU ultracomputer project," in *Experimental Computing Architectures*, ed. J. J. Dongarra, North Holland (1987).

Hummel 1988. S. F. Hummel, "SMARTS — Shared-memory Multiprocessor Ada Run Time Supervisor," Ph.D. Thesis, Courant Institute, NYU (1988).

Kruchten and Schonberg 1984. P. Kruchten and E. Schonberg, "The Ada/Ed system: a large-scale experiment in software prototyping using SETL," *Technology and Science of Information* **3**, pp. 175-181 (1984).

Kruchten 1985. P. Kruchten, "The Ada Machine," Ada/Ed Documentation (1985).

Magnusson 1982. K. Magnusson, "Identifier references in Simula 67 programs," *Simula Newsletter* **10** (2) (1982).

McAuliffe 1986. K. McAuliffe, "Analysis of cache memories in highly parallel systems," Ph.D. Thesis, Courant Institute, NYU (1986).

Pfister *et al.* 1987. G. F. Pfister, W. C. Brantley, D. A. George, S. L. Harvey, W. J. Kleinfelder, K. P. McAuliffe, E. A. Melton, V. A. Norton, and J. Weiss , "An introduction to IBM Research Parallel Processor Prototype (RP3)," in *Experimental Computing Architectures*, ed. J. J. Dongarra, North Holland (1987).

Rosen 1985. J. P. Rosen, "The Ada Task Management Sytem," Ada/Ed Documentation (1985).

Schonberg and Schonberg 1985. E. Schonberg and E. Schonberg, "Highly parallel Ada — Ada on an ultracomputer," pp. 58-71 in *Ada in use — Proceedings of the Ada International Conference*, ed. J. G. P. Barnes and G. A. Fisher, Cambridge University Press (14-16 May, 1985), pp. 58-71.

Schwartz *et al.* 1986. J. T. Schwartz, R. B. K. Dewar, E. Dubinsky, and E. Schonberg, *Programming with sets: an introduction to SETL*, Springer-Verlag, New York (1986).

Shulman 1987. N. V. Shulman, "The semantics of shared variables in parallel programming languages," Ph.D. Thesis, Courant Institute, NYU (1987).

Appendix — An Example of the Calculation of Modified Relay Sets and Shared Sets

```
procedure main is -- MRS_main = { }, 1SS_main = {i, share, ao1, ao2, ao3, ao4, ao5, inc_j, j}
     type at is access integer;
     i, j : integer := 0;
     pragma shared(j);
     ao1 : at;
     ao2, ao3 : at := new integer;
     task t1, t2;
     procedure share(ao4 : in at, ao5 : out at) is -- MRS_share = {i, ao1, ao2}
          procedure inc_i is -- MRS_inc_i = {i}
          begin -- inc_i
               i := i + 1;
          end inc_i;
     begin -- share
          ao1 := ao4;   -- The object that ao4 designates is available to main.
          ao5 := ao2;   -- The object that ao2 designates is available through ao5.
          inc_i;
     end share;
     procedure inc_j is -- MRS_inc_j = {j}
     begin -- inc_j
          j := j + 1;
     end inc_j;
     task body t1 is -- MRS_t1 = {share, i , ao1, ao2 }, SS_t1 = {ao6, ao7, ao8}
          ao6, ao7 : at := new integer;
          ao8 : at;
     begin -- t1
          share(ao6, ao8);
     end t1;
     task body t2 is -- MRS_t2 = {inc_j, j}, SS_t2 = {}
          task t3 is -- MRS_t3 = {inc_j, j}, SS_t3 = {}
          begin -- t3
               inc_j;
          end t3;
     begin -- t2
          inc_j;
     end t2;
begin -- main
     inc_j;
end main;
```

Part 6 Practical Experiences

DESIGNING A FLIGHT CONTROL PROGRAM WITH ADA

Yoram Kol,

MBT, Israel Aircraft Industries, Yahud 56100, Israel

ABSTRACT

When Digital Flight Control (DFC) is implemented in Ada we expect a certain characteristic topology to evolve. An Ada design of a real time flight control program for a missile which reveals such a topology is described in this paper. Without using detailed requirements, a stepwise system decomposition is made, including a System Block Diagram, a Data Flow Chart and a Control Chart. Centralised scheduling is compared with a distributed control and a solution is suggested which takes into account a real time problem of CPU time constraint. Using the terms "point" and "floating" activities serves to combine a thread of serial activities alongside concurrent activities. Finally, a generic package of numeric differential equations is described, allowing the programmer to generate his filters with Laplace Transform (S Domain) parameters, as they are usually defined to him by the control engineer.

1.   INTRODUCTION

There have been some reports on experimental DFC in Ada [2], [3]. Some of the difficulties encountered may be attributed to the fact that the software engineers were not yet fully thinking Ada; however, the main difficulties were due to the real time constraints of the CPUs and Ada compilers in the past.

This paper describes a design of a real time DFC program for a missile which is not mission critical; therefore, no redundancy management or multiprocessing was introduced, greatly simplifying the issue. A new microprocessor and an effective crosscompiler, developed for real time applications [4] were adopted.
    For these reasons the Ada constructs were applied with more freedom perhaps than before, in a way evolved from an object oriented design [5].
It is desirable to implement genuine system processes as active packages. However since context switching between tasks involves extra CPU time, of which we are short, we avoid any unnecessary use of tasks and keep some packages passive.

Since filters constitute a major part of a DFC program, effective development with high reliability may be accomplished by reusability of filters through a generic library.

2.   DESCRIPTION OF THE PROBLEM SPACE

Our Flight Control System (Fig. 1) is divided into two main parts:
a. The missile
b. The Flight Control Computer (FCC) - a 32-bit CPU with an arithmetic floating point unit.
The missile consists of the following subsystems:
a. **THE SEEKER** - comprised of a sensor attached to two gimbals in a way that it can move in elevation and azimuth and search a target. The seeker accepts two types of commands:
    1. SEEKER MODE which determines whether the seeker is in inertial state or is submitted to the FCC commands.
    2. GIMBALS COMMAND to move the gimbals in elevation and azimuth. The seeker produces the GIMBALS POSITION and the TARGET ERROR which is the target position relative to the seeker line of sight.

b. The FLAPS determine the attitude of the missile. They are controlled by the FCC through FLAPS COMMANDS.

c. The RATE GYRO is a sensor which measures the ROLL RATE of the missile.

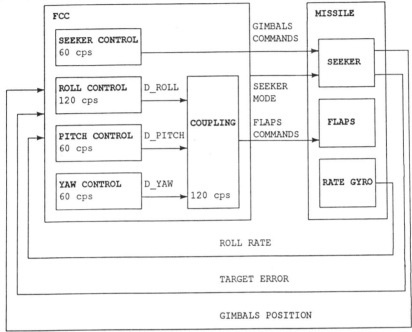

Fig. 1. Block Diagram Description of a Flight Control System

The FCC consists of the following main functions:

a. SEEKER CONTROL which controls the gimbals position through GIMBAL COMMANDS and SEEKER MODE.

b. The ROLL, PITCH and YAW CONTROL, produce the attitude command of the missile in the three spatial axes.

c. The COUPLING function transforms the three axis commands into four FLAP COMMANDS.

A rate of execution, in cycles per second (cps), is defined for each of these functions (Fig. 1).

3.   **BRIEF SYSTEM DECOMPOSITIONS**
       There are two external interrupts that "run" the FCC:
a. A Timer Interrupt at a rate of 120 cps.
b. A Pulse Interrupt from the SEEKER at rate of about 20 cps that informs the FCC of new TARGET ERROR data.

From the system description we distinguish the following DFC objects: SEEKER, PITCH and YAW CONTROL, executed at a rate of 60 cps; ROLL CONTROL and COUPLING, executed at a rate of 120 cps.

At this point we define a LOGIC CONTROL object, which determines the state of the system and leaves the other objects to execute only number crunching functions defined for each particular state.

We complete the system decomposition, by means of a Data - Flow Chart (Fig. 2); the pictorial symbols convention was adopted from Buhr [1]. A box denotes an external device.

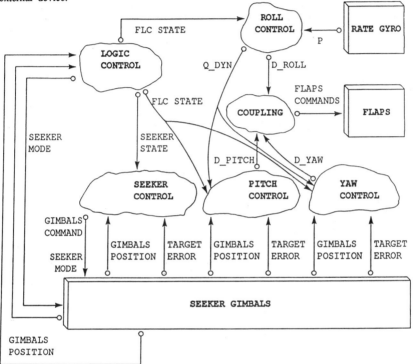

Fig. 2.   Data Flow Chart

4.   SYSTEM TOP LEVEL DESIGN

Let us first consider a centralised scheduling method and then compare it with a distributed activation method.

The centralized scheduling is done by the EXECUTIVE task, which is called by task FAST and then calls the entries of the other tasks at their particular rates according to a certain schedule (Example 3).

The external timer interrupt is first handled by the task FAST which uses the pragma INTERRUPT_HANDLER of the compiler [4]. It serves two purposes:
  a. To ensure that external timer interrupt is not missed.
  b. To allow for occasional minor frame time overflow.

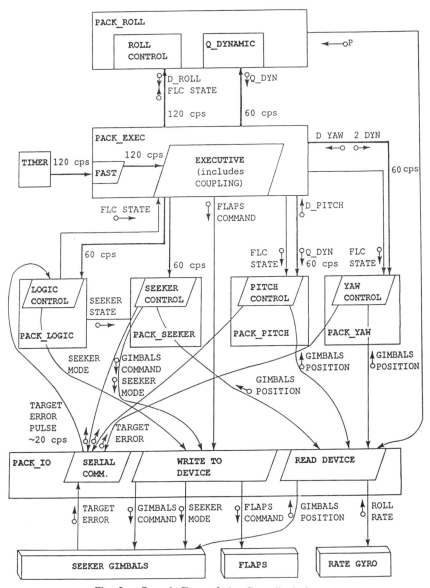

Fig. 3.   Control Chart of the Centralised Control

If a timer interrupt appears while the execution of a minor cycle is not yet completed, the external call is queued up until the EXECUTIVE is ready to accept a new MINOR CYCLE call [3].

The LOGIC, SEEKER, PITCH and YAW objects are implemented as active packages whose main tasks are called by the EXECUTIVE, which therefore turns into a data communication junction (example 4 - task body PITCH_CONTROL).

The COUPLING object is of a 120-cps rate and gets its data from the three axis control units. It is therefore nested as a procedure within the EXECUTIVE.

The ROLL CONTROL object is also of a 120-cps rate and it consists of many packages, procedures and data structures. It is therefore defined as a passive package with its main procedures being called directly by the EXECUTIVE.

The tasks SEEKER, PITCH, YAW and LOGIC CONTROL are called by the EXECUTIVE at a 60 cps rate. The parts which are executed upon a rendezvous are named "point" and are performed serially. These tasks also have other parts which are named "floating" and are performed concurrently (section 6).

Since the LOGIC CONTROL task is not rate-critical, it is called conditionally by the EXECUTIVE and thus gives the system a further adaptivity to reduce CPU load when it gets too high.

To get the freshest input to the various routines and to supply output commands without delay, every unit may execute its own IO but only through the PACK_IO utilities, which includes tasks to read channels write to channels and handling serial communication.

Following is a control chart (with Buhrs' pictorial symbols). A heavier control line denotes routine scheduling calls.

5.   A DISTRIBUTED SCHEME - VS - A CENTRALISED SCHEDULING
In a distributed control scheme the tasks are the same as in the centralised scheduling but the scheme of control is different. The timer serves the tasks SEEKER, ROLL, PITCH, YAW and LOGIC CONTROL through a "delay (NEXT_TIME-CLOCK)" instruction at the top of their loop. When each one of them is ready to transmit its data, it initiates an entry call to the COUPLER - the task that substitutes for the EXECUTIVE.

Following are some aspects of the two control schemes:

- In the centralized scheduling there is only one external Real Time Interrupt, which calls one entry. No other method of timing is necessary. In the distributed control the DELAY construct and the CLOCK construct of package CALENDAR are used whose impact on the CPU load, memory size and program complexity are as yet unknown.

- The centralized scheduling synchronisation is simpler to understand and monitor and is expected to debug better on the target system.

- A distributed system allows the use of independent execution rates for the different tasks. In this respect it may also be more flexible for future changes; however, no design configuration may be regarded as "universal".

In conclusion, it seems more prudent to adopt the centralised scheduling option.

6.   "FLOATING" AND "POINT" TASK ACTIVITIES

In his work on a hard real time executive V. Gagni [6] defines two types of (non Ada) tasks: a point task and a floating task.

In an Ada context we define a point activity as an activity that has to be completed before its caller can proceed. Obviously it is the part that is executed upon a rendezvous. As mentioned before, the point activities are scheduled by the EXECUTIVE.

The floating activities are executed after the rendezvous has been completed and are concluded by the next time a rendezvous takes place. They are not known to the EXECUTIVE and may be used in two ways:

a. Preparing calculations that do not have to be completed between input and output, for the next cycle, in difference equations ("filters") as in the following example (1):

```
Example 1: To solve the digital difference equation

  Y0 = C0*X0 + C1*X1 + C2*X2 + D1*Y1 + D2*Y2

two procedures are used:

a. IMMEDIATE : Y0: = C0*X0 + S

b. PREPARE:      S: = C1*X1 + C2*X2 + D1*Y1 + D2*Y2
```

b. Preparing less time critical parameters for the axis control functions. Example 2 demonstrates further the use of the point and floating parts.

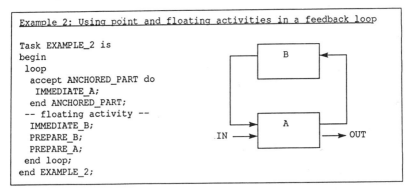

```
Example 2: Using point and floating activities in a feedback loop

Task EXAMPLE_2 is
begin
 loop
  accept ANCHORED_PART do
   IMMEDIATE_A;
  end ANCHORED_PART;
  -- floating activity --
   IMMEDIATE_B;
   PREPARE_B;
   PREPARE_A;
  end loop;
end EXAMPLE_2;
```

The point and the floating activities marked by comments in examples 3, 4.

Example 3: Package PACK EXEC

```
package body PACK_EXEC is
   :
 test body FAST is
 begin
  loop
   accept INTERRUPT
   EXECUTIVE.MINOR_CYCLE
  end loop;
 end FAST;
   :
 task body EXECUTIVE is
 begin
  loop
   select
    accept MINOR_CYCLE do--Called by FAST INTERRUPT at 120 cps
--------- point activity ---
     COUNT_TIME;                                 -- 120 cps
    end;
-------- floating activity ----
    IMMEDIATE_ROLL(FLC_ST,D_ROLL);               -- 120 cps
    if EVEN_CYCLE
     Q_DYNAMIC(Q-DYN);                           --  60 cps
     PITCH_CONTROL.CYCLE(Q_DYN, D_PITCH);        --  60 cps
     YAW_CONTROL.CYCLE(Q_DYN, D_YAW);            --  60 cps
     COUPLING;                                   -- 120 cps
    else        -- if not EVEN_CYCLE
     COUPLING;                                   -- 120 cps
     SEEKER_CONTROL.CYCLE;                       --  60 cps
     select
      LOGIC_CONTROL.CYCLE(TIME_COUNTER);--60 cps conditional
     else
      null;
     end select;
    end if; -- EVEN_CYCLE
    EVEN_CYCLE : = not EVEN_CYCLE
    PREPARE_ROLL                                 -- 120 cps
   or
    :
   end select;
  end loop;
 end EXECUTIVE;
   :
end PACK_EXEC;
```

```
Example 4: task body PITCH CONTROL

task body PITCH_CONTROL is
begin
loop
 select
          :
 or
  accept CYCLE (Q_DYN: in float; DEL_PITCH: out float) do
-------- point activity ---
          :
   case FLC_STATE is
   when launch =>
    IMMEDIATE_APA;
   when pursuit =>
          :
   end case; -- FLC_STATE
          :
  end CYCLE;
 -- floating activity --
  case FLC_STATE is
  when launch =>
   PREPARE_APA;
  when pursuit =>
          :
  end case; --FLC_STATE
 end select;
 end loop;
          :
end PITCH_CONTROL;
```

7.   THE TUSTIN LIBRARY

The GENERIC construct is very useful since it allows reusability of filters that are so frequent in DFC.

Control engineers usually design a flight control system in the S domain. Although there are methods to design discrete systems in the Z domain, they are not as easy. We also have to bear in mind that DFC systems are hybrid.

Later the prgrammer transforms the S domain parameters into discrete parameters using the Tustin transformation, a useful method because of its relative simplicity and fidelity [7]. Traditionally it is done with the help of a special interactive tool. Then manual coding including comments to identify the filter in the S Domain is done, followed by tests. Major changes in filter definitions are not rare even at the stage of flight tests. Therefore it is helpful if the filters are programmed directly in the S domain, which is what PACK_TUSTIN enables us to do.

For example, a generic filter of second order consists of a package which includes procedures IMMEDIATE, PREPARE and INITIALIZE.

The IMMEDIATE procedure is a fast response procedure designed to accomplish minimum time delay between input and output. It is often called by the point activity of a task.
However, a second order filter cannot work without the PREPARE procedure, which prepares the filter for the next cycle. The PREPARE procedure is usually executed at the floating part of the task.

If IMMEDIATE is called without first preparing the filter, a TUSTIN_ERROR exception is raised. The same thing would happen if PREPARE is called without first executing the IMMEDIATE procedure. This may help discover either a programming error regarding a particular filter, or a malfunctioning in the control scheme.

The INITIALIZE procedure intialises values of the state variables according to a selected steady state. If the input and output of a filter are of the same units, all the state variables get the same value, which is specified as a desired output value (example 6). If they are of different units, as in the case of INTEGRATOR then two initial parameters are defined.
A typical use of a filter is demonstrated in the folllowing example (5):

```
Example 5: Typical use of PACK TUSTIN

with PACK_TUSTIN; use PACK_TUSTIN;
package body EXAMPLE_5 is
 package A is new FILTER_G_ZW (G=>2.0,  Z=> 0.6, Wd=>100.0
          Ws=>120.0, UPPER_LIMIT=>1.5, LOWER_LIMIT=>-1.5)
  task body TIME_RESPONSE is
  begin
   loop
    accept ANCHORED_PART do
 --- point activity -----
     A. IMMEDIATE (X_IN, Y_OUT)
    end ANCHORED_PART; -- entry
 --- floating activity --
    A. PREPARE;
   end loop;
  end TIME_RESPONSE; --task
end EXAMPLE_5;     --package body
```

```
Example 6: A Generic Filter from PACK TUSTIN

 package PACK_TUSTIN is
  TUSTIN_ERROR: exception;
        :
  -- filter G/ (Z,WD) = G/(1+S*Z/WD+S**2/WD**2) --
  generic
  G : in float : = 1.0;
  Z : in float;
  Wd in float;
  Ws in float;
  UPPER_LIMIT : in float : = 1.0;
  LOWER_LIMIT : in float : = -1.0;
  package FILTER_G_ZW is
     procedure IMMEDIATE (XIN: IN FLOAT; YOUT: OUT FLOAT);
     procedure PREPARE;
     procedure INITIALIZE(Y_INIT: IN FLOAT: =0.0);
  end FILTER_G_ZW;
        :
 end PACK_TUSTIN;
```

8.   SUMMARY

A missile DFC program design based on a centralized scheduling task is represented. It executes the point activities of the control tasks sequentially, while concurrency takes place by means of the floating activities.

A generic filters library enables the programmer to implement a digital filter using S domain parameters. The filters are designed to give a minimum time delay between their input and output, by means of the IMMEDIATE and PREPARE procedures.

ACKNOWLEGEMENT

Much gratitude to my wife Sara for the editing and all her support, and to my colleagues - Braude E., Gafni V., Kadary V., Rotman Y. and Weinkleir R. for their helpful advice.

REFERENCES

[1]   R.J.A Buhr, System Design with ADA.

[2]   T.G. Lahn, S.E. Minear, J. Murray of Honeywell Military Avionics Div., Some view on the use of Ada for Digital Flight Control Systems, Proceeding of the IEEE/AIAAA 7th Digital Avionics Systems Conference, Oct. 1986 Forth Worth, TX, USA, pp 455-460.

[3]   Keith D. Pratt and Royl. Sherrill of Boeing Military Airplane Company at Seatle, Wash., Experience with development of a real Time Multiprocessor Executive in Ada, Proceedings of the IEEE 1985 National Aerospace and Electronics Conference NAECON, Dayton, Ohio, U.S.A, pp 672-678.

[4]   DDC-I Ada Compiler System User's Guide for DACS-80386, DDC International A/S Lundtoftevej 1c, DK-2800 Lyngby Denmark.

[5]   G. Booch, Object Oriented Development, IEEE Transactions on Software Engineering, Feb. 1986, Vol. SE-12.

[6]   Vered Gafni, MBT/IAI Israel., A Model for a Hard Real Time System Executive, Proceedings of the 15th IFAC/IFIP Workshop on Real Time Programming, May 1988, Valencia, Spain.

[7]   Katz Paul, Digital Control Using Microprocessors, Prentice Hall Int. Inc., 1981.

THE USE OF JSD AND ADA ON THE SUBMARINE COMMAND SYSTEM PROJECT

John R. Lawton
SUCCESSOR Systems, CAP Scientific Ltd., LONDON.

INTRODUCTION

CAP Scientific are sub-contracted to develop and supply the software for a new Command System for a variety of Royal Navy submarine classes. The system, known as the Submarine Command System (SMCS), is a complex embedded system with a large software content.

SMCS is believed to be the largest Ada project for an embedded system (at this stage of development) in Europe, and CAP Scientific have estimated that over two hundred man-years of effort will be required to develop the software. This development is being undertaken using the Jackson System Development (JSD) method, with Ada and Occam being the implementation languages.

JSD is a method that is gaining in popularity with software developers as a valuable means of rigorously specifying the functional behaviour of real-time software systems. One of its major strengths is the relatively small set of well-defined constructs that are used in a specification. The formal semantics of these constructs allow simple transformations to be applied to a JSD specification to produce software designs for which source code can be automatically generated.

Because most of the software for SMCS will be specified using JSD and implemented in Ada, CAP Scientific have had to derive a development strategy that successfully integrates the two different representations. In particular, we have been keen to exploit the possibility of defining the specification language and the transformation from specification to implementation, in a sufficiently precise form such that automatic translation from a software specification into Ada source code becomes a feasible option.

This paper describes a strategy for the use of Ada as an integral part of a software specification language and the subsequent transformation of such specifications into Ada source code. The

experiences of the SMCS development team in applying this strategy are
also outlined. It should be noted that the ideas described in this paper
are currently in use and deliverable binary code is being produced.
However, the approach is undergoing refinement as we gain more experience
of its use.

THE SUBMARINE COMMAND SYSTEM

The main functions of SMCS are to compile an accurate 'tactical
picture' for presentation to the submarine command team, and to assist in
tactical weapon deployment. SMCS is required to be tolerant to hardware
failures, to respond in real-time to a wide range of external stimulii,
and to be capable of adapting easily to changes in operational
requirements.

The SMCS hardware architecture is based on the concept of
clusters of loosely coupled micro-processors, distributed around a Local
Area Network. Industry standard 32-bit micro-processors are used
throughout, each with a substantial amount of local RAM. A number of
specially designed MMI consoles provide a user-friendly interface to the
system for the operators. In order to provide resilience to single points
of failure, all of the key hardware components are duplicated.

The software for SMCS is divided into three main categories,
Application Software, Support Software and Foundation Software.

Application Software is intended to meet most of the user
required functionality of SMCS, assuming that the hardware environment is
an 'ideal' machine. In this way, the Application Software takes no account
of any peculiarities of the underlying hardware architecture; in
particular, the Application Software ignores issues related to SMCS
hardware failure.

The Support Software roughly corresponds to a distributed
operating system and it is this software that provides a 'clean'
environment in which the Application Software can execute. Aspects such as
fault tolerance, database distribution and inter-processor communications
are provided as part of the Support Software.

The Foundation Software comprises a set of low-level, machine
specific, functions such as device drivers and the Ada Run-time Support
Environment.

This paper discusses only the approach adopted on SMCS for the
development of Application Software that is to be implemented in Ada.

THE JACKSON SYSTEM DEVELOPMENT METHOD

A full description of JSD is beyond the scope of this paper, this section provides just a brief overview. Jackson (1983) and Cameron (1986) provide a more comprehensive description of JSD.

A fundamental concept underpinning JSD is the strict division of the development life-cycle into two major phases - specification and implementation. In the specification phase a rigorous executable specification is produced. In the implementation phase the specification is transformed into an efficient implementation.

Specification

The specification phase is split into two sub-phases - the modelling phase and the network phase.

In the modelling phase a number of model processes are defined that model, or simulate, the dynamic behaviour of entities in the subject matter of the system, in terms of the actions that they perform or suffer over time. In the network phase, a network of communicating sequential processes is composed by connecting function processes to the model.

Figure 1 gives a simple example of a model process. Note that structure chart notation, as described by Jackson (1975), is used to represent the internal sequence, iteration and selection structure of the process. The example is not taken directly from SMCS, but is representative of the type of structure, and the classes of actions (events), that would be modelled in a real-time system.

Figure 1   A Simple Model Process

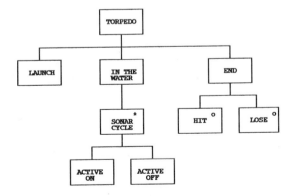

The product of the specification phase is a rigorously defined network of communicating sequential processes. Each process manages its own set of private data, called its 'state vector'. Only the 'owning' process has update access to its state vector. The use of parallel processes as a specification notation encourages the developer to naturally represent the parallelism in the subject matter, for example hundreds of tracks in a command system, or millions of accounts in an on-line banking system.

Figure 2 gives an example of a simple network of processes. In this example, TORPEDO is a model process, and ACTIVE_SONAR and PASSIVE_SONAR are function processes. The three processes communicate via simple FIFO data streams.

Figure 2   A Simple Network of Processes

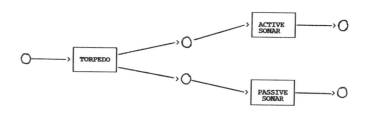

Thus a typical JSD specification is highly parallel, containing perhaps hundreds of process types, with thousands of process instances, all of which exist in parallel and which communicate with each other via well-defined connections.

It is worth noting that a completed JSD specification provides a level of detail that can be equated to the level of detail that might be found in what is traditionally termed 'detailed design'. However, the detail that is defined at this stage is concerned only with the functional behaviour of the system, no implementation detail is permitted.

Implementation

The specification could in theory be directly executed if a 'JSD Specification Engine' were available. Direct execution using the same number of real processors as are present in the specification, or virtual processors (for example Ada tasks), is usually impractical or would result in a system that would be very slow.

The implementation phase in JSD makes use of a number of simple, automatable, transformations that can be used to turn the specification into an efficient implementation. The main transformations are **inversion** and **state vector separation**, which significantly reduce the parallelism present in the specification, and hence reduce the number of real or virtual processors needed for execution. As an example of the power of these transformations, consider the fact that a specification defining the existence of thousands of parallel processes can usually be transformed to run as a single Ada task.

From this brief introduction it should be apparent that JSD is very different to many of the other well known methods. Some of the major differences being that it is a true <u>method</u> with a number of well defined steps, it really does separate specification from implementation, it is not 'top-down', and it allows a developer to specify entity descriptions which capture <u>behaviour</u> and <u>state</u> information in a coherent and co-ordinated manner. In some respects, JSD is similar to Object-Oriented Design and this similarity is explored in Birchenough (1988).

THE USE OF ADA IN SMCS SPECIFICATIONS

To permit SMCS specifications to be precise and unambiguous, a specification language has been derived to complement both the JSD method and the Ada programming language. This specification language includes a subset of Ada. The principal use of Ada within the specification language is as a notation for :

i)   Primitive operations as part of process structures. Note that the use of JSD prescribes that control structures are restricted to the 'structured' constructs of sequence, selection and iteration, and tools are used to allow process internals to be developed as tree structures. 'Fragments' of Ada code, (usually simple assignment statements, or operations on abstract data types), are attached to specific leaves of the tree structures to indicate **when** the operations are to be performed.

ii)   Data items. Ada's extensive type definition facilities are used to rigorously define the data attributes of state vectors and data stream records. The ability to specify abstract types via packages specifications is particularly useful at this stage.

Figure 3 gives an example of the specification language for the
internals of a single process instance. The internal structure
of the process is defined by the use of a structure chart,
while operations on data items (and communication with other
processes) are defined through the use of 'fragments' of Ada
code.

Figure 3   The Use of Ada in Process Specifications

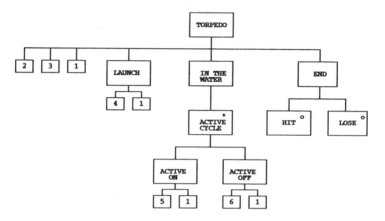

OPERATIONS

1. READ (IN_RECORD);

2. TOTAL_ACTIVE_TIME := 0;

3. IN_THE_WATER := FALSE;

4. IN_THE_WATER := TRUE;
    TIME_OF_DISCHARGE := IN_RECORD.TIME;

5. WRITE (ACTIVE_SONAR, ON_RECORD);
    WRITE (PASSIVE_SONAR, OFF_RECORD);
    TIME_GOING_ACTIVE := IN_RECORD.TIME;

6. WRITE (ACTIVE_SONAR, OFF_RECORD);
    WRITE (PASSIVE_SONAR, ON_RECORD);
    ACTIVE_TIME := IN_RECORD.TIME - TIME_GOING_ACTIVE;
    TOTAL_ACTIVE_TIME := TOTAL_ACTIVE_TIME + ACTIVE_TIME;

Generally, the specifiers use 'fragments' of Ada code, (linear
code sequences), for primitive operations as a means to define,
unambiguously, the functional behaviour of the system. Ada adds a degree
of rigour to a JSD specification that might otherwise have been specified

in English or some form of pseudo-code. The resultant specification can be (and is) truly 'executable', and is more amenable to automatic implementation transformations.

THE USE OF ADA IN SMCS IMPLEMENTATIONS

The SMCS development team have been somewhat cautious in their approach to the use of the Ada language for the implementation of SMCS software. There are a number of perceived problems with Ada that we have tried to avoid.

In particular, the Ada tasking model has been criticised by many users, for example Burns et al (1987), because of its impact on run-time performance. For a Command and Control system that must respond rapidly in a deterministic fashion to real-world events, the use of unconstrained Ada tasking is not recommended and its use is controlled on SMCS. We also control the deployment of exceptions and dynamic allocation.

There are a number of different implementations schemes, such as those described in Cameron (1987), each with their advantages and disadvantages. The scheme adopted as the default implementation strategy for all SMCS Application Software is that described in Lawton & France (1988). This scheme is a derivative of Cameron (1987) and imposes a policy that alleviates many of the potential problems associated with Ada, ensuring for example that Ada tasking is used in a controlled way to remove most of the adverse effects of the Ada tasking model.

Each process type is transformed by inversion into a procedure. Inversion is a language independent implementation of the co-routine concept. Each read operation in the specification of the process is replaced by code that stores the current 'program counter' value (i.e. a label in the process text) and then performs an exit from the procedure. When the procedure is re-entered, a small prelude causes execution to resume at the position in the text just beyond where the procedure performed an exit on its previous invocation.

Using these techniques, a set of instances of a given process type can be transformed into one inverted procedure and a table of state vectors. Hence there is a direct transformation from the specification view of a collection of concurrent processes to the 'traditional' implementation view of a procedure updating a file or a database table.

By connecting the inverted processes together into a procedure calling hierarchy, and implementing each required thread of control as an Ada task, the parallelism present in the specification can be

significantly   reduced,   and   the   need   for   inefficient   inter-process
communication mechanisms (e.g. Ada Rendezvous) is eliminated. Use of these
simple transformations typically result in only a handful of Ada tasks per
processor.

SMCS EXPERIENCE OF JSD AND ADA

An   advantage of using Ada 'fragments'   in the specification is
the   increased   degree   of   rigour   that   this   brings   to   the behavioural
specification of the system. It is now possible to compile and execute the
specification   using a   simple   default transformation. This   allows early
verification   of   the   functional behaviour   of the   system, although   the
resulting   code   generated   for   such   prototype implementations   is often
somewhat inefficient.

The   customer has quickly come   to terms with the   JSD style of
specification.   It seems to provide a good   compromise between the need to
specify   behaviour in a 'formal'   and unambiguous fashion, while   offering
good user accessibility. In particular, the construction of a model of the
subject   matter of the system is very helpful in clearly defining abstract
concepts   from the user domain. For example, on SMCS, we were surprised to
learn   the   extent   to   which   different   users/developers   had   differing
interpretations   of the abstract concept of 'track'. The use of a rigorous
JSD   model   helped   to   define   the   'track'   concept   and   eliminated all
ambiguity.   The modelling phase has also helped to   free both the user and
the developer from the more traditional function-oriented approach, and to
concentrate on 'what the system is about', before considering the system's
functions.

It is worth noting that the full set of Ada constructs are used
on   SMCS.   We   have   not   restricted ourselves to only   a subset   of Ada.
Packages,   variant   records,   tasking, generics,   private data   types, and
Ada's   strong typing,   are   all heavily utilised.   What we have   achieved,
however,   is a clear definition of **when**   in the development lifecycle each
of the different Ada constructs is to be used.

Since   the only Ada used in the specification is in the form of
'fragments'   of sequential code, the   implementor can choose to   transform
the   specification   in   a   number   of   ways,   following   well-defined
transformation techniques to produce efficient code. This permits a number
of different 'designs' to be constructed from the same specification, with
each   design offering different performance   characteristics. For example,
two   or   more   processes in   the specification   can have   their structures

integrated into a common structure. This causes no problems since the Ada
'fragments' can be easily removed from their position in the original
process structure, and re-inserted into alternative structures, (JSD
'dismemberment'), although clearly it is important that the semantics of
the original structures are preserved in the transformation process.

Given the unambiguous nature of SMCS specifications, it is
relatively easy to develop Ada code generation tools to transform
specifications into efficient implementations. The SMCS project has
invested in just such a programme and we have already generated a
significant amount of deliverable Ada code by this method. Note however,
that the principal use for Ada code generation is for the construction of
compilation units and procedure calling hierarchies; the Ada 'fragments'
from the specification remain unchanged during implementation.

One view of the overall strategy is that the specification
determines what has to be done, in what order, while the implementation
introduces the necessary control structures to permit efficient
implementation. For example, while linear Ada code sequences are defined
during specification, the tasking arrangement and subprogram calling
hierarchy is defined during implementation. Swann (1988) has drawn a
comparison between the 'traditional' view of compilation of source code to
produce object code, with the SMCS view of transformation of a
specification to produce Ada source code.

The rigour of the specification has also improved the testing
of SMCS software. Testing of both individual processes and a set of
processes is facilitated since the generation of test harnesses and test
data is amenable to automation. We have developed a number of tools to
help with this activity. As might be expected, the use of tools has
largely eliminated certain classes of errors that are often introduced
between specification and Ada source code.

SUMMARY
CAP Scientific have evolved a practical approach to the use of
the Ada language in the embedded systems domain. The overall strategy for
development of SMCS software is to specify the required behaviour of the
software using the JSD method with a well-defined specification language,
largely ignoring implementation detail, and to implement in Ada, avoiding
known language problems. Certain Ada language constructs are used in the
specification to define what needs to be done in what order. Control
structures are added during implementation to allow the specification to

be realised on the available hardware.

Whilst the specification of the software may be highly parallel, the level of parallelism in the implementation can be controlled to meet the constraints imposed by the target hardware configuration. Multiple parallel processes in the specification can be reduced to a single Ada task if necessary.

The combined use of a number of techniques, including separation of specification from implementation, process inversion, state vector separation, automatic code generation and controlled use of certain features of Ada, allow all of the benefits of both JSD and of Ada to be realised.

ACKNOWLEDGEMENTS

The author wishes to acknowledge the contribution of a number of people to the ideas expressed in this paper, my thanks go to all the SMCS software development team, in particular to Norman France and Tim Swann, and to Alan Birchenough and Alan Moore of Michael Jackson Systems Ltd. CAP Scientific is a division of SEMA Group plc.

REFERENCES

Birchenough, A. & Cameron, J.R. (1988). JSD and Object-Oriented Design. Proceedings of 7th Ada (UK) Conference.

Burns, A., Lister, A.M. & Wellings, A.J. (1987). A Review of Ada Tasking. Springer-Verlag.

Cameron, J.R. (1983). JSP & JSD : The Jackson Approach to Software Development. IEEE Computer Society Press.

Cameron, J.R. (1986). An Overview of JSD. Trans on S.E. Feb. Vol SE-12, No 2,1986

Cameron, J.R. (1987). Mapping JSD Specifications into Ada. Proceedings of 6th Ada (UK) Conference.

Jackson, M.A. (1975). Principles of Program Design. Academic Press, Inc.

Jackson, M.A. (1983). System Development. Prentice Hall International.

Lawton, J.R. & France, N. (1988). The Transformation of JSD Specifications into Ada. Ada User, Jan-88.

Swann, T.G. (1988). Code Generation for a Large Command System. AGARD Working Group on Automatic Code Generation, Geilo, Norway.

CORADA: An Expert System Compiler into Ada.

D. Chouvet, D. Kersual, B. Lemaire, D. Meziere, J.Y. Quemeneur
SYSECA 315 Bureaux de la colline
92213 SAINT-CLOUD CEDEX FRANCE

ABSTRACT:
We present CORADA(Rule Optimizing Compiler into Ada), an expert system compiler, which enables one to transform an expert system into an Ada module easily integrable into an Ada application. The knowledge base language, used by CORADA, enables one to write rules with a powerful syntax similar to those of the expert system development tools available in a standard Lisp environment.
The strong typing aspect is the main feature of this language. Using typed declarations enables us to perform a type checking at the rule language level which guarantees a more reliable knowledge base. The rule declarative language is open: it is possible to reuse Ada user-defined types, functions and procedures. The expert-module and the Ada application will thus be strongly integrated.
In addition to the expert system development tool, a tool such as CORADA can be used to solve the problems of expert systems integration and portability.

1 INTRODUCTION

Expert systems are now reaching maturity, and their industrial use presents the two fold problems of integrating them into a software and/or hardware environment and of their communication within this environment. Expert systems appear as a means of increasing the efficency and intelligence of software systems. Thus, an expert system may be seen as an intelligent software component.

It is increasingly important to integrate expert systems into complex applications. To perform such an integration, the expert system must be available in a language which is not specific to artificial intelligence applications and which can be linked to the other application components. The expert system must also be able to run on a multipurpose target machine.

We describe in this paper the CORADA rule compiler which transforms an expert system into an Ada module integrable in any Ada application.

In addition, an expert system embedded into an application must exchange data with the application's environment. If the application is a real time system, the data on which the expert system is to work is produced in a random manner in relation to the expert system inference cycle. The communication process must therefore contain an asynchronous mechanism. The new piece of data produced by the application's environment during each inference cycle is stored in memory, and then asserted in the inference engine at the end of the cycle.

2 CIME PROJECT AND CORADA

The CORADA compiler, developed by a SYSECA team within the framework of a Strategic Artificial Intelligence Project supported by THOMSON-CSF company, tries to provide a solution to these problems. The expert system written in a production language is transformed by CORADA into a set of Ada procedures.

The CORADA compiler is a part of a bigger project: CIME (for Expert Module Integrator and Conceptor)(CHEHIRE et al. 89). The CIME tool provides a powerful and easy to use development environment designed for conception and fast prototyping, a knowledge base optimizer and a rule compiler into Ada (CORADA). CORADA produces an expert module which is integrable and can cooperate with the other application modules.

The CIME tool enables the user to design and validate a knowledge base, produce an integrable expert module and maintain the knowledge base. The CIME language in which a knowledge base is described has been specially designed to be independant of the development environment language (Lisp) and of the target environment language (Ada).

In this paper we only consider the CORADA compiler.

3 CORADA AND ADA

The CORADA compiler is written in Ada and generates Ada code. Ada has been chosen for the following reasons :

- Ada is a modular and portable language. This ensures the portability of the CORADA tool   and the generated Ada expert modules. Thus an expert system processed by CORADA can be run on any target computer with an Ada environment. The integration of an expert module into a larger application is simplified due to the modularity of the language.

- Ada tasking mechanism offers all the required primitives to implement the communication processing between the expert module and the other application's modules. This enables an expert system written in Ada to be embedded into a larger real-time system.

4 CORADA FUNCTIONALITIES
4.1 Production language

The production language, used to describe the knowledge base, has been designed to simplify the integration of an expert system into an Ada application. As any production language, it provides the statements to describe the rules. But it also provides statements to define the application types, functions and procedures which are used by the inference mechanism.

Thus, the expert system can easily infer on application's data and process them with specific application code inside the inference mechanism. Finally this production language is a typed language, such an approach is consistant whith the use of a strongly typed target language (Ada).

CORADA compiler supports those functionalities:

- Forward-chaining rules :
A rule can be fired, i.e the actions described in the right hand side of the rule are executed if all the conditions of the left hand side are satisfied.

- AND,NOT,EXISTS and JOIN operators
- OR,FORALL,CASE and SPLIT macrooperators :
These operators and macrooperators are used to describe the conditions of a rule. They may be nested and combined all together.

- Logical dependencies:
This functionnality implements a truth maintenance system for the assertion of facts. A fact which is logically supported by another fact is automatically retracted from the fact data base since its support vanishes.

- Synchronous and asynchronous communications with the outside environment:
The communication mechanism will be described in a forthcoming section.

- Symbolic debugging facilities at the rule level:
Each expert system executable image generated by CORADA contains a rule level symbolic debugger. It enables the user to inspect the fact data base and the agenda of the instantiated rules between two inference cycles, and to trace their modifications during the inference cycle.

The strong typing aspect is the main feature of this language. It supports the simple types: integer, float, fixed, boolean, character, string, symbol and enumerative types. It also supports composed types (record, constrained and unconstrained array) and access types.

Any fact of the knowledge data base must be typed, the two main parts of a fact are the relation name and the value which is itself implemented by a simple or composed type. A specific type must be defined for each relation, the user has only to specify the type implementing the value part.

These type declarations enable us to perform a type checking at the rule language level. The data typing ensures a more readable and reliable knowledge base.

Any type defined in this language has a corresponding Ada type declaration. Thus, it is easy to translate the rules into Ada code. The type declaration statement allows the user to specify that a type has to be implemented by a user-defined type in the Ada code.

Examples:
If the user's application contains those declarations in the package user_types:

type position array (1..3) of real;
type color is (orange, blue);
type mobile_structure is
  record   -
    name : symbol;
    color : color;
    position : position;
  end record;

A CORADA's expert system must contain those declarations in ordrer to use the mobile_structure type:
(defarray position (integer 1 3) :type real
            :exec (:name "user_type.position"))

(defenumerative color (orange blue)
        :exec (:name "user_type.color"))

(defrecord mobile_structure
        (^color :type color
         ^name :type symbol
         ^position :type position)
      :exec (:name "user_type.color"))

To define the relation mobile, whose value-type is mobile_structure, the user adds this declarative statement:
(defrelation mobile :type mobile_structure)

4.2 The left hand side language
The left hand side language is used to describe the patterns, which are the templates of the facts. The set of facts, which instantiate a rule, match the patterns of the rule declaration.

The first element of a pattern must be a relation name. The other elements define constraints on the data fact value. A pattern component can be of any previously declared type (simple type, record, array). Like in Ada, the language supports positional association or named association. In the named notation, the component name or the index value must be prefixed by an '^' character. You can use both notations in a pattern with the same restrictions as Ada.

Examples:
Constant declaration:
(defconst ?*security-distance* :type float = 10000.)

Rule declaration:
```
(defrule prevent-collision
    (mobile blue ?name-blue ( ?xb ?yb ?))      ;;; with positional association
    (mobile ^color orange                      ;;; with named association
            ^name ?name-orange
            ^position ( ^1 ?xo ^2 ?yo))
    (test (and ((abs (?xb - ?xo)) < ?*security-distance)
               ((abs (?yb - ?yo)) < ?*security-distance))))
    =>
    (assert (proximity-alarme ?name-orange ?name-blue))
)
```

The equality of the diagonal terms of a 3x3 matrix can be specified by the pattern:

(matrix ^(1 1) ?x ^(2 2) ?x ^(3 3) ?x)

4.3 The procedural language
The procedural language defines a set of control statements which are only available in the right hand side part of a rule (if, while, for).

A set of predefined operators is also defined to write expressions used on both lhs and rhs part of a rule (boolean, arithmetic operators).

This procedural language gives specific statements to handle facts in the rhs part: retract a fact from the data base, assert a new fact into the data base, modify a fact of the data base.

These fact handling facilities are also available outside the expert module, specific procedures are given to the user to be included in it's application code. For example, a module cooperating with the expert system module can add or supress facts.

Finally, two declarative statements enable one to define a function or a procedure which is implemented by an Ada user-written subroutine. Once declared, such a function or procedure can be used in any statement of the procedural language.

Example:
```
(deffunc distance
    (^position1 :type position ^position2 :type position )
    :out float
    :exec-name "package_3d.euclid_distance" )
```

This declaration defines a distance function, whith two arguments of type array of real, which is implemented by the Ada function euclid_distance defined inside the package Package_3d. This distance function can be used in the following rule:

Constant declaration:
(defconst ?*short-security-distance* :type float = 5000.)

Rule declaration:
(defrule prevent-collision-bis
    (mobile blue ?name-blue ?p1)   ;;; with positional association
    (mobile ^color orange   ;;; with named association
           ^name ?name-orange
           ^position ?p2)
    (test (distance ?p1 ?p2) < ?*security-distance*)
    =>
    (if (distance ?p1 ?p2) < ?*short-security-distance* then
        (assert (proximity-alarme ?name-orange ?name-blue))
    else
        (assert (proxinity-warning ?name-orange ?name-blue))
)
)

The rule declarative language is open: it is possible to reuse Ada user-defined types, functions and procedures. The expert-module and the Ada application will thus be strongly integrated.

4.4 Memory management

In real-time processing context , memory management is an important feature. In standard Lisp environment a garbage collection mechanism is available and implicitly used, but it can interrupt the execution of any process at any time without any process control. With such a garbage collection mechanism, it is impossible to guarantee a response time.

The search of efficency and of a high degree of portability led us to implement a specific memory manager. In fact, the Ada standard doesn't guarantee that the memory released by the primitive UNCHECKED_DEALLOCATION is reusable by the Ada application, this feature depends on Ada compiler implementation. Our memory manager is based on the principle of continuously counting references. This method requires an additional management during each assignment or freeing of pointers, but completely removes the need of a separate garbage collector process. So, the execution of the expert system produced by CORADA will not be interrupted by uncontrolled garbage collecting operations.

4.5 Compliling rules

Since the aim of the CORADA compiler is to generate fast code, while respecting the fonctionalities of the production language, a complete compilation of the rules into high-level procedural language has been adopted.

The recognized efficiency of the RETE algorithm led us to use it in the CORADA compiler(FORGY 82; ART 87). The compilation of the left-hand side of the rules is therefore based on this algorithm. It is carried out in two phases:
    - Transformation of rules into a RETE network.
    - Transformation of each node of the RETE network into an Ada procedure.

The compilation therefore translates all the rules into Ada code, and only the facts become data structures.

4.6 Communication between expert module and application's environment

Two communication mechanisms are available: a synchronous one and an asynchronous one.

Synchronous communication can be used for example to obtain information from an operator interface. During such a synchronous communication process the expert module execution is suspended. This mechanism is simply implemented by calling any function or procedure in the rhs or lhs part of a rule.

The asynchronous communication permits data transfer between the expert module and the application, control of the expert module by the application's environment and control of application's modules by the expert module. This communication mechanism is implemented with the Ada tasking mechanism.

The expert module is itself an Ada task (SE), the application is itself implemented by one or more tasks (TU-i). To communicate data and control between these tasks, specific mailbox tasks (BAL-SE, BAL-TU-i) are automatically written by CORADA according to specific declaration given by the user (i.e. the types of the data to be transferred, the source and the target tasks).

Figure 1: asynchronous communication mechanism

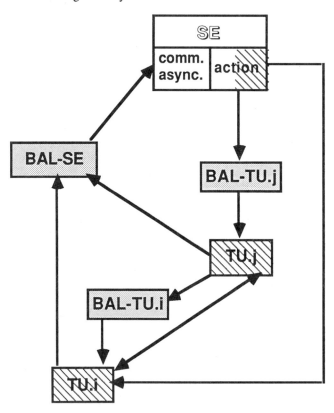

user code

CORADA generated code

Figure 2: Generation of an expert system executable image using CORADA

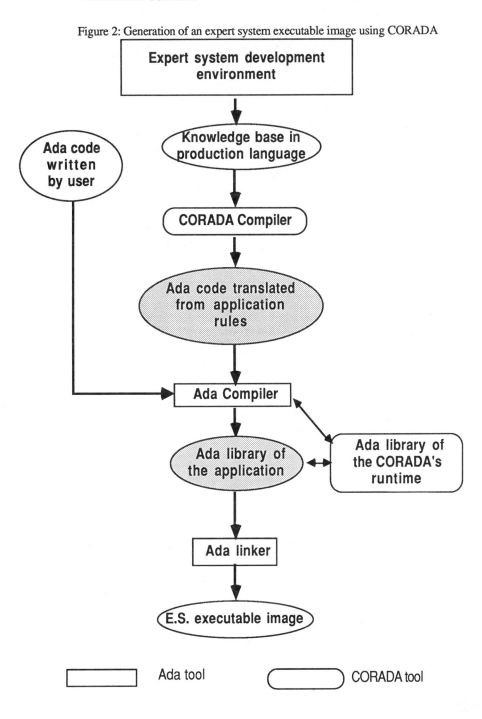

A mailbox task BAL-X is associated to the target task X. The mailbox task BAL-X receives asynchronously any information and control sent to the task X by any other task, it delivers these informations to the task X when X requests a rendez-vous with it.

At the end of each inference cycle, a communication procedure is executed which makes a rendez-vous with the BAL_SE task in order to allow the expert-system task SE to handle the informations asynchronously sent to it during the previous inference cycle.

The integration of the expert system in the application is flexible: the system expert task can be a slave of an application's task or it can be the main task. In any configuration some tasks can be the slaves of the expert system task, it is a way to implement a real-time control process monitored by an expert system in an Ada application.

4.7 Creation of an executable image

The mechanism of production of an executable image by CORADA is shown on figure 2. CORADA is mainly composed of two parts: the CORADA compiler and the CORADA runtime library.

Firstly, the CORADA compiler produces Ada source code corresponding to the rules. Secondly, this code is compiled in Ada library which inherits the CORADA runtime library and user application's specific units. Finally the application executable image can be linked.

5 CONCLUSION

Today, expert systems enter an industrial phase. Their operational use is becoming generalized. Applications in which an intelligent module exists and is integrated into a traditional data processing environment are starting to appear.

In addition to the expert system development tool, a tool such as CORADA can be used to solve the problems of expert systems integration and portability.

The use of a typed declarative language to describe the knowledge base ensures the reliability of the knowledge base and allows to directly infer on data types of the application. This and the possibility of calling user defined procedures and functions inside the rules make the expert system easier to integrate into an Ada application.

Once developed, the expert system is compiled into Ada and becomes an intelligent module, which can be embedded into an Ada application on a conventional computer. CORADA is a representative of a new type of software tool: integrable expert module generators.

References

ART 87   ART reference manual version 3.0, Inference Corp, 1987

CHEHIRE W., COMBASTEL A., CHOUVET D., QUEMENEUR J.Y., ZERR F.
CIME: une approche coherente pour developper, integrer et optimiser des modules experts dans un milieu operationnel.
(submited to 9th Int. Workshop Expert Systems & Their Applications AVIGNON 89)

FORGY C.L. RETE/ a fast algorithm for the many pattern / many object pattern match problem , Artificial Intelligence, vol 19, Sept 82

Observations on Portable Ada Systems

David Emery
The MITRE Corporation, MS A156, Bedford, MA, 01730 USA
(emery@mitre.org)

Karl Nyberg
Grebyn Corporation, P.O. Box 1144, Vienna, VA, 22183 USA
(karl@grebyn.com)

Abstract: This paper presents observations from the authors' experience porting large Ada software systems. Software is ported to reproduce its functionality on a new machine/operating system. The basic reason for porting software is that it is (supposed to be) much less expensive than developing new software with the same functionality. We present eight 'lessons learned' with examples from our experience. Our primary finding is that highly portable systems have a strong model of their underlying host environment. These models are adaptive and are well documented and tested. Finally, we provide recommendations to software designers and software project managers to make the software porting task easier, and thereby much more cost-effective.

What is Software Portability?

We define portability as the relative effort required to get a piece of software running on one host to run on another. A 'host' in this sense consists of at least the underlying computer architecture, the operating system, and the Ada compilation system (both compiler and runtime environment) on which the software is intended to execute (Kaindl 1988). Specifically, portability is a characteristic of software measured by the effort to implement the required functionality on a new host from scratch compared to the effort to rehost the software onto the new host. 'Perfectly portable' software would require no more than recompilation to get it running on the new host.

There is a strong, but not well-defined, relationship between software portability and software reuse. We make the following distinction: porting is moving an entire system to a new host environment while preserving functionality; reuse is using a system (or parts of a system) to achieve different functionality. Portable software and reusable software share many of the same characteristics; portable software is probably easier to reuse, and reusable software is probably easier to port.

It is our experience that there are two kinds of systems for which porting is difficult. The first kind requires small changes in many places. Such systems are hard to port because of the large number of units that must be identified and changed. The many disparate changes are an indication that these systems do not have well defined virtual layers, and that the separation of concerns between the various layers has not been identified. The second kind are those where there may be only one package containing all system dependencies, but porting this package requires substantial work. In some cases, it is all but impossible to port this package to the new host, and the entire port fails. This failure may be due to some necessary element that is not provided by the new system (e.g., a real–time clock with sufficient resolution) or because providing the necessary service is prohibitively expensive (in terms of effort to get the software to run, or in terms of execution costs).

Simply using Ada is not sufficient to produce portable systems. Ada has done much to reduce compiler dependencies, but Ada does not cover many host services required by software systems. Command line parameters, process creation (running another program) and in particular file naming are required by most software systems that we have ported. Ada's emphasis on modularity and its support for abstraction provide linguistic assistance for limiting host dependencies (Nissen & Wallis 1984). Ada does not mandate that the programmer use these features to support portability. As has been observed, "It is possible to write bad code in any language!"

Observations from Our Experience

1.   *Portable Software has a* **Strong** *Model of its Host*

The common feature of portable software is its understanding of the host environment. Systems that are easiest to port have a clear understanding of their existing host, possible future hosts, and their requirements for executing on a host. Specifically, portable software uses (either on purpose or by accident) a model of the host environment that both meets the needs of the software and that is feasible on a significant set of hosts (Bardin 1987). This may be achieved by determining a "weakest implementation" (Pappas 1985) or "lowest common denominator" (KIT (no date)) for existing and potential hosts. Developing a model of the underlying host is different from simply encapsulating system dependencies. The difference is one of consistency and completeness.

There are often implicit dependencies on the host that are not expressed in a SYSTEM_DEPENDENCIES package. One example is a program that needs to know if a certain file exists in the current directory, or in some other specified directory. If the only operation on files is OPEN, there is no explicit concept of "directory," or "current directory." This can create problems when porting to a system that does not support hierarchical directories, or whose syntax for naming directories is different. The SYSTEM_DEPENDENCIES package does not present a complete model of the system's requirements and assumptions about the underlying file system.

Developing these models is clearly a design activity. Software architects have to determine how to meet their requirements on a particular host system and also consider potential future hosts. The goal is to produce a model of the host environment that meets the requirements of the software, and that is easy and efficient to implement on the current host as well as on future hosts. Unfortunately, such design is still a bit of "black magic" (Lampson 1984).

We observed a "good" model when trying to port a programming environment from VMS to Unix. Most programming environments need to provide a mechanism for invoking a "foreign tool" whose command line parameters are not known when the environment is developed. In this programming environment, the designers came up with a model for tool parameters that consisted of two parts, 'parameters' and 'options.' This was apparently inspired by the syntax used on VMS, the initial development host. This model proved to be a very useful one, because it could be used in a variety of situations. It turned out that most programs can support this distinction, including Unix tools that get some of their information from Unix 'environment variables.'

When the environment was ported to Unix or a similar system that does not differentiate between command line parameters and options, this model is still valid. Most Unix tools support the distinction between parameters and options via a convention (options, called switches in Unix terms, are prefixed by the '–' character, but the Unix shell does not enforce this convention). Unix tools could be easily integrated into the programming environment's model. Constructing a 'command builder' that can interpret the programming environment's "call" and translate that into a operating system specific invocation is easy to do.

This model has the additional value that it can be used to support Unix 'environment variables', which are a special case of 'options.' The 'command builder' can interpret some options as a request to set a specific environment variable, rather than providing the value via an actual operating system command line element.

An example of a "bad" model occurred in the same programming environment. One of the services provided by the programming environment was intended to be a machine–independent (and hopefully portable) 'virtual' file naming syntax. This system was initially developed on top of VAX/VMS, but was expected to be portable to Unix and to MS–DOS.

VMS provides a primitive file version numbering system. In general, whenever a file is accessed on VMS, the file is not updated in place. Instead a new version of the file is created. Versions are numbered sequentially, starting with 1. By default, if no version number is specified, VMS retrieves the version of the file with the greatest version number (which is presumed to be the most recent version.) This facility is directly implemented by the operating system, and the syntax for naming versions is built into the file system.

The designers of the environment decided to adopt the VMS model for sequential versions of files. Their syntax for 'virtual file names' included an optional sequential version number. The file naming syntax was presented to the rest of the environment as a model of the host system's file system. The interpretation of these names was performed by system–dependent code.

Consider how this model can be implemented on a system that does not support version numbering and also has a fixed format for file names, such as MS–DOS. On VMS, the model can be implemented using a one–to–one mapping between 'virtual file name' versions and specific VMS version numbers of a file. On some versions of Unix, this could be implemented by adding the version number to the 'virtual file name' to produce a Unix file name. However, on MS–DOS, there must be a much more complex mapping function between the 'virtual file name,' and the version number of that name, to an MS–DOS file. This mapping must itself be maintained on disk, because it must be shared among various processes and survive system shutdowns. Such a system can be implemented on MS–DOS, but its performance is poor, because of the cost of interpreting the mappings followed by the cost to actually retrieve the appropriate MS–DOS file.

The designers presented a coherent model of the system, but the model was not efficiently implementable on one of its likely targets. Porting this software to MS–DOS required a substantial amount of work to implement the sequential version abstraction.

2.   *Portable Software Verifies its Models*

It is not sufficient for portable software to identify a model of its host. This model must be correctly implemented. Portable software should verify that its host interfaces are correctly implemented. Testing is one approach to this. Portable software should provide test suites for its models of the host. Ideally, these tests should be self–diagnosing, in that they should report success or failure. Test data for a model also helps to further document the expected behavior of the model. Another way to verify (and document) host interfaces is to use a formal specification system such as Anna (Rosenblum 1988, Luckham et al 1987).

The original release of the Ada binding to X Windows (Hyland & Nelson 1988) contained no test programs, not even a simple Hello_World program. It was difficult for us to determine if our port had been successful. When we developed a test program for the binding and it failed, we were unsure if this reflected a problem in the binding, in our test program, or in our X Windows library. The next release of the binding came with several sample programs. Although not a comprehensive test suite, these tests at least provided us with some confidence that the port was successful.

The Intermetrics Ada Integrated Environment (AIE) contains a significant number of tests for the important system interfaces (Intermetrics 1987). These tests would report failure, and in some cases the tests also reported the cause of the failure. One important set of tests is the stress tests, particularly those that test multiple access to the program library. File system dependencies often contain implicit assumptions about concurrent access to the same file by different programs, and the AIE stress test ensures that the software behaves correctly in the face of concurrent users.

3.   *Portable Software is Adaptive*

"Software, port thyself!" Some of the most portable systems have performed their host analysis to the point that they are almost self–porting. Many problems occur at the point where the software exchanges data with the host. One topic for adaptive software is how to translate its data into the host's format. Ada provides excellent support for adaptability through the intelligent use of data type attributes when coding.

Another place for adaptive software comes in system tuning and performance monitoring. Portable software should come with instructions and code that analyze the performance of the software and identify hot spots for tuning during the porting process. Portable software follows the general 90%–10% rule for software, in that 90% of the time is spent on 10% of the code, and this is the code that should be tuned.

The Intermetrics AIE contains several examples of adaptive software. One of the best examples occurs in a software structure that emulates virtual memory. In this system, a reference to a virtual location is interpreted as a page number, and an offset to a location within that page. When porting the software, the user can tune the system by adjusting the page size, and the software will automatically derive the optimal packing of information on a page.

Given a page size of N storage units, the problem is to define a page as an array of integers. In Ada terms, this can be calculated as follows:

```
        -- First define a type whose size is System.storage_unit
        -- This is usually a byte or a word, depending on the
        -- architecture. This type definition should be checked for
        -- each new implementation
type stored_unit is range –2 ** (System.storage_unit  –1)
                      .. 2 ** (System.storage_unit – 1) –1;
for stored_unit'size use System.storage_unit;
        -- next figure out how many storage_units per integer
storage_units_per_integer : constant := integer'size /
                                System.storage_unit;
        -- then how many integers fit on a page of N storage_units
integers_per_page : constant := N / storage_units_per_integer;
        -- and how much is left over
leftovers_per_page : constant := N –
                (integers_per_page * storage_units_per_integer);
        -- now we know enough to correctly define a page
        -- of virtual memory
type page_array_type is array (1..integers_per_page) of integer;
type overflow_array_type is array (1..leftover_storage_units) of stored_unit;
type page is record
    data : page_array_type;
    overflow : overflow_array_type;
end record;
for page'size use N;  -- this now serves as an "assertion check"
```

Notice that the only thing that must be verified to port this software to another machine is the type definition for Stored_Unit. In particular, this will work for any value of N (greater than or equal to storage_units_per_integer). Different values of

N can be provided during performance analysis to determine the optimum value for N for a given machine.

Another excellent example of adaptability occurs in GNU Emacs. GNU Emacs uses the Unix make (Feldman, 1979) facility for tailoring GNU to different hosts. To construct Emacs for a specific machine, there are a few 'macros' that the user provides. The makefile does conditional compilation based on the values of these macros. For example, default pathnames to Emacs library files can be provided as a makefile macro. Machine dependencies are also stored in specific C header files, and the makefile selects the appropriate file for the target machine. All these machine dependency files follow a pattern, so constructing Emacs for a new Unix machine requires producing a new header file for that machine, based on the existing header files, and instructing make to use that header file when compiling and linking Emacs. Unfortunately, Ada does not fully support this technique, because there is no equivalent to the C pre–processor (used to insert a string from the environment at compilation time into the source code).

4.   *Portability has an Effect (both Positive and Negative) on Performance*

The claim has been made that portable software is inherently less efficient than software that has not been designed with portability in mind. Portability has an effect on performance, but it is not necessarily negative. Adaptive software can provide the compiler with more information, because the compiler is expected to figure out a data layout, or array bounds, for instance. Given this additional information, a good compiler can perform more optimization, making the software perform better on both the current and any future host.

Performance is also directly affected by the model of the host used by the software. Choose the wrong model, and the host interface becomes a substantial bottleneck (as shown previously). On the other hand, a good model can facilitate (but not guarantee) substantial performance enhancements.

Practical experience indicates that most portable software initially exhibits some degree of inefficiency, usually because the ported software duplicates some service performed by the host (Mendal 1988). However, if this service is identified, then replacing the ported software's implementation by the host's implementation should be very easy to do, and cause significant performance improvement.

The Intermetrics AIE presents three models of its Host Interface (HIF). The External Interface is used by the rest of the software to obtain HIF services. Below it sits the Indexed–Sequential Access Method (ISAM) Interface, so the external interface software is implemented in terms of ISAM files. Below this interface is an implementation of ISAM that uses fixed–size file pages. This lowest layer is implemented in terms of Ada's DIRECT_IO. This software provides its own buffering scheme, which can be eliminated if the host's implementation of DIRECT_IO provides efficient buffering. However, should the new host operating system provide an equivalent ISAM, it is very easy to replace the implementation of the ISAM model with calls to the host's ISAM facility, eliminating calls to the Ada DIRECT_IO package.

5.   *Portable Software Uses Standards*

There is an obvious gain in portability from using directly applicable standards. But there are other uses for standards in portable software. Designing a good interface is hard work. Most standards have undergone substantial rigorous public review, and represent a clear model of their underlying system. Often the model embedded in a standard can be used as the basis for defining the software's model of a different host.

POSIX (the IEEE Standard Portable Operating System Interface based on Unix) presents a clear example of this. Both Microsoft and DEC have announced that they will implement the POSIX interface on OS/2 and VMS (respectively). There is at least one proposal (Harbaugh 1988) for a common file naming package that uses a variation on the Unix file naming scheme. Software that uses a Unix style of file naming should be easily ported to a wide variety of systems that support hierarchical directories.

Another example of this is illustrated by the many compilers that use some variant of DIANA (Evans et al 1983) as their internal representation. Almost every compiler vendor has modified DIANA to meet his individual requirements (so no two DIANA implementations are the same). Several implementors have publicly acknowledged the savings by adapting DIANA, rather than developing a new representation from scratch (Milton 1983, Mendal 1988).

6.   *Portable Software Comes with a Porting Manual*

The hardest part of the porting process is identifying system dependencies. Therefore, software that is expected to be portable should come with a Porting Manual that identifies these dependencies.

Here is a suggested Table of Contents for a Porting Manual:

1. Overview of This Manual
2. The Porting Process
   a. Resources Required
   b. Sequence of Events
   c. Estimated Schedule
3. Structure of the Software
   a. Compilation Order
   b. Compilation Dependencies
   c. System Dependencies
4. Modifying Dependent Units
   · for each unit
      1. System Dependencies
      2. Porting this Unit
      3. Performance Considerations
5. System Test and Integration
   a. Overview of Test and Integration Process
   b. Unit/Subsystem Test Suites
   c. Integration Test Suites
6. Performance Monitoring and Tuning
   a. Overview of Performance Monitoring and Tuning

b. Potential Performance 'Hot Spots'
c. Tuning Parameters
d. Performance Tests and Tuning Suites

This Porting Manual identifies the system dependencies, permitting the person doing the port to concentrate on those units (and ignore other units). The required model of the interface is documented, both on paper and also through the use of tests that provide an 'operational verification' of the behavior of the model. The manual identifies the sequence of operations needed to port a complex system to the new host, and should provide resource and schedule estimates. The manual provides information to support the task of tuning and adaptation needed to make the system perform adequately on the new machine, factors that are often ignored when trying to get software to compile on the new host.

7.   *Porting Software Stresses Compilers*

An amazing number of compiler bugs and dependencies can be found when moving code from one mature compiler to another, even on the same computer and operating system. Ada has gone a long way towards reducing the number of implementation dependencies, and the ACVC tests try hard to ensure conformance with the language Standard. However, what works on one compiler often breaks another.

There are several different categories of language problems that porting can uncover. First are implementation freedoms in the language, such as the order of evaluation of expressions. Another class of problems are compiler bugs. These usually occur as a result of interactions of Ada features. Finally there are the set of issues that concern **pragma** INTERFACE and similar services. Some compilers do not support **pragma** INTERFACE at all, while others place restrictions on the subprograms that may be called from Ada. Passing data across an inter–language procedure call can also cause problems.

We observed several examples of implementation freedoms when porting the X Ada binding. For instance, the following compiled correctly on several compilers, but generated a compilation warning on another:

type X_Integer **is range** –2**31 .. 2**31 –1;
type X_Natural **is new** X_Integer **range** 0 .. 2**31 –1;

The compiler flagged the definition of X_Natural, warning that evaluating the upper bound on the range of X_Natural would yield a value (2**31) out of the range of X_Integer. In this case, there was an implicit dependency on evaluating an expression.

Another example from the X Binding concerns **pragma** INTERFACE. Most Unix–based compilers provide the ability to specify the linker name of an 'interfaced' subprogram, but they do it differently. One compiler supports an optional third parameter to **pragma** INTERFACE, and others support a separate pragma, called INTERFACE_NAME. Compiling one version of the binding on another compiler causes these pragmas to be rejected but the compilation itself succeeds.

This then causes an error when trying to link a program using the X Binding packages.

8.   *To Prove Portability, Deliver on Multiple Hosts*

If portability is a major concern, then the best (and perhaps only) way to achieve it is to require delivery on multiple hosts. This is an approach that was taken in the early STARS work, and appears to be effective (STARS 1988). STARS contractors are required to deliver code that executes on multiple host configurations using compilers from different vendors. There are two approaches to multiple deliveries. The first way is to develop on one host, and then port the software to another host. This is commonly the way software is developed and, as a result, ported (Bowles 1988). The other way is to require parallel development and delivery.

There are benefits to developers from the parallel development approach. By using two different hosts, a failure (e.g., compiler bug) on one does not stop development. Bad design decisions can be identified early on, particularly via prototyping interfaces on both hosts. Additionally, the use of multiple hosts forces the designers to deal with two possibly different systems as current hosts for the software, and not unknown potential future platforms. This will help in the development of appropriate models of the execution environment through practical experience. Finally, one of the hosts may prove to be a much more cost–effective development host, providing some real financial benefits to the project (Carstensen 1987).

Recommendations

Recommendations to Designers

Know your hosts. Spend the time to develop a good model of your requirements on the host. Use standard interfaces, even if it requires some work to implement your specific requirements on top of the standard. Prototype the models on several machines. Document these models from a portability perspective. Include portability as a topic during Design Reviews.

Use the capabilities of Ada and adaptive algorithms to let your software port itself to a new host. Adopt design and coding standards and guidelines that emphasize portability. Develop tests of your interfaces that are both comprehensive and self–diagnosing. Identify performance 'hot spots' in the interfaces.

Recommendations to Managers

Plan to spend much more time during design to support portability. Provide the resources to design, prototype and evaluate host models. Try to use multiple systems during development; do parallel development if possible. Be prepared for compiler problems. Deliver a Porting Manual.

Conclusions

Portable software starts with portable architecture and designs. Thus the emphasis is upon the software designer, not the implementor. The key technical issue in portability is producing the right model of the host(s) to which the software will be targeted. This is not something that can be solved by coding standards or style guides, but is a design (perhaps even a requirement analysis) activity that needs to be undertaken before coding.

Management has its role in portability, too. Management must decide to pay the additional up-front cost and schedule to achieve a high level of portability. The best way to develop portable software is to do parallel development on multiple hosts. This requires management commitment, in terms of time and money.

Our experience indicates it is possible to develop software systems that are easy to port. Ada assists in this by providing facilities to help the designers and implementors, but Ada is not sufficient. This paper presents some observations from our successful porting efforts. We hope software developers will apply these observations, to make our next software port easier.

Acknowledgments: We would like to thank Geoff Mendal for sharing his experiences porting the Anna toolset and his review of this paper. Rich Hilliard, Marlene Hazle, Chris Byrnes, Anthony Gargaro, and Olimpia Velez also provided valuable comments. Finally, we would like to recognize the Intermetrics AIE design team. This paper started as an attempt to understand what makes the AIE so portable.

References

Bardin, B. (1987). Layered Virtual Machines + OOD – a Balanced Refinement Methodology. Boston: Proceedings AIAA Computers in Aerospace VI.

Bowles, K. (1988). Lessons Learned in Ada Developments. Washington: Presented to ACM DC Local SIGAda.

Carstensen, H. (1987). Magnavox Lessons Learned from AFATDS. Boston: Presented to Ada Expo.

Evans, A. et al. (1983). Descriptive Intermediate Attributed Notation for Ada (DIANA) Reference Manual Revision 3. Pittsburgh: Tartan Labs, Inc.

Feldman, S. (1979). Make – A Program for Maintaining Computer Programs. Software – Practice & Experience, vol 9, no 4.

Harbaugh, S. (1988). Universal FileNames Package. in Proceedings 1988 STARS Workshop. Washington: STARS Joint Program Office.

Hyland, S. & Nelson, M. (1988). The Ada Binding to X Window System. Princeton: Presented to ACM SIGada.

Intermetrics, Inc. (1987). Rehost/Retarget Manual for the Ada Integrated Environment (IR–MA–826–0). Cambridge: Intermetrics, Inc.

Kaindl, H. (1988). Portability of Software. ACM SIGPLAN, vol 23, no 6.

KAPSE Interface Team (KIT). (no date). Ada Tool Transportability Guide. Washington: Ada Joint Program Office.

Lampson, B (1984). Hints for Computer System Design. IEEE Software, vol 1, no 1.

Luckham, D. et al (1987). Anna – A Language for Annotating Ada Programs. Berlin: Springer Verlag

Mendal, G. (1988). Experience Porting Anna. personal communication.

Milton, D. (1983). Lessons Learned from Developing the Verdix Ada Compiler. Tinton Falls, NJ: Presented to ACM Princeton Local SIGAda.

Nissen, J.C.D. & Wallis, P.J.L. (1984). Portability and Style in Ada. Cambridge: Cambridge University Press.

Pappas, F. (1985). Ada Portability Guidelines (ESD–TR–85–141). Waltham: SofTech, Inc.

Rosenblum, D (1988). Design and Verification of Distributed Tasking Supervisors for Concurrent Programming Languages, PhD. Thesis. Stanford: Stanford University.

Stallman, R. et al. (1987). GNU Emacs Documentation. Cambridge: Free Software Foundation.

STARS (1988). Proceedings 1988 STARS Workshop. Washington: STARS Joint Program Office.

Additional Bibliography on Ada Portability

Brosgol, B. & Cuthbert, G. (1987). The Development of the Ada Binding of the Graphical Kernel System. Ada UK Ada User, vol 8 suppl.

Brown, P.J. ed. (1972). Software Portability. Cambridge: Cambridge University Press.

Emery, D. (1988). Experience using Pragma Interface. Princeton: Presented to ACM SIGAda.

Fisher, G. (1983). A Universal Arithmetic Package. ACM Ada Letters, vol 3, no 6.

French, S. (1986). Transporting an Ada Software Tool: A Case Study. ACM Ada Letters, vol 6, no 2.

Gargaro, A. & Pappas, T.L. (1987). Reusability Issues and Ada. IEEE Software, vol 4, no 4.

Genillard, Ch. & Ebel, N. (1986). Reusability of Software Components in the Building of Syntax–Driver Software Tools in Ada. Cambridge: Cambridge University Press.

Goodenough, J. & Probert, T. (1983). Designing and Testing Interfaces for Portable Software: Ada Text_IO as an Example. in Ada Software Tools Interfaces, P.J.L. Wallis, ed. Berlin: Springer Verlag.

Goodenough, J. (1980). The Ada Compiler Validation Capability. ACM SIGPlan Notices, vol 15, no 11.

Koh, J. & Sym, G.T. (1984). A Proposal for Standard Basic Functions in Ada. ACM Ada Letters, vol 4, no 3.

Kurtel, K. & Pietsch, W. (1986). A Portable Ada Implementation of Indexed Sequential Input/Output. ACM Ada Letters, vol 6, nos 2 and 3.

Lecarme, O. & Pellisier Gart, M. (1986). Software Portability. New York: McGraw–Hill.

Matthews, E. (1987). Observations on the Portability of Ada IO. ACM Ada Letters, vol 7, no 5.

Nyberg, K. (1988). Porting Ada Applications Between a PC and a VAX. Washington: Presented to Capital Area PC Users Group Special Interest Group for Ada.

Rehmer, K. (1987). Development and Implementation of the Magnavox Generic Ada Basic Math Package. ACM Ada Letters, vol 7, no 3.

Vines, D. & King, T. (1988). Gaia: an Object–Oriented Framework for an Ada Environment. ACM SIGMOD Record, vol 17, no 3.

Willman, H. (1982). APSE Portability Issues – Pragmatic Limitations. Boston: Presented at ACM AdaTEC.

SYNTHESIZING SOFTWARE DEVELOPMENT USING ADA

Anthony Gargaro
Computer Sciences Corporation, Moorestown, NJ, USA

Christian Romvary
Computer Sciences Corporation, Moorestown, NJ, USA

Abstract. *This paper describes the use of Ada to synthesize the different phases of software development; namely, requirements analysis, preliminary design, and detailed design. The experience of using Ada in the demonstration of a military command and control system is cited to illustrate the use of Ada in these phases.*

PROLOGUE

The potential contribution of Ada to software design was recognized during the test and evaluation of Ada. Since then Ada has been used as a precise formalism for detailed design and as a foundation for design paradigms. In addition, a plethora of text books and tools have promoted Ada beyond its original role as a programming language. This paper presents the view that Ada is an adaptable formalism for supplementing contemporary software development practices prior to programming.

Until an integrated approach towards formally specifying requirements, design, and implementation is available, Ada can be used to mitigate the difficulties of transitioning among the respective specification practices. Typically, these practices are derived from an informal methodology supported through a set of autonomous tools. It is within such a methodology that Ada contributes to synthesizing multi-disciplined software development practices to achieve an improved degree of product consistency, formality, and rigor. This perspective has been partially substantiated by using Ada in a recent demonstration of an application. The demonstration's software development strategy is amplified to address the conference theme that Ada is the design choice.

BACKGROUND

The referenced application was a demonstration of the enroute mission monitoring for the Military Airlift Command (MAC) Command and Control (C2) Information Processing System (IPS). The demonstration served a dual purpose: to evaluate the operational capabilities of the proposed MAC C2 IPS hardware and software, and to validate the proposed Ada software development methodology for the full scale development. The demonstration required the use of Ada as the program design and implementation language. Furthermore, the software was to be developed to comply with the software development product requirements specified in the United States Department of Defense (USDoD) DOD-STD-2167 (1985).

The system comprised multiple PC-based workstations networked with dual minicomputers typically resident at an IPS operational site. The accompanying software provided a contemporary graphical workstation interface, maintained local and centralized data bases, and supported the local network of workstations. A variety of timing constraints were imposed on system response time and the software had to be resilient to system failures, damage, and threats. In addition, commercially available non-developed item (NDI) software components, e.g., a relational data base management system, were needed to reduce the risk associated with building a system from entirely new components.

SOFTWARE DEVELOPMENT STRATEGY

The software development strategy was influenced by several objectives. These objectives included: compatibility with the in-house Digital System Development Methodology (DSDM) as described in Steppel et al (1984), compliance with DOD-STD-2167 (2167), and exploitation of an Ada-based design language. These objectives raised potential conflicts; in particular, the first two objectives were perceived as threats to successfully achieving the third objective. This was because both DSDM and 2167 imply a development methodology using structured design principles to derive a hierarchical functional decomposition of the software. The literature provided persuasive arguments to suggest that such a development methodology was incompatible with preferred Ada design. In addition, there was no consensus of the Ada community on mapping an Ada design to the 2167 static structure, although a well-reasoned compromise was subsequently proposed by Gardner et al (1988).

After evaluation of the alternatives, the following development strategy was adopted. Ada was established as the principal formalism to specify a process-orientated software development methodology consistent with DSDM and 2167. The rationale was that Ada represented the most consistent, permanent, and rigorous form of expression available and that its introduction after requirements analysis would reduce the perceived risk that a hierarchical functional design would compromise the effective use of Ada. Furthermore, in terms of resources, i.e., staff and tools, Ada was the optimal communication medium. A consequence of this strategy was that all information for the mandated 2167 design products for preliminary and detailed design was included as a part of the compilable Ada formalism. In essence, Ada was established as a Software Development Language (SDL) similar to the Ada Design Language Continuum outlined by Pincus (1986). While Ada was not the basis for the software development methodology, it became the syntactic and semantic "glue" for the DSDM/2167 hybrid methodology.

REQUIREMENTS ANALYSIS

Requirements analysis is often combined with preliminary design when requirements are straightforward. For the demonstration, although the application domain was well-understood, a comprehensive requirements analysis was performed for the enroute mission monitoring component separate from preliminary design. This was necessary to identify additional requirements vital to a practical competitive demonstration. In addition, it was essential to propose a rational transition from requirements analysis to an Ada preliminary design. There was continuing concern that unless some form of object-orientated requirements analysis was adopted, the subsequent design would be compromised to the extent that many Ada constructs would be misused or not used effectively.

Composite Specification Model

The Composite Specification Model (CSM) was used to guide requirements analysis. CSM as described by NASA (1987) provided sufficient flexibility that its outputs were compatible with both DSDM and 2167. In addition, CSM had been developed recognizing that Ada would be a potential design and implementation language. CSM stipulated three mutually orthogonal, but complementary, specifications of requirements: entities and relationships (contextual), transition of control (dynamic), and transformation of data (functional). For the demonstration only dynamic and functional specifications were pursued; a contextual specification was abandoned early because its orientation appeared to yield a less commonly understood presentation of requirements. Initial emphasis was on developing a functional specification because the demonstration requirements were essentially driven by the processing and transformation of mission monitoring data.

Functional analysis was compliant with DSDM and 2167 recommendations since requirements were presented as Data Flow Diagrams (DFDs) derived using structured specification techniques and tools similar to those advocated by Hatley and Pirbhai (1987). The preliminary DFDs and accompanying Data Dictionary (DD) were then available to conduct dynamic analysis. At this point, the dynamic specification was deliberately adapted to introduce Ada. This adaptation resulted in a preliminary software architecture rather than a design-independent dynamic perspective of requirements. For example, the specification introduced knowledge of the hardware architecture. This apparent violation of requirements analysis eventually lead to a functional specification that was design independent. The dynamic specification served to identify design properties that should not be deductable from the DFDs. The DFDs were continually refined to ensure their design independence and to audit the evolving dynamic specification. The transition from requirements expressed as DFDs to a dynamic specification became crucial to the ultimate success of synthesizing software development using Ada. The resulting Ada formalism was the basis for design and the generation of the 2167 design documentation.

Abstract Partitions

In the absence of any formal guidelines for constructing the dynamic specification using Ada, an approach was developed based upon the notion of abstract partitions. The approach allocated requirements to aggregations of Ada library units; an aggregation was termed an abstract partition. The allocation was determined by perceived foci of control and interfaces necessary to support the functional specification on the prescribed processing resources. Rules for composing abstract partitions were influenced by the Virtual Node (VN) concept as described by Atkinson et al (1988), namely that a VN encapsulates resources local to a processor. In this context, an abstract partition comprised a root procedure that withed library and template units as defined by the referenced VN concept. For the initial dynamic specification, precise details such as inter/intra-node communication were deferred; therefore, VN-style interface units were omitted from the partitions.

The advantages of using abstract partitions were an early allocation of functional requirements amenable, as subsequently described, to the 2167 static software structure, and a specification of library units suitable for developing a distributed Ada design. Accordingly, as preliminary design proceeded, design information from additional Ada units became incorporated into the static structure for design product generation. In this way, the danger of compromising the Ada design by the static structure was controllable. Abstract partitions were carefully refined to express control and synchronization, and the resulting Ada units were incorporated within the context of the 2167 static structure. Abstract partitions served the dual role of 2167 Top-Level Computer Software Components (TLCSCs) for design documentation generation and as VNs for guiding the design and implementation. A corollary of these roles was that Ada library units constituting abstract partitions became units in the context of the 2167 static structure and a separate TLCSC comprised template units.

The above approach was an informal procedure. The transition from the functional DFDs to abstract partitions was akin to a craft, and was performed without the use of automated tools. This made it difficult to provide requirements consistency and traceability between the functional and dynamic specifications. The DFD representation of requirements was not readily perspicuous in the composition of abstract partitions. This difficulty was mitigated to a limited degree by cross-referencing DFD processes and Ada units. Each Ada unit identified DFD processes it supported; similarly, the DD process entities referenced the corresponding Ada unit(s). The important contribution was that the abstract partitions provided a satisfactory expression of a dynamic specification for requirements analysis and expedited the transition to design.

PRELIMINARY DESIGN

The abstract partitions derived from requirements analysis established the basis for preliminary design. In 2167 terms, abstract partitions were logically grouped as TLCSCs to form Computer Software Configuration Items (CSCIs). For the demonstration, CSCIs were identified with the software for the Communications Processor, File Server, and Workstations. These CSCIs had been promulgated by the MAC C2 IPS system specification; however, until completion of requirements analysis and preliminary design, no functional allocation had been determined for them. The functional allocation to the File Server resulted in six abstract partitions shown in Figure 1 (prefixed by AP and cast in preliminary design roles as VNs and TLCSCs).

Figure 1: File Server - Abstract Partitions

```
--| role: VN Abstract Partitions          --| role: TLCSC Abstract Partitions
                                           package File_Server_CSCI is
with AP_APF, AP_DBC, AP_DLD,                 package APF_TLCSC is ... end;
  AP_EMF, AP_MSG, AP_WSM;                    ...
procedure File_Server is                     package WSM_TLCSC is ... end;
  task VN_APF_Task;                        end File_Server_CSCI;
  ...                                      package body File_Server_CSCI is
  task VN_WSM_Task;                          package body APF_TLCSC is separate;
  task body VN_APF_Task is                   ...
  begin                                      package body WSM_TLCSC is separate;
    AP_APF;                                end File_Server_CSCI;
  end VN_APF_Task;                         separate (File_Server_CSCI)
  ...                                      package body APF_TLCSC is
begin                                        --| include:
  null;                                      --| withed AP_APF library units
end File_Server;                             procedure AP_APF is ... end;
                                           end APF_TLCSC;
                                             ...
```

While for the demonstration the File Server CSCI shared a single processing resource, the constituent partitions did not preclude the CSCI from being distributed among the separate processing resources of the network. However, performance efficiency considerations of the NDI software components outside of the abstract partitions warranted that the VNs be designed as individual Ada main programs.

Program Development Language

The use of Ada as a program development language began with the composition of abstract partitions and continued with the refinement of the corresponding dynamic specification. Refinement was complete when all Ada library units necessary to achieve the exact requirements, i.e., the lowest level expressed in the DFDs and DD, had been specified. During refinement, communication and synchronization among and within the partitions was formalized, e.g., entry calls or remote procedure calls. These calls were not encapsulated by a VN-style interface unit, but by the template units. In addition, critical objects and types to the partition, were identified and packaged. This latter activity was similar to object-orientated development as outlined by NASA (1986). The resulting design was compilable and was consistent with the specified requirements.

Software Top-Level Design Documentation

The principal product of preliminary design was the Software Top-Level Design Document (STLDD) as prescribed by 2167. Intrinsic to the STLDD was the 2167 static structure whereby each TLCSC comprised Lower Level Computer Software Components (LLCSCs) and units. Because of the commitment for all documentation to be included as compilable Ada, an Ada documentation tool was used to automatically generate the STLDD. Use of this tool required that the Ada SDL resulting from the refinement of the abstract partitions be carefully adapted to the constraints of the static structure. Several Ada constructions that do not necessarily contribute to approved or efficient programming practices were found particularly useful in building a 2167 software development shell. These constructions included generics, nested packages, overloaded subprograms, renames statements, and use clauses. In many instances, their application resulted in a clear and succinct design.

The shell normalized the abstract partitions into a canonical static structure. To accomplish this normalization the shell provided the necessary syntactic camouflage for the Ada documentation tool to process the library units within the abstract partitions as a static hierarchy of Computer Software Components (CSCs). This camouflage was carefully contrived to ensure that the semantics of the Ada design were not compromised. For example, to comply with the 2167 documentation requirements for objects with global, local, input, or output attributes, generic units were introduced to artificially reference these objects; the respective instantiations of these units were used to create the illusion of these attributes as required.

In addition, the shell permitted the introduction of units that provided improved visibility into the preliminary design. The purpose of these units was to facilitate subsequent detailed design. The units were clearly identified as design artifacts that required refinement and possible redistribution of their constituent parts when formally developed as units within the abstract partitions. For example, Figure 2 illustrates a simple design requirement (with all formal design commentary removed) for the interface to the Nodal Data Network (NDN) to be specified through a private type, *Link_Type*, defined in a template library unit.

The interface subprograms were specified in terms of a generic instantiation referencing *Link_Type*. A package encapsulating the renamed subprograms was then located to comply with the hierarchic static structure. In this way, it was possible to create the necessary handle for design documentation without compromising the subsequent detailed design requirements for developing the interface.

Figure 2: NDN Interface Development Shell

```
package Design_Types_Package is ...
   type Node_Type is (CP_Node, ...);
   type Link_Type (Node : Node_Type := Default_Node) is private;
   ...
   generic
      type Design_Input_Type is private;
      procedure Generic_Design_Input (Input : in Design_Input_Type);
      procedure Design_Input (Input : in Link_Type);
   ...
end Design_Types_Package;
package body Design_Types_Package is ...
   procedure Design_Input (Input : in Link_Type) is
      procedure Local_Design_Input is new
            Generic_Design_Input (Design_Input_Type => Link_Type);
   begin
      Local_Design_Input (Input);
   end Design_Input;
   ...
end Design_Types_Package;
with Design_Types_Package;
package File_Server_CSCI is ...
   package File_Server_Template_TLCSC is
      package NDN_IO_Unit is
         use Design_Types_Package;
         procedure Link_Input (Input : in Link_Type)
               renames Design_Input;
         ...
      end NDN_IO_Unit;
      ...
   end File_Server_Template_TLCSC;
   ...
end File_Server_CSCI;
```

DETAILED DESIGN

The library units comprising the abstract partitions and the Ada SDL used to generate the STLDD during preliminary design established the basis for detailed design. The principal objective of detailed design was to identify any remaining library units, to ensure that all unit interfaces were completely specified, and that the dependencies among and composition of all units were finalized. In addition, units were refined to express critical algorithmic processing as required by 2167. For example, since Ada tasking was to be used within units of the abstract partitions, the tasks were defined as clients, servers, etc. Finally, during detailed design the use of NDI components was completely specified with respect to the interfaces that were to be made available. These interfaces were for low-level graphic processing, database manipulation, and network communication.

Program Design Language

The use of Ada as a program design language was consistent with commonly advocated practices discussed in NAC (88). Except for guidelines pertaining to the inclusion of specific text necessary for generating 2167 documentation, there were no formal guidelines other than those established for a style of programming that promoted reusability as described in CompSci (1987). Commentary of the design was informal and relied on the names and structure of the Ada text to provide the necessary degree of formality. The resulting design was compilable and was ready for mock-up execution.

The ability to perform mock-up execution was essential since the software was designed to execute in a loosely-coupled execution environment using heterogeneous hardware and software. Therefore, early assurance was required that the proposed software distribution was reasonable. In addition, it was important to detect incompatibilities from binding Ada to the NDI software components. Towards this objective, Ada provided the necessary formalism to express a design suitable for mock-up execution. In this context, Ada synthesized the NDI software to the detailed design. For example, the remote procedure call facility of the File Server design imported the functionality provided by the NDI inter-program communication software by defining an abstract type for mailboxes in a template unit. This abstraction was used to provide the communication interface among the abstract partitions. Whenever feasible, the detailed design maintained NDI transparency to increase the portability of the abstract partitions.

Software Detailed Design Documentation

The production of the software detailed design document (SDDD) as prescribed by 2167 was generated from the Ada SDL prepared for detailed design. The shell developed for the STLDD was revised to include more detailed commentary and to replace all body stubs in the static structure by references to the unit bodies developed in the detailed design. Conversely, body stubs were introduced into the Ada SDL to replace actual bodies. This apparent regression was necessary because the detailed design contained information for mock-up execution that had to be restricted from incorporation in the SDDD. The reason for this was twofold; unless restricted, the information would have exceeded the constraints of the Ada documentation tool and, inappropriate detail would have infiltrated the design documentation. For example, the binding to an NDI software component necessarily included profuse use of target compiler-dependent features bordering the semantic fringes of the language. These features were not recognized by the Ada documentation tool and had to be removed.

EPILOGUE

The use of Ada as a SDL contributed to a successful demonstration of the IPS enroute mission monitoring. It comprised 54,000 lines of design and implementation code. The demonstration was completed in less than 6 months by a staff that varied from 8 to 15. The extrapolation of productivity metrics was not a meaningful evaluation because of the intensive effort typical of a competitive procurement; similar conditions would not prevail in a full-scale development activity.

The most important evaluation was that the demonstration surpassed all performance requirements. After two days of operational testing only one significant flaw occurred. This followed the introduction of a deliberate failure to validate the workstations' standalone capabilities. A further evaluation came from the software development documentation that accurately specified the requirements and design for the demonstration. In tracing the cause of the above flaw, the documentation showed a requirement identified in the functional model was lost in the transformation to the design. This inconsistency between requirements analysis and design was not surprising since the transformation was not a disciplined practice. The absence of a disciplined transformation indicated that a software development methodology must be derived from a more formal basis than this approach.

The efficacy of using an Ada object-orientated development methodology was not determined. The difficulty encountered in developing a contextual specification reduced the opportunity for object-orientated requirements analysis. The approach confirmed that Ada can be used to construct a top-level design using more traditional process-orientated techniques without necessarily precluding the subsequent application of object-orientated design and programming.

In retrospect, the software development strategy included a design process reminiscent of the perceptions forwarded by Parnas and Clements (1986). Towards achieving such a process, Ada provided an adaptable formalism.

ACKNOWLEDGEMENTS

The authors are pleased to acknowledge the referee commentaries received on the abstract for this paper. In addition, the authors are indebted to the staff that contributed to the successful demonstration.

REFERENCES

Atkinson, C. et al. (1988). Ada for Distributed Systems. Ada Companion Series, Cambridge University Press.

CompSci (1987). Ada Reusability Handbook. Computer Sciences Corporation, Technical Report SP-IRD 11.

Gardner, M. R. et al. (1988). Software Engineering, Ada Development, and Acquisition

Streamlining Under DOD-STD-2167. The MITRE Corporation, MTR-88W00006.

Hatley, D. J. & Pirbhai, I. A. (1987). Strategies for Real-Time System Specification. Dorset House Publishing.

NAC (1988). Ada Language Processing for Ada-Based Design Languages. Proceedings of the Ada-Based Design Languages Workshop. United States Naval Avionics Center.

NASA (1986). General Object-Oriented Software Development. National Aeronautic and Space Administration, SEL-86-002.

NASA (1987). Guidelines For Applying the Composite Specification Model (CSM). National Aeronautics and Space Administration, SEL-87-003.

Parnas, D. L. & Clements, P. C. (1986). A Rational Design Process: How and Why to Fake It. IEEE Transactions on Software Engineering, Vol. SE-12, No.2, 251-257.

Pincus, S. (1986). Software Development Experiences with DOD-STD-2167. ACM SIGAda Meeting Presentation, Pittsburgh, PA.

Steppel, S. et al. (1984). Digital System Development Methodology (DSDM[R]). Computer Sciences Corporation.

USDoD (1985). Defense System Software Development: DOD-STD-2167. United States Department of Defense.

Ada Mechanisms To Obtain Concurrency In GKS

F. Pérez, J. Carretero, L. Gómez, A. Pérez, J. Zamorano.
Dep. de Arquitectura y Tecnología de Sistemas Informáticos.
Facultad de Informática. Universidad Politécnica de Madrid.
Campus de Montegancedo.
28660 Boadilla del Monte. Madrid. SPAIN.

Abstract. *Many tools suitable for sequential programming are not adequate for the development of concurrent applications. This paper analyses the use of the Graphical Kernel System (GKS) together with concurrent languages like Ada, showing the inherent problems that arise with GKS in a multitasking environment. These problems are solved by means of a system, called "Concurrency Manager", which is described in this paper. The standard GKS-Ada binding has been preserved and a set of parameters makes the system adjustable.*

INTRODUCTION.

The increasing use of concurrent programming and sophisticated man-machine interfaces produces new problems when someone wants to specify, design and implement software, by using tools that do not fit this kind of programming. One of those tools is the **Graphical Kernel System (GKS)**, a graphical standard defined by the Graphics Working Group of ISO with the code IS7942 and whose Ada binding was proposed in 1986.

This work derives from a project[†] whose original objective was to build a concurrent application with interactive graphical interfaces, that should be portable, and easily maintainable and readaptable to other applications.

The size of the project and the need of concurrency made Ada a natural choice. Other good reasons to choose Ada were the simplicity of its concurrency mechanisms, its modularity, its wide usage and the possibility to make reusable software. The constraint of portability guided us to look for a widely used graphical support, with available Ada binding. Due to these reasons GKS was chosen.

Early in the design process, the need of concurrent access to GKS was identified. Every task using GKS should be able to run without disturbances in its inner vision of graphical characteristics. But GKS prevents the simultaneous execution of more than one task. Therefore, in order to create a virtual environment in which every task would see its own independent GKS, the **Concurrency Manager (CM)** was developed. This is the main problem to be analysed and solved in this paper.

Final implementation of CM should support:

- Transparency. The final system should present the tasks with the original GKS-Ada binding.
- Flexibility. The system should allow the definition at compile time of the application characteristics.

---

† This project was partially supported by SEIDEF S.A. (Spain)

- Efficiency. The introduction of CM should not increase excessively the execution time of the application.

Finally, the set of solutions developed should be general enough to fit other non concurrent tools with similar concurrency problems to GKS.

First of all, this paper presents some of the problems that arise using GKS in a multitasking environment. Then a solution to these problems is analysed. Finally, some considerations concerning CM and the conclusions derived from its design and implementation are presented.

PROBLEMS WITH GKS.

GKS is a graphical standard oriented towards sequential programming. It maintains global characteristics shared by all the tasks working with it. From now on, we will identify those characteristics as the "global graphical state".

The result of the execution of a GKS primitive depends on the current "global graphical state" at the time of execution. In a multitasking environment, every task should have its own graphical state. When a task is going to use GKS, the global graphical state must be a copy of the graphical state of the task, otherwise problems like the one presented in figure 1 may arise. In this figure, it can be seen that task 1 executes its GKS primitives with the graphical state associated with task 2.

The global graphical state includes the following information items:

- Active workstations.
- Selected normalization transformation.
- Graphical attributes.
- Open segment (if any).

Under GKS the term "workstation" refers to any kind of graphical device. A workstation presents one of two different states: Active or non active. The execution of every graphical output primitive will have an effect on every active workstation. Then, every time a GKS graphical output primitive is executed one has to make sure that only the activated workstations are those used by the current task.

Normalization transformation and graphical attributes (colour, line width, fill style, etc.) are also specific to every task, so they should be considered as part of the graphical state of the task and become active when a task is to be executed.

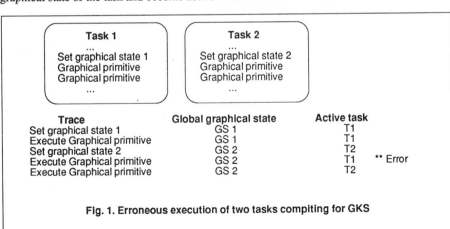

Fig. 1. Erroneous execution of two tasks compiting for GKS

GKS segments are used to store graphical information. While a segment is open, every graphical primitive of every task is stored inside it. Therefore, it is important to prevent graphical primitives generated by a task from ending up in a segment opened by another task.

Another problem with GKS is that some graphical resources (such as workstations, segments, transformations, etc.) need to have a unique identifier across the whole system. In a multitasking environment it would be very helpful to manage the allocation of resource identifiers in such a way that the same identifier cannot be used by two tasks simultaneously.

Finally, problems with GKS input may arise. GKS provides three input modes: REQUEST, SAMPLE and EVENT.

- REQUEST MODE. In order to get an input in this mode, input devices have to be specified by the application tasks. When an input is requested, the whole system is locked until an explicit input command arrives from the user. In a multitasking environment, only the task that requests input should be locked.
- SAMPLE MODE. In this mode inputs are read in a non locking fashion without waiting for an explicit command from the user.
- EVENT MODE. This mode allows the user to get inputs concurrently from several active devices. It maintains a single FIFO queue for the whole system, where GKS stores all the input items. In a multitasking environment, an input queue for every task in event mode is needed.

IMPLEMENTATION.

The solution developed attempts to solve the problems mentioned above. Figure 2 shows a global scheme of CM, composed of the following elements:

- The **Scheduler** deals with the problems that concern mutual exclusion and graphical states.
- The **Input manager** fits GKS input mechanisms to a multitasking environment.
- The **GKS resource manager** solves the problem of allocating unique identifiers to the GKS resources that require them.

Any implementation that solves the previous problems should provide mutual exclusion to access GKS and set the graphical state of the task to be executed. Ada's more natural way to implement this is by means of a task that schedules the application tasks and controls context switching. This task, called scheduler, is the core of the solution presented here.

The scheduler uses a preemptive round-robin policy with different levels of priority, emulating the behaviour of an operating system scheduler, with the GKS primitives as atomic operations. Therefore the GKS scheduler context switching is only done at the end of the execution of the GKS primitives.

An application task that is about to execute GKS primitives must request access to the scheduler, specifying the priority of execution. When the use of GKS is finished, the task must send notice to the scheduler. The scheduling policy operates as follows: An executing task will be swapped out whenever it spends its time slice and there is another task with the same priority waiting for execution, or when another task with higher priority arrives. Due to Ada's communication mechanism between tasks (*rendezvous*), the scheduler cannot interrupt the execution of a task unless it explicitly asks to be swapped out; the task should execute a *rendezvous*. This should be done at the end of every GKS primitive execution.

In order to avoid the presence of all this convoluted code in the application tasks, the GKS binding has been adapted in such a way that, instead of invoking directly a GKS primitive a modified one is invoked. This modified primitive executes the original one and then asks the scheduler whether the task should be swapped out or not. The interface with the modified binding is identical to the original. In the new binding, two aditional primitives have been included to inform the scheduler: GKS START and GKS END. This mechanism allows the scheduler to be transparent to the application. A redefined GKS primitive will have a structure like the one presented in figure 3.

The operations related to the swap out of a task are: Graphical state gathering and storage; deactivation of associated workstations; and closing of the open segment (if any). GKS_INQUIRE primitives are used to gather the graphical state, this includes active workstations, graphical attributes, normalization transformations and the identifier of the open segment (if any). The scheduler uses the reverse procedure to restore the graphical state associated with the task to be swapped in: it restores its graphical attributes and associated transformation, and activates its associated workstations. If the task had an open segment, it was closed before when its graphical state was saved; but closed segments cannot be reopened, so the scheduler uses an auxiliary segment and the Workstation Independent Segment Storage (WISS) to restore the open segment associated with the task.

A scheduler task body skeleton can be seen in apendix A. This skeleton shows the main actions associated with each *rendezvous* of the scheduler.

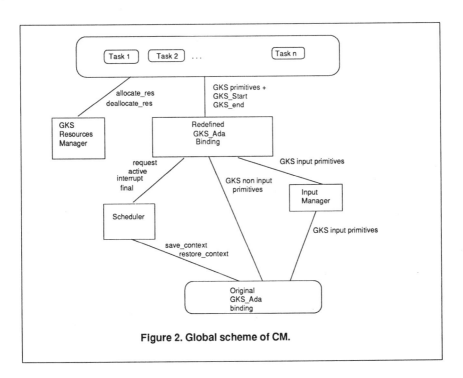

Figure 2. Global scheme of CM.

With this scheme, if an application task takes control of GKS and it does not invoke any GKS primitive, the scheduler will never be able to swap it out. In the same way, if an application task takes control of GKS and never executes the GKS END primitive, lower priority tasks will never be able to take control of GKS.

An application task can be structured like a sequence of code with some non GKS bursts (calculations, non GKS input/output,etc.) and some GKS bursts. Setting a GKS START at the begining of a GKS burst and setting a GKS END at its end, is the correct way to use this scheduler.

It should be noticed that for this scheduler a GKS primitive is not the atomic operation. The actual atomic operation consists of the piece of code from the end of a GKS primitive to the end of the next one, since the control variable exported by the scheduler is tested after the execution of a GKS primitive. A control variable is used instead of executing *rendezvous* with the scheduler in order to get more efficiency.

The scheduler behaviour depends on several tunable parameters such as:

- Maximum number of tasks.
- Priority levels.
- Context switching procedures.
- Basic round-robin quantum.
- Number of basic round-robin quanta by task.

In order to get more flexibility, the scheduler can be implemented like a generic package. By giving adequate values to the former parameters it can be tailored to different applications. Within this generic approach, it is not the scheduler, but the package instanting it, that includes the context switching procedures. Then, the scheduler remains absolutely independent from GKS; thus compilations are avoided and it is possible to use the scheduler for other applications. This generic scheduler specification can be seen in figure 4.

```
procedure GKS_START(TASK_ID: in TASK_TYPE; PRIORITY: in PRIORITY_TYPE) is
begin
    SCHEDULER.REQUEST(TASK_ID,PRIORITY);
    SCHEDULER.ACTIVE(TASK_ID);
end GKS_START;

procedure GKS_Primitive(...    ) is
    TASK_ID: TASK_TYPE;
begin
    ORIGINAL_GKS-Ada_BINDING.GKS_Primitive(...    );
    if SCHEDULER.INTERRUPTION then
        SCHEDULER.INTERRUPT(TASK_ID);
        SCHEDULER.ACTIVE(TASK_ID);
    end if;
end GKS_Primitive;

procedure GKS_END is
begin
    SCHEDULER.FINAL;
end GKS_END;
```

Figure 3. Redefined GKS-Ada binding structure.

Up till now, only tasks dealing with graphical output have been considered. However, the interaction with a system using graphical interface requires some kind of graphical input processing.

The **input manager** is the part of CM that deals with GKS graphical input. It is composed of a set of modules that solve the problems formerly mentioned. This manager provides procedures to deal with the three GKS input modes (request, sample and event) in a multitasking environment. Input management involves two different actions: getting the input and giving the input items to the requesting task. Provided that the requested devices input mode and the identity of the task using each device are known, it is possible to assign input items to the appropiate tasks. The way of getting the input items depends on the input mode used since, in a multitasking environment, each mode has its own problems.

- Sample mode. This mode presents no problems when working in a multitasking environment. The original GKS primitives can be used.
- Event mode. Input is managed distributing the original GKS event queue among tasks that have requested this type of input. Each task has an assigned queue in the input manager that holds its input items.
- Request mode. The input manager does not use the original GKS request input mode. The main reason is that request mode locks the whole system while the input is being made. This is not possible in a multitasking environment, where the only task to be locked must be the one that requests input. Therefore, the input manager implements the request input mode simulating it with the event mode.

The **GKS resources manager** is a useful tool, but it is not essential. This module simplifies the allocation of unique identifiers to the GKS elements used by the tasks (workstations, segments, and normalization transformations), avoiding possible troubles arising when two resources have the same identifier. An implementation of the system which does not use the resources manager could be very dangerous if one is not very careful in giving each task a set of unique identifiers. Furthermore, the fact that each task is using only

```
generic
    type TASK_TYPE is (<>);
    type PRIORITY_LEVELS is (<>);
    type TASK_STATUS is private;
    type PRIORITY_LEVEL_QUANTUM_TYPE is array (PRIORITY_LEVELS) of positive;
    -- Basic round robin quantum
    QUANTUM: duration;
    PRIORITY_LEVEL_QUANTUM:    PRIORITY_LEVEL_QUANTUM_TYPE;
    -- Context switching procedures specification
    with procedure SAVE_CONTEXT (STATUS: out TASK_STATUS);
    with procedure RESTORE_CONTEXT (STATUS: in TASK_STATUS);
Package SCHEDULER is

    -- Exported variables definition
    -- Scheduler procedures specification

end SCHEDULER;
```

Figura 4. Generic Specification of the Scheduler.

its own resources identifiers, would mean that it had to be controlled along the execution to avoid erroneous behaviour.

IMPLEMENTATION FEATURES.

Efficiency. Graphic context switching procedures are the main reason for the overhead introduced by the concurrency manager. The scheduling efficiency will depend on the number of context switches and the time spent on each. This time is determined by the graphical state size, which depends on the number of active workstations, whether an open segment exists or not, etc. Furthemore, scheduler parameters and application tasks characteristics strongly affect the number of context switches. Efficiency measurement is very difficult in these kinds of systems because the performance is highly dependent on the application. The practical results obtained with the application developed have shown that the loss in performance caused by the CM can be easily tolerated.

Transparency. The original GKS-Ada interface has been strictly maintained. Only two primitives (GKS_START and GKS_END) have been added to specify concurrent access to GKS. GKS can be used concurrently by just inserting those two new primitives in the body of the tasks every time a GKS burst appears.

Flexibility. The concurrency manager can be tuned with several parameters, adapting it to the application needs (maximum number of tasks, priority levels, etc.). The functions for context switching are generic parameters, which makes it possible to have a scheduler which is absolutely independent of GKS. This scheduler can be used to provide concurrent use of other tools by providing the particular context switching functions.

CONCLUSIONS.

A system which permits the use of GKS with concurrent programs has been developed. This paper outlines the problems found when building concurrent graphical applications with GKS. The proposed solution uses a standard GKS implementation plus a simple set of Ada components. The original GKS-Ada binding is maintained, with the only addition of two new primitives. The scheduler is the core of the concurrency manager developed. It can be tuned up with a set of parameters to fit a variety of applications.

Other different applications can be developed using this scheduler. An example could be to use CODASYL Data Bases in an Ada multitasking environment.

BIBLIOGRAPHY.

- J. G. P. Barnes, "Programming in Ada", Addison-Wesley. 1984.
- P. Bono, I. German, "GKS Theory and Practice". Springer-Verlag 1987.
- G. Booch, "Software Engineering with Ada". The Benjamin/Cummings Publishing Company Inc.1983.
- R. Buhr, "System Design with Ada". Prentice Hall. 1984
- F. R. A. Hopgood, D. A. Duce, "Introduction to the Graphical Kernel System". Academic Press. 1983.
- ISO "Information Processing systems, Computer Graphics -GKS- Functional Description". ISO IS 7942.
- V. Milanese, "Ada and Nil: Two Concurrent languages for GKS". Computer Graphics Forum. Vol. 6, No. 3, pp 219-234. 1987.
- R. F. Puk, "Report on the Meeting of Computer Graphics Language Bindings". Ada Letters. Vol. 8, No. 4, pp 83-96. 1988.

APENDIX A: Skeleton of the scheduler.

```
task SCHEDULER_TASK is
    entry REQUEST (TASK_ID: in TASK_TYPE; PRIORITY: in PRIORITY_TYPE);
    entry INTERRUPT (TASK_ID: out TASK_TYPE);
    entry ACTIVE (TASK_TYPE);
    entry FINAL;
end SCHEDULER_TASK;

task body SCHEDULER_TASK is
    begin
        -- initialize
        loop
            select
                accept REQUEST (TASK_ID: in TASK_TYPE;
                                PRIORITY: in PRIORITY_TYPE) do
                    -- task_id to queue orderer by priority
                end;
                while REQUEST'COUNT > 0 loop
                    accept REQUEST (TASK_ID: in TASK_TYPE;
                                    PRIORITY: in PRIORITY_TYPE) do
                        -- task_id to queue orderer by priority
                    end;
                end loop;
                if ACTIVE_TASK then
                    INTERRUPTION:=FIRST_QUEUE_TASK_PRIORITY>ACTIVE_TASK_PRIORITY;
                else
                    -- remove task from queue and set context
                    ACTIVE_TASK:=true;
                    accept ACTIVE(FIRST_QUEUE_TASK);
                end if;
            or
                accept INTERRUPT (TASK_ID: out TASK_TYPE) do
                    TASK_ID:=ACTIVE_TASK_ID;
                end;
                INTERRUPTION:=false;
                -- task_active to queue, remove task from queue and context switch.
                accept ACTIVE (FIRST_QUEUE_TASK);
            or
                accept FINAL;
                INTERRUPTION:=false;
                -- save context
                if QUEUE_EMPTY then
                    ACTIVE_TASK:=false;
                else
                    -- remove task from queue and set context
                    accept ACTIVE (FIRST_QUEUE_TASK);
                end if;
            or
                delay QUANTUM;
            end select;
            if not INTERRUPTION then
                if NEW_TASK_ACTIVE then
                    -- recalculate quantum
                else
                    if FINISHED_QUANTUM then
                        if not EMPTY_QUEUE then
                            INTERRUPTION:=ACTIVE_TASK_PRIORITY=
                                          FIRST_QUEUE_TASK_PRIORITY;
                            -- recalculate quantum
                        end if;
                    else
                        -- recalculate quantum
                    end if;
                end if;
            end if;
        end loop;
    end;
```

LIST OF AUTHORS

C. Atkinson

G. Auxiette

R. Bayan

A. Burns

D. W. Bustard

J. F. Cabadi

C. Cardigno

J. Carretero

D. Chouvet

A. Crespo

P. de la Cruz

N. W. Davis

C. Destombes

R. B. K. Dewar

A. Di Maio

C. M. Donaldson

K. S. Ellison

T. Elrad

D. Emery

A. Espinosa

S. Flynn-Hummel

J.P. Forestier

C. Fornarino

P. Franchi-Zannettacci

J. L. Freniche

A. García-Fornés

A. Gargaro

R. J. Gilinsky

J. B. Goodenough

L. Gómez

A. D. Hutcheon

M. Irving

J. van Katwijk

D. Kersual

Y. Kol

B. Krieg-Brückner

J. R. Lawton

J. E. Lee

B. Lemaire

D. Meziere

C. W. McKay

P. M. Molko

M. T. Norris

K. Nyberg

R. A. Orr

M. R. Palmer

A. Pérez

F. Pérez

A. Pérez-Riesco

J. A. de la Puente

J.-Y. Quemeneur

P. Rehbinder

J. Robinson

C. Romvary

S. H. Saib

E. Schonberg

L. Sha

H. Toetenel

J. Zamorano

A. J. Wellings